Alternative Urban Futures

Alternative Urban Futures

Planning for Sustainable Development in Cities throughout the World

Raquel Pinderhughes

ROWMAN & LITTLEFIELD PUBLISHERS, INC.
Lanham • *Boulder* • *New York* • *Toronto* • *Oxford*

ROWMAN & LITTLEFIELD PUBLISHERS, INC.

Published in the United States of America
by Rowman & Littlefield Publishers, Inc.
A wholly owned subsidiary of The Rowman & Littlefield Publishing Group, Inc.
4501 Forbes Boulevard, Suite 200, Lanham, Maryland 20706
www.rowmanlittlefield.com

PO Box 317
Oxford
OX2 9RU, UK

British Library Cataloguing in Publication Information Available

Library of Congress Cataloging-in-Publication Data
Pinderhughes, Raquel.
   Alternature urban futures : planning for sustainable development in cities throughout
the world / Raquel Pinderhughes.
      p. cm.
   Includes bibliographical references and index.
   ISBN 0-7425-2366-7 (hardcover : alk. paper) — ISBN 0-7425-2367-5 (pbk. : alk.
paper)
   1. Urban ecology. 2. City planning—Environmental aspects. I. Title
   HT241.P556 2003
   307.76—dc21   2003013133

Printed in the United States of America

∞™ The paper used in this publication meets the minimum requirements of American
National Standard for Information Sciences—Permanence of Paper for Printed Library
Materials, ANSI/NISO Z39.48-1992.

CONTENTS

v

ACKNOWLEDGMENTS

It gives me great pleasure to acknowledge and thank the people who contributed to the development of this book. First and foremost, research assistants extraordinaire: Glenna Anton, Shannon Raider, and Jill Stapleton. Their contributions to this book were significant, and I am very fortunate to have them in my life as students and colleagues. I want to especially thank Glenna for hanging in with me to the end; I would not have met my deadlines without her help. Second, as is clear from the text, this book draws on the ideas and work of scholars across many disciplines. Although I cannot mention them all by name, I must explicitly acknowledge the excellent work of the scholars who edited and contributed to a special journal issue of *Environment and Urbanization* on sustainable cities; of David Drakakis-Smith's three part series Sustainable Urban Development in Third World Cities; of William Rees, particularly his article "Understanding Sustainable Development"; Kameshwari Pothukuchi and Jerry Kaufman's article entitled "The Food System: A Stranger to the Planning Field"; and Catherine Murphy's work on urban agriculture in Cuba, particularly her monograph *Cultivating Havana*. Next, all of the students who have taken my urban environmental planning and policy courses and with whom I have had my most challenging discussions about how to make the world a better place. Colleagues in Havana, Cuba, particularly Catherine Murphy, Eugenio Fuster Chepe, Roberto Mesas, and Humberto Valdez; in Curitiba, Brazil the staff at IPPUC, particularly Sheyla Santos. I would also like to thank the Lazar family for giving me a home base in Curitiba. In the United States, staff at the Institute for Food and Development Policy (Food First), who facilitated my international study abroad seminars in Havana, Cuba, particularly Peter Rosset; colleagues at the Ecology Center in Berkeley and at San Francisco State

ACKNOWLEDGMENTS

University, particularly Christina Vallero, Miriam Knof, and Erin Ro-
driguez. Thanks to Bhavna Shamasunder for reviewing the first draft,
Hugh Lovell for his excellent photographic work, Brian Romer and
Ginger Strader at Rowman & Littlefield for editorial assistance. I would
also like to acknowledge and thank the staff at two local community organizations—KPFA radio and La Pena Community Center—and the
farmers who bring their produce to our local farmers markets, for nourishing my soul and body throughout the years during which I wrote this
book.

On the home front there are many people to thank: my parents, for
love, guidance, and inspiration. They edited the manuscript, but more importantly, they taught me the importance of critical thinking, working for
social justice, teaching, and optimism. My mother-in-law, for love, en-
couragement and support. My brothers and sisters, friends, comadres, co-
padres, and godchildren. *Mil gracias* to Donna for always being there.
Much love and thanks to you all. My husband took much time away from
his own research and writing to allow me to pursue mine, and his feedback throughout the writing of the manuscript made it significantly better; ours is a lifelong journey of mutual support and love—thank you for
every single day. Our children were consistently supportive of my writing;
rather than complaining about the time I spent at the computer, they encouraged and inspired me with their love and music. This book will always
be associated in my mind with the song they composed and sang to me on
the day I completed the manuscript. This book is dedicated to you both
and to your generation.

Photograph by Hugh H. Lovell

PREFACE

We live on one planet, connected in a delicate, intricate web of ecological, social, economic and cultural relationships that shape our lives. If we are to achieve sustainable development, we will need to display greater responsibility—for the ecosystems on which all life depends, for each other as a single human community, and for the generations that will follow our own, living tomorrow with the consequences of the decisions we make today.

—Kofi Annan, secretary general of the United Nations, public remarks leading up to the World Summit on Sustainable Development in Johannesburg, South Africa, August 2002

This book addresses one overarching question: how can planners and policymakers manage urban infrastructures in ways that are less damaging to the natural resource base, produce less waste, and prioritize human needs? The focus is on planning and management of the urban infrastructure in five areas: (1) waste management, (2) water supply and management, (3) energy production and use, (4) transportation, and (5) food systems. The book was written to provide readers with information they will need to challenge existing models of unsustainable urban development and promote sustainable urban development.

As noted by the editors of a special issue of the journal *Environment and Urbanization* devoted to sustainable cities, the vast majority of contemporary social and environmental problems are the product of infrastructures and economic activities that have been designed and implemented with little or no regard for environmental impacts, livelihood, housing needs, transport distances, and/or local and regional natural conditions; this has resulted in dispersed and unbalanced patterns of natural resource and energy consumption and increased social and economic inequality (Anonymous 1992). With few exceptions, the processes and systems that have been put into place to deliver the basic services that people need create, rather than resolve, social and environmental problems. Models of growth and development are based on ever increasing inputs of energy and other natural materials that simply cannot be sustained (Goodland, Daly, and El Serafy 1991). Modern infrastructure systems designed to deliver water, waste, energy, transportation, and food services rely on nonrenewable energy sources, utilize water and energy inefficiently and wastefully, and produce air, water, and ground contamination as well as toxic and hazardous waste. The highly technical infrastructure management and design systems, which rely on fossil fuels, synthetic chemicals, and industrial equipment to deliver clean water, collect and dispose of waste, deliver energy and transportation services, and provide people with food, are wreaking havoc on local and global ecosystems and are damaging human health (Anonymous 1992). Worldwide hegemony of the conventional urban development paradigm has meant that despite differences between nations and levels of development, every city in the world now suffers from problems related to air and water contamination, solid waste accumulation, chaotic growth patterns, traffic congestion, decreasing open space and farmland, environmental degradation, declining environmental quality, increasing socioeconomic inequality, lack of food security, and poverty (Couch 1990; Gossaye 2000).

In the last five decades, as the world economy has grown fivefold and world trade has increased by a factor of fourteen, social and income inequalities have increased significantly (UNEP 2003). Despite substantial increases in economic growth and per capita income in wealthy nations, an estimated 1.2 billion people in developing countries, including half the population in Africa, are living on less than one U.S. dollar a day (UNEP 2002, UNEP 2003). More than one billion people are without safe drinking water. Two billion people have no access to modern energy services. "Globally, more than one billion people breathe unhealthy air and 3 million people die each year from air pollution—two thirds of them are poor people, mostly women and children, who die from indoor pollution caused by burning wood and dung" (Moosa 2002, 14).

As the debt service repayments of developing countries increase, national governments are increasingly susceptible to the overexploitation of natural and human resources in the pursuit of economic growth. The last five decades of international development policy have shown that economic growth achieved through pillaging the planet's natural resources or through social exclusion can be neither economically or socially sustainable (Fox Quesada 2003). It will not be possible to improve quality of life for the billions of people around the world whose basic needs are not being met, and for future generations, without substantially decreasing both the impact of economic activities and urban development on the environment and social inequalities between and within nations and cities.

As noted by the United Nations Centre for Human Settlements, the call for sustainable development is not simply a call for environmental protection.

Instead, sustainable development implies a new concept of economic growth—one that provides fairness and opportunity for all the world's people, not just the privileged few, without further destroying the world's natural resources and without further compromising the carrying capacity of the globe. Sustainable development is a process by which economic, social, environmental, fiscal, trade, energy, agricultural, industrial, and technological policies are designed and are mutually supportive in such a way as to bring about development that is economically, socially, and environmentally sustainable. Current consumption cannot be financed by incurring economic debts that others must repay in the future; investments must be made in the health, housing, basic services, and environmental infrastructure of today's population so as not to create a social debt for future generations; and natural resources must be used in ways that do not create ecological debts by over-exploiting the carrying and productive capacity of the earth (United Nations Centre for Human Settlements 1994).

In an essay entitled "Understanding Sustainable Development," planners Bernd Hamm and Pandurang Muttagi point out that, fundamentally, sustainable development is not about the environment but rather about the capacity of human society to enact permanent reforms in order to safeguard the delicate balance between humans and their natural life support system (1998). To promote sustainable development, planners and policymakers will have to reject paradigms and processes that are based on exploiting resources far outside an urban area's administrative and geographic boundaries and structured around economic activities designed and implemented with little or no regard for environmental or social impacts, and adopt approaches and technologies that are designed to promote economic activities and deliver infrastructure services in ways that are more ecologically and socially responsible. To do so, planners and policymakers must be well informed about paradigms, processes, and appropriate technologies that are less resource-intensive and damaging to human beings; much of the information they need is presented in this book.

Obviously, modern cities are not closed systems (Rees 1998). Urban infrastructure services and urban people will always depend on raw materials from distant lands as well as on the natural resources in their surrounding regions and, after utilizing those resources, much of the waste and pollution generated from urban growth will leave the city (White and Whitney 1992; Rees 1998). Thus the goal of sustainable urban development, and its associated approaches and appropriate technologies, is to promote planning and policy that can significantly *reduce* the negative environmental and social impacts of cities (Anonymous 1992).

Promoting sustainable cities will require planners and other urban authorities to focus on the impact of urban development on water quality and availability, waste output and disposal, energy resources, air contamination, open space, farm land, improvements in the ecological quality of local and regional areas, land uses, public health, and meeting human needs (Priemus 1999). Translating sustainability goals into everyday management practices will require planners and policymakers to support and promote integrated processes and approaches that go way beyond how most urban authorities and planners currently conduct business; this refers to both the way authorities carry out administrative and management tasks as well as to the paradigms, systems, and technologies that authorities employ to manage infrastructure and deliver public infrastructures and services (Jensen et al. 2000).

Urban planners and policymakers will have to promote land uses and land use policies principally developed to shape the urban environment in ecologically responsible ways and enhance the livability of human settlements. They will need to support processes and technologies that are explicitly designed to use fewer resources and produce less waste; reduce inefficient patterns of production, distribution, and consumption; use water more efficiently; reduce dependency on nonrenewable resources; and increase reliance on renewable energy sources. They will need to reorganize government subsidy and tax systems so that they reward sustainable development and create disincentives for unsustainable economic activities (i.e., to increase reliance on mass transit and biking and reduce reliance on cars). They will have to promote and support international policies and financing strategies that assist developing countries in utilizing appropriate technologies and sustainable management strategies to develop strong urban infrastructures that deliver basic services to all residents (i.e., clean water, sanitation services, reliable energy, affordable mass transit, adequate housing).

Structure and Content

This book is organized in seven chapters. The opening chapter introduces readers to the concepts of development, urban development, and sustainable development. The next five chapters focus on water quality, supply, and management (chapter 1); waste disposal, collection, and management (chapter 2); energy supply and management (chapter 3); transportation planning and management (chapter 4); and urban food production (chapter 5).

Chapters 1 through 5 are structured similarly. Each begins with a description of the infrastructure service on which the chapter is focused (water, waste, energy, transportation, and food). This is followed by a critical analysis of the conventional approaches and technologies urban planners employ to deliver and manage this particular infrastructure service, with an emphasis on examining how and why these approaches and technologies promote unsustainable urban development. This leads to a discussion of alternative planning approaches and appropriate technologies that can be used to deliver infrastructure services in ways that are more ecologically and socially responsible and support sustainable urban development. Detailed information is provided about all of the alternative processes, approaches, and technologies presented in each chapter so that readers will have a thorough understanding of what is required to put these alternatives into place.

Each chapter uses examples from cities around the world to illustrate how urban planners and policymakers are utilizing alternative planning approaches and appropriate technologies to minimize their city's impact on the environment and provide residents with the infrastructure and services they need to sustain a high quality of urban life. These examples provide readers with concrete examples of how sustainable development planning and policy approaches have been successfully implemented in cities throughout the world. Examples were collected from over forty nations and more than one hundred cities around the world.

Together, these five chapters provide readers with an understanding of planning and policy approaches and technologies that can be utilized to manage urban infrastructures in ways that are less damaging to the natural resource base, produce less waste, and prioritize human needs. Each chapter ends with a chapter summary, accompanied by a list of questions that can be addressed with the information provided in that chapter. Chapter 6, entitled "Toward Sustainable Development Planning in Cities," summarizes planning and policy changes that will need to be put into place to support sustainable development in cities throughout the world.

INTRODUCTION: PLANNING FOR
SUSTAINABLE URBAN DEVELOPMENT

From the crust of the earth, we take minerals; from the forests, timber; from the farms, grain and meat; from the oceans, fish; and from the rivers, lakes, and aquifers, fresh water. The average resident of an industrial country consumes 3 times as much fresh water, 10 times as much energy, and 10 times as much aluminum as someone in a developing country. The ecological impacts of [this scale of consumption] reach into the local environments of the poor. Our appetite for wood and minerals, for example, motivates the road builders who open tropical rain forests to poor settlers, resulting in the slash-and-burn forest clearing that is condemning countless species to extinction. High consumption translates into huge impacts. In industrial countries, the fuels burned release perhaps three fourths of the sulfur and nitrogen oxides that cause acid rain. Industrial countries' factories generate most of the world's hazardous chemical wastes. Their military facilities have built more than 99 percent of the world's nuclear warheads. Their atomic power plants have generated more than 96 percent of the chlorofluoro-carbons that destroy the earth's protective ozone layer.

—Alan Durning, *How Much Is Enough*, 1992

Development and the Environment

The international policy statement that formally linked development and the environment was the 1987 Brundtland Report written by the United Nations World Commission on Environment and Development, in which sustainable development was introduced as a new development paradigm. Brundtland defined *sustainable development* as "development that meets the needs of the present without compromising the ability of future generations to meet their own needs" (World Commission on Environment and Development 1987, 43).[1]

The concept emerged in reaction to the disturbing social and environmental consequences of economic activities and development processes. Since World War II, world economic activity has increased fivefold, producing an increasingly integrated world economy of enormous scale (Rees 1996). The production of human-made goods and services has increased at an unprecedented pace, and the magnitude of the processes involved is remarkable; societies are using extraordinary amounts of natural resources and energy per person per year (Adriaanse et al. 1997). It took all of human history to grow to the $60 billion scale economy of 1900; today the world economy grows by this amount every two years (Goodland 1991; Rees 1996). The sheer scale at which humans are withdrawing natural resources, burning fossil fuels, emitting pollutants, disposing of wastes, and modifying the landscape to pursue social and economic activities has been accompanied by a profound and unprecedented destruction of the environment which could impact the planet's ability to support human life (Adriaanse et al. 1997).

One of the greatest tragedies of the development paradigm and its associated processes, programs, and technologies is that immense increases in economic activity and industrial development around the world have benefited only a very small proportion of the world's population. The richest one fifth of the world's population consume 75 percent of the world's economic product, while the poorest one fifth of the world's population consume less than two percent. Approximately one quarter of the world's population living in industrialized countries consume more than 80 percent of the world's nonrenewable resources and most of the world's food products, while billions of people around the world are deprived of basic needs (i.e., food, shelter, safe potable water, sanitation and waste services, reliable energy sources, health care, and employment) (Tinbergen and Hueting 1991). As the economy has become ever more global, natural resources are increasingly extracted and processed in one country, transformed into products in another, and consumed in yet another. Since industrialized countries import the vast majority of the material resources they need, people in industrial nations benefit from consuming imported resources while the environmental cost of producing them falls on others, most often the poor developing countries and people that supplied them in the first place (Adriaanse et al. 1997).

In developing countries, social and environmental problems stem from the failure of five decades of development planning to "substantially lessen the proportion of the population living with unmet basic needs" (Anonymous 1992, 4). An estimated 600 million urban residents in developing countries live in life- and health-threatening environments because of unsafe and/or insufficient water, unsafe and/or inadequate housing sites, poor quality and often overcrowded shelter, inadequate provisions for sanitation, lack of garbage collection and drainage, malnourishment, and lack of health care. At least 250 million urban residents have no regular access to safe piped water; 400 million lack sanitation (United Nations Centre for Human Settlements 1994). Almost two thirds of the urban populations in Africa, Asia, Latin America, and the Caribbean have no hygienic means of disposing of human waste, and an even greater number lack adequate means to dispose of waste waters (Human Settlements Programme 2001). More than one fifth of the world's population lack access to safe drinking water. From 30 percent to 50 percent of urban solid waste in developing countries is left uncollected. In some large cities, the daily outpouring of industrial wastes into water bodies reaches millions of cubic meters, and public health risks from hazardous waste are severe; in some countries, as little as 2 percent of municipal sewage is treated. Electric power has yet to reach two billion people. Between 30 percent to 60 percent of the urban population in developing countries lack adequate housing with sanitary facilities, drainage systems, and piping for clean water (Global Environmental Outlook 2000). Approximately 1.3 billion people living in developing countries live in areas that do not meet World Health Organization (WHO) standards for airborne dust and smoke; about one billion people live in cities that exceed WHO standards for sulfur dioxide.

In the past four decades, as economic growth has increased significantly, the number of people living in cities in conditions of absolute poverty has continued to increase. More than 300 million people have incomes so low they cannot fulfill even the most basic nutritional and housing requirements. Even after spending the bulk of their income on food, people in poverty suffer from undernutrition. Children living in poverty are generally below average weight for their age and suffer from impaired development, which jeopardizes their ability to be gainfully employed as adults. Average death rates and infant and child mortality rates are higher among the poor (Commission on Sustained Development 1997). When piped water or sanitation services are lacking, urban residents are extremely vulnerable to health problems and environmental hazards; about half of the urban population in Africa, Asia, and Latin America suffer from one or more of the main diseases associated with inadequate provisions for water and sanitation (Human Settlements Programme 2001).

Any consideration of sustainable development in developing countries must focus on basic infrastructure development related to lack of safe water supply, sanitation, and drainage; unreliable and unsafe energy supply;

inadequate solid and hazardous waste management; uncontrolled emissions from motor vehicles, factories, and low-grade domestic fuels; illnesses linked to congestion and crowding; housing needs; the occupation and degradation of environmentally sensitive lands; and lack of food security; as well as the relationships among these problems (Bartone et al. 1994).

In industrialized countries, problems stem from the immense scale of resource and energy use, waste, pollution, greenhouse gas emissions, and environmental inequities (Anonymous 1992). People in industrialized countries consume and control most of the world's natural resources. Composing approximately one quarter of the world's population, people in industrialized nations consume the vast majority of the world's nonrenewable resources, eat 45 percent of the meat and fish, use more than 80 percent of the paper, and use over five and a half times more energy per person than people living in developing nations. North Americans *alone* use about ten times as much energy per person than Africans, Asians, and Latin Americans; the entire continent of Africa uses less than three percent of worldwide commercial energy (Petesch 1992). In 1996, developing countries averaged fifteen passenger cars for every one thousand people, compared to an average 326 per one thousand in industrialized countries; North America had the highest consumption, with 484 cars per one thousand people (World Resource Institute 2001). In 1997 world average motor gasoline consumption was 48 gallons (182 liters) per person. In industrialized countries the average was 165 gallons (626 liters) per person, more than eleven times the 14.5 gallons (55 liters) per person average in developing countries (World Resource Institute 2001). North America is far and away the biggest consumer of gas per capita, with 432 gallons (1,637 liters) per person consumed in 1997; this is almost five and a half times greater than petrol consumption in Europe (World Resource Institute 2001).

Another tragedy of the development paradigm is that consumption at such an enormous scale, and its associated waste, are possible only because of chains of exploitation and production that reach all over the planet (Ryan and Durning 1997). As authors John Ryan and Alan Durning reveal in the book *Stuff: The Secret Lives of Everyday Things*, for the majority of people living in wealthy industrialized nations, the social and environmental impacts of productive and consumptive chains of production are hidden from view—in rural areas, fenced-off industrial locations, and low-income communities (1997). Immense scales of consumption and waste are facilitated by industrialized nations transferring much of the social and environmental costs of their production and consumption to developing countries (Puckett et al. 2002). Examples include industrial countries (a) benefiting from selling environmentally harmful products such as pesticides, which are illegal in many industrial countries yet exported to developing countries, and (b) exporting hazardous wastes to developing nations (Reid et al. 1988; Puckett et al. 2002). Any consideration of sustainable development in industrialized countries must focus on infrastructure development and patterns of production and consumption that perpetuate inefficiency and waste by not utilizing processes and technologies that are less damaging to the natural resource base, produce less waste, and do not pose a threat to human and environmental health.

Paradigm Shifts

Conceptually, the term *development* is used to refer to processes that lead to improvements in the living conditions of people. The rationalization undergirding the development paradigm is that the benefits of accelerated economic growth will be shared with low-income populations based on the assumption that as wealth is created it will trickle down to the poor in the form of employment opportunities and wages.

In practice, the development paradigm is associated with a systematic set of economic capacity-building processes and strategies that are supported by loans, aid packages, and international agreements. The paradigm emerged after World War II, when the United States led a movement to form five new international organizations whose collective goal would be to move forward the development of nations. These organizations were the Nations Monetary and Financial Conference (1944), the International Monetary Fund (1944), the International Bank for Reconstruction and Development (1944), the United Nations (1945), and the World Bank (1946). The principal goal of development projects is to provide nations with the capacity to develop an infrastructure and political environment that encourages capital investment based on the explicit utilization of a nation's natural resource and human capital base leading to increased economic growth as measured by increases in gross national product (Rees 1998).

The first series of international loans made by the World Bank established the process of development in principle and action. These loans were used to reconstruct European infrastructure that had been damaged during the war and to fund infrastructure development and industrial processes that would explicitly move forward the goals of economic growth in Latin America, Africa, and Asia. The World Bank's first loan to a developing country was in 1948 to fund hydroelectric development in Chile. In 1950 the World Bank made a loan to Ethiopia to fund the maintenance of a road system. In 1953 the World Bank made the first of three loans to Japan to support power (energy) development (World Bank Group 2002).

As William Rees points out in his essay "Understanding Sustainable Development," the economic system at the heart of the development paradigm focuses exclusively on the productive, consumptive, and accumulative activities that create a flow of goods and services between the systems (1998). In the development paradigm, the *environment* (consisting of natural, human-made, and social components) is seen as important and necessary to facilitate economic growth, but it has no essential natural essence, no inherent value in and of itself (Rees 1998). Based on this presumption, the development paradigm leads to the conclusion that in order to develop, nations must aggressively pursue economic growth strategies that fully exploit their natural resource base and human labor force. Workers are seen as benefiting from employment opportunities no matter how low the wages or how poor the conditions of labor. It is precisely this combination—of natural resource and labor exploitation—that attracts investment (typically foreign investment from prosperous nations), leading to industrial processes being introduced into rural and urban sectors. This leads to economic growth (measured by increases in gross national product and corporate profits), which, in turn, provides a basis for development staff working in international development agencies and institutions to conclude that a nation is developing.

The concept of *economic growth,* measured by growth in the production capacity of a nation using increases in gross national product (GNP), gross domestic product (GDP), and other indicators of material wealth, such as number of freeways, autos, and trucks and number of nuclear energy plants, is essential to the development paradigm. As Rees points out, in the process of counting all monetary transactions as economic activity, measures like the GNP fail to distinguish between monetary transactions that genuinely add to well-being and those that diminish it, ignoring the social costs of labor exploitation and the environmental costs of economic activities without accounting for the depletion of natural resources used to produce goods and services or activities that create pollution (1998). Increases in GNP can come from increased money circulating due to oil spills, earthquakes, and wars. Social indicators, such as health indicators, levels of education, unemployment figures, and poverty/income figures are not used as measures of development. The emphasis is exclusively on capital accumulation and production for sale, trade, and consumerism (Rees 1998). Progress toward development is measured by the amount of money circulating in an economy, not by increases in the well-being of the population and the ability of the population to rely on its natural resource base to sustain itself over generations (Rees 1998).

In the 1970s, development specialists working for institutions like the United Nations and World Bank acknowledged that despite two decades of development efforts in Asia, Latin America, and Africa, the trickle-down effect was not succeeding in alleviating poverty or increasing the well-being of the vast majority of the people living in developing countries. In fact, in many countries poverty and social inequality increased throughout the 1970s, as did civil rights violations; ironically, many of these violations were directly connected to social movement struggles to raise wages and benefits for workers. By 1972 the World Bank was financing urban development projects specifically focused on addressing the social and environmental problems that had resulted from two decades of unsuccessful development policies, unsuccessful in the sense that these policies were not leading to improvements for the vast majority of people. This recognition led the World Bank to define what it called its "brown agenda," an agenda focused on the critical urban problems in developing countries—lack of water supply, sanitation, and drainage; inadequate solid and hazardous waste management; uncontrolled emissions from motor vehicles, factories, and low-grade domestic fuels; accidents linked to congestion and crowding; and the occupation and degradation of environmentally sensitive lands (Bartone et al. 1994).

In the 1980s, development specialists affirmed that the strategies they were using to promote rapid economic growth were resulting in the rapid degradation and destruction of the natural resource base of developing countries. Concrete examples included forests cut down to make way for settled agriculture; the extraction of raw materials for industrial production; construction leading to deforestation, erosion, habitat destruction, cultural devastation, and species extinction; oceans being fished for export products to the point of species extinction; coral reef destruction and elimination of fishing as a means of income and way of life for whole cultural groups; rivers dammed to create hydroelectric projects for industrial production facilities, resulting in communities being forced to move from their homelands as well as species extinction; industrialization of rural agriculture and animal husbandry, leading to large amounts of chemical inputs contaminating soil and drinking water; and rapid urban and periurban development, resulting in squatter communities without infrastructures for water, waste, adequate housing, energy, education, and health care (World Commission on Environment and Development 1987). At the 1987 United Nations World Commission on Environment and Development conference, development specialists explicitly confronted the fact that development policies and practices were leading to increases in both poverty and environmental degradation around the world; it is in this context that they identified the need for a new development paradigm and introduced the paradigm of sustainable development (World Commission on Environment and Development 1987).

Whereas the *development paradigm* is based on degrading the world's natural resources, exploiting human labor, and compromising the carrying capacity of the globe and the health of humans and other species, the *sustainable development paradigm* rejects policies and practices that support current living standards by promoting social inequality and depleting the natural resource base, leaving future generations with poorer prospects and greater risks (Repetto 1986). In stark contrast to the development paradigm, the sustainable development paradigm brings together a concern for controlling or limiting the harmful impacts of human activities on the environment (the *sustainable component*) with a concern for meeting human needs (the *development component*) (Anonymous 1992).

Pragmatically, sustainable development is distinguished from development because the policies and practices promoted by sustainable development are intentionally and explicitly designed to minimize the use of environmental resources and reduce the impact on environmental sinks by using processes and technologies that simultaneously improve the economy and people's quality of life (World Commission on Environment and Development 1987). Sustainable development implicitly acknowledges that development must be based on a strong sense of equity and social justice wherein large differentials in income and wealth globally and within industrialized nations are not compatible with the principle of living within environmental capacity limits (Smith et al. 1988).

Urban Development

Urbanization has become the dominant trend in the growth and distribution of the world population. Cities are the place where most of the human population now resides and where most of the resource consumption and waste production take place. In 1800 three percent of the world's population (25 million people) lived in cities; by 1980 the figure had reached 40 percent of the world population; by 2000, more than half of the world's population (3.3 billion people) lived in cities (United Nations Population Fund 2001). According to United Nations projections, six billion of the world's nine billion people will be living in cities by 2020, tripling the urban population over current levels in just two generations. In cities as geographically diverse as Delhi, Jakarta, Bogotá, and Baghdad, more than half of the population is composed of children under the age of fifteen (Drakakis-Smith 1995). Urban areas are growing three times faster than their rural counterparts. Ninety percent of the expected population increase in the next two decades will occur in cities. Most of this increase (90 percent) will take place in developing countries, where 77 percent of the world's population currently resides; where the impacts of environmental deterioration on the quality of life are already severe; and where the urban infrastructure is already failing to provide basic services to the majority of the population (Commission on Sustainable Development 1997).

Urban development exerts tremendous pressure on local urban environments and their surrounding regions and natural resource base, creating immense and growing problems related to water supply, sewage, solid waste, fossil fuel dependency, greenhouse gas emissions, air and water pollution, land degradation, loss of green and natural spaces, urban sprawl, land contamination, transport, traffic congestion, noise pollution, social inequalities, and public health problems (United Nations Environment Programme 2002). As they are currently structured, patterns of urbanization and urban growth pose enormous challenges which if not addressed will lead to profound environmental degradation, the collapse of basic services, and social conflict (Basiago 1999).

Infrastructure is an essential element of urban development. *Infrastructure* refers to the long lived engineered structures, equipment, facilities, and services that are used in economic production and by households (World Bank 1994). It includes services that are derived from the set of public systems traditionally supported by the public sector to enhance residential and nonresidential consumption and production, such as water systems, waste systems, solid waste management, drainage and flood protection, roads, mass transit, energy installations, food systems, and telecommunications.

As cities grow in size and population, local governments are challenged to develop infrastructure that can meet the needs of the population for housing, access to clean water, waste disposal, energy, transportation, food, health care, and education. Infrastructure planning and development have a dramatic impact on a city's local and regional land and natural resource base, on the global ecosystem, and on people's daily lives. Since spatial and environmental policies are intricately linked, decisions related to land use, investments in land development, infrastructure, and capital improvements fundamentally influence the form and quality of urban development for decades (Rees 1996; de Roo and Miller 2000). Good infrastructure services are essential to economic activities, to cope with density and population growth, improve living standards, reduce poverty, raise productivity, protect the environment, and promote social and environmental equity (Ingram and Kessides 1994; Drakakis-Smith 1995). Adequate infrastructure includes provisions related to both the physical infrastructure (i.e., water supply, sanitation facilities, drainage, urban roads, solid waste disposal facilities, and land management) and the social infrastructure (i.e., food, education, and health care facilities) (Drakakis-Smith 1995). Properly designed and managed investments in urban infrastructure development can reduce adverse social and environmental impacts within a city and its periphery, leading to improvements in public health, the natural resource base, economic development, standard of living, and well-being for urban residents (Choguill 1996). Badly designed and poorly managed urban infrastructures contribute to poverty, social inequality, and environmental degradation (Drakakis-Smith 1995).

INTRODUCTION

Sustainable Urban Development

The concept of sustainable urban development directly addresses the social and environmental problems caused by urban development. The economic, social, and environmental planning practices embodying the concept of sustainable urban development are proposed as antidotes to social and environmental problems in cities (Basiago 1999). Within contemporary urban planning circles, sustainable urban development is the concept and buzz word that appears to be the guiding principle for a global society entering the new millennium, superseding almost all others (Turner 1997). The popularity of the concept indicates that planners and policymakers understand that if improvements are to be made to the urban environment it will be essential to design and manage urban infrastructures using processes and technologies that are less damaging to the natural resource base, produce less waste, and increase the well-being of individuals and communities (Anonymous 1992).

Yet despite the rhetoric about the importance of sustainable urban development, most planners and policymakers continue to support an almost constant replication and expansion of unsustainable economic activities, infrastructure development, and consumption patterns (Basiago 1999). As noted by Andrew Basiago, in an article entitled "Social and Environmental Sustainability in Development Theory and Urban Planning Practice," environmental problems are increasing precisely because planners continue to promote and support projects that increase a city's use of natural resources and production of wastes (1999). By not adequately taking the value of the environment into account, the vast majority of urban planning practices and procedures continue to foster the division between economic activities and nature. The result is increasing environmental degradation at every level juxtaposed by increasing rhetoric about the immediate need to protect precious environmental resources and a commitment to sustainable development. As Basiago states eloquently, "It is as if city and regional planners have seized upon the ideal of sustainability as a tangible goal, a particular societal end-state, rather than properly viewing it as an organizing principle governing activity at all levels of an urban system, a process for selecting urban alternatives that will yield vitality" (1999, 148).

Articulating sustainability in any setting as a goal of planning and public policy is not difficult or controversial; the challenge lies in admitting that urban growth and development exceed what is sustainable and committing to doing something about it (Goddard 1999). Current human settlement patterns in cities located in the developing world create the need for more raw materials, energy, and economic development to overcome basic social and economic problems and meet the needs of local populations. It will not be possible to provide the material resources needed to sustain a decent standard of living for the world population in environmentally acceptable ways if present economic growth processes and approaches continue. Planners and other officials must explicitly support planning and policy designed to reduce a city's use of natural resources and production of wastes while simultaneously improving its livability so that it can better fit within the capacities of local, regional, and global ecosystems (Newman 1999). The challenge is to advance planning and policy that promote ecologically and socially responsible "sustainable" urban development. In the chapters that follow, readers are provided with information needed to take on this challenge.

Note

1. The concept of sustainable development was introduced into the international development arena in 1980 by the IUCN publication *World Conservation Strategy*, but did not receive worldwide attention until after the U.N.'s World Commission on Environment and Development published its report *Our Common Future*, which came to be known as the Brundtland Report (de Roo and Miller 2000).

CHAPTER ONE

URBAN WATER QUALITY, SUPPLY, AND MANAGEMENT

Sustainability implies that the supply of "natural capital" is maintained. The use of renewable sources—such as water—should not exceed the rate of renewal, the use of nonrenewable resources—like fossil fuel— should be such that they will not be exhausted before alternative sources are available, and fundamental ecological processes and structures should be maintained.

—Water 21 Project, 1999

Water

Water is essential to life. Without water, most species cannot exist. Fresh water is critical to human survival, settlement, and development; without access to fresh water, human evolution cannot continue. Although fresh water is often viewed as an inexhaustible resource with unlimited renewable capacity, it is in fact a finite resource, limited by availability constraints, affected by socioeconomic developments, population growth, and polluting activities (Postel 1997). An aerial view makes it appear as if the earth is full of water, but only about 2.5 percent of all the water on earth is fresh and two thirds of that supply is locked in glaciers and ice caps. In an article entitled "Dividing the Waters," Sandra Postel, director of the Global Water Policy Project, describes how the renewable fresh water supply on land, made available year after year by the sun-powered hydrologic cycle that creates precipitation, equals only 0.0008 percent of all the water on earth; this supplies all the water needed for forests, grasslands, rain-fed agricultural lands, and all other nonirrigated vegetation (1997). Nearly two thirds of this renewable supply returns to the atmosphere through evaporation or transpiration (the uptake and release of water vapor by plants which condenses and returns to the earth in the form of precipitation). The one third of the supply that remains on the earth's surface after rainstorms or snow melt is runoff (the flow of fresh water from land to sea through rivers, streams, and underground aquifers). This supply is the source of almost all human withdrawals of water and diversions of water used for irrigated agriculture, industry, households, and in-stream water services, which include the dilution of pollutants, transportation of goods, sustaining of fisheries, and the generation of hydroelectric power. This delicate natural balance is affected by factors such as population growth, accelerated climate change, huge water diversion projects, and economic and political interests which continue to override water availability; as a result, water is being used at a rate beyond which it is being replenished; this pattern of use threatens the delicate balance of water upon which humans depend (Godrej 2003).

A significant dimension of the problem of fresh water supply is related to the fact that the geographic location of fresh water is not distributed equally, easy to access, or available on demand. Water-rich countries such as Brazil, Canada, and the former Soviet states stand in stark contrast to countries located in arid zones in the Middle East and Africa. Canada alone contains 20 percent of the world's fresh water, while nine out of fourteen countries in the Middle East are chronically water short and must continually contend with unreliable precipitation patterns. Asia has 36 percent of global runoff but is home to 60 percent of the world's population. South America has 26 percent of the world's runoff but supports only six percent of the world's population (Postel 1997). Much of the river flow in tropical and high latitude locations is difficult and expensive to access.

For centuries, human intervention has impacted natural hydrological cycles and dynamics (Anton 1993). The story of settled agriculture, the growth of cities, and the rise of early empires is to no small degree a story of controlling water in order to make the land more prosperous and habitable (Postel 2000). As humans have altered the course of the land through deforestation, farming, excavation, and the disposal of earth and debris through construction, water flows and water dynamics have been severely affected. Evaporation, erosion, water quality, flooding, drying, salination levels, and the rising and lowering of water tables have all been severely impacted by human activities.

In an article entitled "Thirsty Cities," Danilo Anton discusses how human intervention, leading to modern urbanization in the form of cities, has strongly affected water dynamics (1993). In stark contrast to natural processes, urbanization results in large portions of ground being covered with relatively impermeable barriers of various paving materials that prohibit infiltration, evaporation, and most precipitation runoff.[1] Rather than infiltrating into the ground, most water runs over the land surface and captures pollution, which it then carries into both freshwater sources and saltwater bodies.

Human settlements and industrial processes in urban areas place severe strains on existing water resources and environmental protection capacities. As human populations increase, so do their water and wastewater disposal requirements. As cities get larger and human activities in urban areas expand, populations require more water for drinking, personal hygiene, household uses, landscape and agricultural irrigation, industrial uses, wastewater treatment, recreation, and other land uses (Anton 1993). Hydrological cycles are affected as land is excavated, removed, or buried under fill materials. Water dynamics are affected as structures are inserted into or laid on top of ground surfaces, and as these structures collect precipitation on roofs and other surfaces, they obstruct surface or groundwater flow. The construction of cities modifies watersheds and the obstruction of nutrient transport between ecosystems (Gleick et al. 2002). Increases in local population increase competition for limited regional water supplies and industrial processes and human activities contaminate freshwater sources. All together, the way in which urban development has unfolded has caused major problems in water resources, among them changes in the flow of streams, changes in the hydrological patterns of streams, changes in the amount of suspended sediment, sedimentation and silting of reservoirs, excessive draw down of groundwater levels, contamination of surface waters and groundwater, flooding, erosion, and difficulties in recycling potentially limiting resources such as phosphorus from wastewater back to agriculture (Anton 1993).

According to the United Nations, "Disruption of hydro-geologic systems can easily threaten food security, drinking-water supplies and the environment or cause massive poverty even when the amount of water physically available remains comparatively large" (Grey et al. 1995, 12, 3). Postel states it succinctly: "Water may seem to be everywhere, but for a rising portion of the world's population, there may soon be hardly a drop to drink or to use for growing food, supporting industries and cities, and preserving life-giving ecosystems. . . . A growing scarcity of fresh water is now an impediment to global future food security, health of aquatic ecosystems, and social and political stability" (1997, 54–55).

Environmental and Social Impacts of Conventional Water Planning and Distribution Approaches

Municipal authorities are responsible for urban water management and for providing urban residents with adequate water supply, acceptable water quality, as well as basic wastewater, sewage, and flood drainage services. Urban water management involves the fields of water supply, water purification, prevention of flooding, urban drainage, wastewater treatment, and sludge handling. The decisions that water management authorities make impact water flow, water supply, access to fresh water, and water quality. While most cities import water from underground sources or from long distances to support their water needs, many cities rely on both strategies. Water is taken from streams, lakes, rivers, oceans, and aquifers and diverted through many strategies, including extensive damming projects, and brought to the surface through pumping and wells. In most cities, factors such as urban sprawl, the expansion of agricultural production into periurban areas, and the inefficient design and management of domestic water supply systems have induced profoundly unsustainable patterns of groundwater use, and authorities are facing serious problems related to water supply, water quality, and wastewater treatment (Anton 1993; Postel 1997). Consequently, urban authorities are increasingly challenged to promote effective management of limited sovereign and shared freshwater resources.

In cities throughout the world, water problems are getting worse. A United Nations assessment, prompted by the U.N.'s International Drinking Water Decade of the 1980s, concluded that a global water crisis could easily be caused by the capacity of the hydrological cycle to supply water being outstripped by the volume of human demands, pollution of water resources, and poor water management (United Nations Department of Economic and Social Affairs 2000). Increasing population growth may result in as many as 5.5 billion people living in areas that suffer from severe water stress, resulting in two out of every three people facing water shortages by 2025 (Tearfund 2001; Earth Summit Watch 2002).[2] Increasing scarcity of fresh water threatens global food security, social and political stability, the health of aquatic ecosystems, and human health.

The problem of the inequitable distribution of water resources presents a major challenge for urban authorities. While easy access to clean water at affordable prices is the norm in wealthy industrialized countries, in the poorest countries residents struggle to survive on a daily ration equal to less than a bucket of water (Tearfund 2001). While people in the United States and England have access to an average of eighty gallons (303 liters) and forty gallons (150 liters) of clean water a day respectively (enough to wash fifteen cars), access to clean drinking water is still a dream for people in many parts of the world. More than one billion people (about one fifth of the world's population) lack access to safe drinking water. According to the United Nations Environmental Program's *Global Environment Outlook Report*, polluted water negatively affects the health of 1.2 billion people and contributes to the annual death of 15 million children younger than five years of age; every eight seconds a child dies from a diarrhea-based disease, such as diarrhea, typhoid, cholera, amoebic infections, or bacillary dysentery caused by contaminated water (United Nations Environment and Development Programme 2000). Without adequate water quality and sufficient access to water, billions of people will continue to suffer from illnesses arising from inadequate access to water, unsanitary environments, and polluted water (Earth Summit Watch 2002).

Limitations on access to water through municipal systems and traditional shallow wells have led to the emergence of water markets. Poverty and social inequality are deepened when low-income residents without access to clean water are forced to purchase water from private suppliers who transport it into cities, where they sell it at high cost to consumers. Purchasing water is a major expense for low-income households in developing countries.

Water Markets

In the city of Ta'iz, Yemen, stratified water markets have emerged in which price varies with water quality. Low-quality water (sometimes taken directly from the sewage lines) is sold to be used *only* for washing and cleaning uses, *not* for cooking or drinking. Medium-quality water is supposed to be used for cooking, the expectation being that it will be boiled to get rid of pathogens. High-quality purified water (typically supplied from small, private treatment plants) is to be used for drinking. Low wage earners can spend as much as a full day's wages just to purchase low-quality water. Under these conditions, households are forced to use low-quality water for cooking or drinking, which can lead to severe public health problems.

Groundwater

Ninety-seven percent of the planet's liquid fresh water is stored in aquifers. Groundwater plays a critical ecological role as the primary source of base flow into rivers and streams and as the major water source for most surface vegetation communities and wetlands. Groundwater sustains the flow of rivers and streams and maintains riparian and wetland ecosystems. Aquifers function as sinks for land-based sources of pollution and accumulate waste products over time.

Humans have tapped into underground water sources for centuries. The strategy functioned well when local populations were relatively small and dispersed throughout a region. But as populations have increased, cities have become more densely populated, economic activities more diverse, and technological processes more advanced, humans have gone deeper and deeper into the earth to collect groundwater (Anton 1993). Until very recently, groundwater was treated as a ubiquitous and reliable source of high-quality water that was either replenishable or based on reserves so great that human withdrawals would not be significant (Anton 1993; Postel 1997). But over the last half century, aquifer characteristics and groundwater flow properties have been rapidly depleted and degraded as a consequence of unsustainable development planning and unsustainable management of the natural resource base. The rapid spread of energized pumping technologies enabling rapid groundwater development and the emergence of socioeconomic systems dependent on its reliability have resulted in a scale and intensity of abstraction and pollution so great that, under current recharge regimes and pollution intensity, much of the damage to groundwater sources is irreversible (Postel 1997). Formerly renewable sources of groundwater are becoming nonrenewable because of overdraft in which rates of abstraction exceed rates of recharge.

In addition to abstracting water, pumping changes water flow patterns; this often results in the migration of pollutants and low-quality water into aquifers. Pumping also results in sedimentation buildup in aquifers as sediment settles on the sides and bottom of underground storage areas. The single largest cause of land subsidence (the gradual settling or sudden sinking of the earth's surface owing to subsurface movements of earth materials) is the compaction of unconsolidated aquifer systems caused by excessive groundwater pumping. The draining of aquifers causes sediments to compress, reducing the total storage capacity of the aquifer system and lessening its capacity to store water (Brown et al. 2001; United States Geological Survey 1999).

In almost every region in the world, the groundwater resource base and the social, economic, and environmental systems dependent on it are under threat from overabstraction by pollution caused by huge increases in the use of agrochemicals in both rural and urban areas, and by the discharging of untreated industrial and domestic waste directly into the ground. Minor and major spills of industrial chemicals, such as organic solvents, have resulted in large-scale groundwater contamination (Grey et al. 1995). The contamination of groundwater by excessive pumping and industrial and inadequate waste removal systems is particularly troublesome, because unlike streams, aquifers cannot be rejuvenated. As Godrej points out, "We produce industrial contaminates so toxic they can only be diluted to safe levels by millions of times their quantity of water. Yet 60 percent of liquid industrial waste in the United States is injected straight into deep groundwater in the fond hope that none of it will ever bubble up into the water people actually use" (2003, 11). Natural purification processes are limited underground; thus contaminated water remains underground in the same state it was in when the pollutants were introduced. Complicating matters is that, in contrast to surface water, underground networks are hard to track, so scientists cannot easily predict where pollutants in groundwater will end up.

Agriculture is the largest abstractor of groundwater, but groundwater is also a critical source of water supply for municipal uses and is essential to meet large-scale, global needs for urban drinking water supply, food security, water for manufacturing, and wastewater treatment systems. Groundwater is now the primary source of drinking water for 1.5 to two billion people worldwide, one third of the world's population (Brown et al. 2001). Some of the largest cities in the world, including Jakarta, Lima, and Mexico City, depend on aquifers for almost all of their water. At least half of the megacities estimated to have populations over ten million are heavily dependent on groundwater (Brown et al. 2001). Some cities, like New Delhi, India, which have large populations that are not served by the municipal water system, rely on groundwater as their primary source of supply (Grey et al. 1995). Over half the population of the United States meets all or part of its drinking needs from groundwater. Groundwater accounts for one third of water extracted for public supplies in England and Wales (Grey et al. 1995). Although tapping into underground water sources has become acceptable practice in cities throughout the world, current practices are ultimately unsustainable because groundwater is located in deep aquifers that take thousands of years to replenish, and depleting aquifers causes many serious social and environmental problems.

Large Diversion Schemes

As national and local governments exhaust water sources in local areas, they are forced to search farther and farther away for new sources of water. This has led to large water diversion schemes that transport water over great distances, often spanning across several river basins or watersheds. The California aqueduct, from which the city of Los Angeles gets its water, is so extensive that it can be seen from space. Large diversion schemes profoundly disturb stream systems, resulting in wetlands and lakes disappearing, creating rivalries between later and earlier growing cities, and impacting habitat and wildlife (Godrej 2003). Ninety percent of California's wetlands have been lost as a result of various water projects used for such purposes as irrigation, industrial processes, and to serve energy and water needs in cities. This has had a huge impact on birds, fisheries, and water quality. River deltas, where fresh water and salt water meet, are the location of some of the richest, most fragile ecosystems; the diversion of river water upstream has caused the salinization of these delicate environments.

The social implications of dams are equally profound; they include displacement, public health problems, and neglect of local community needs. Most often, the displaced are members of marginalized groups to whom governments are not accountable and the areas to which people are "resettled" are frequently not suited to the ways in which they have traditionally lived. In some areas, year-round standing water in reservoirs and accompanying irrigation canals can increase the risks of waterborne disease. Large bureaucracies frequently neglect the needs of local communities as they develop schemes to control, transport, and store water (Godrej 2003). The Three Gorges Dam in China will displace and resettle 1.3 million people (McCully 1996).

The endless quest to find new sources of water has also led to the introduction of more invasive pumping technologies, going deeper and deeper beneath the surface of the earth to extract groundwater. This has resulted in the lowering of water tables and salt water intrusion into aquifers, threatening to turn renewable resources into nonrenewable resources as groundwater reserves are depleted. A project in Libya designed to draw water from an aquifer beneath the Sahara desert and transfer it 3,500 kilometers through a network of giant pipelines threatens to deplete the aquifer completely since the area receives very little annual rainfall (Godrej 2003).

Access to Sufficient and Clean Water Supply

The ability of municipal authorities to provide populations in their jurisdictions with access to sufficient and clean water supply and wastewater services depends heavily on the material and economic resources public authorities have to allocate to this challenge. Industrialized nations have the privilege of using public and private sector resources to create an infrastructure that brings clean water for drinking, cooking, and personal hygiene to residents twenty-four hours a day and at relatively affordable prices (Anton 1993). With ample financial resources, governments in industrialized nations have been able to provide their urban populations with an abundant, consistent, affordable water supply. Ample financial and technological resources allow water to be carried from long distances, treated, stored, and routed to residents and institutions through a piping system that allows clean water to be used for various purposes and then disposed of as wastewater (Anton 1993). After human use, water is disposed of (treated or untreated) in a much different state than when it was originally extracted. Storm water that falls on streets and roofs is collected in culverts, canals, and pipes, removed through a network of pipes, and carried outside the area.

It is important to point out that while ample financial and technological resources enable municipal authorities to create strong water infrastructures and deliver clean water to populations, they do not prevent authorities from putting inadequate or degraded water delivery and removal systems into place in urban settings that deplete, waste, and contaminate freshwater sources in prosperous nations. Storm drains that are poorly designed for many of the types of waste people put into them, leaky sewer systems, and leaky landfill sites that seep toxins into groundwater are only three examples of how urban water management systems in wealthy, industrialized countries degrade water quality, change water quality, affect water volume, and impact groundwater levels and flows. Ironically, ample financial and technical resources in prosperous, industrialized nations have resulted in the waste of a huge amount of fresh water which could be captured and reused (Anton 1993).

The situation is very different in the vast majority of developing countries, where the water infrastructure is much less developed and, in many residential areas, access to clean fresh water or to any fresh water is limited, irregular, or nonexistent. The provision of water has been identified as one of the most urgent problems facing urban authorities in developing countries (Drakakis-Smith 1995). As stated earlier, at least 250 million urban residents have no regular access to safe piped water and more than one fifth of the world's population lack access to safe drinking water. In most developing countries, municipal authorities are currently facing serious problems related to providing a reliable and clean water supply for human uses and adequately treating wastewater; yet nearly all of the projected population increases in the next fifty years will take place in low-income, developing countries that are already experiencing water shortages and where people currently lack sufficient water to drink, satisfy hygienic needs, and produce food (Biswas 2000).

Economic constraints pose the most substantial barrier to the provision of water and sanitation infrastructure and public services at the local level. In most developing countries, water management services are the responsibility of the public sector for which access to internal funding to create a water supply and disposal infrastructure is severely limited (Biswas 2000). The provision of clean drinking water and safe disposal of wastewater to the rapidly growing centers is constrained by the high cost of creating a water supply and disposal infrastructure, financing and management problems, and water scarcity. In these countries, rapidly growing urban populations, expanding manufacturing activities, and the needs of the agricultural sector compete for freshwater access under conditions of weak infrastructure; this leads to inadequate water supply, poor water quality, and poor quality or nonexistent wastewater treatment systems (Biswas 2000). The funding situation is made more difficult in the context of infrastructure and management problems that result in inadequate construction, pricing, and billing systems, leading to considerably fewer funds generated to finance operating and expansion costs of the water infrastructure. Examples of such problems include the city of Calcutta, which has no metering system whatsoever, and cities like Beijing, Hanoi, and Bombay, where subsidized water prices encourage high consumption and waste among those who are fortunate enough to have regular access to fresh water (Biswas 2000). Because investments in water supply and sanitation have not kept pace with the growth of urban populations, urban inhabitants are increasingly not being served by the municipal water supply and/or sewage systems and, in many parts of the world, many residents depend on shallow wells and community pumps to meet their domestic water needs. Declines in water level frequently cause shallow wells to go dry, forcing people to wait many hours to obtain water from limited municipal tap stands and/or purchase water. Purchasing water is an expense that very low-income families simply cannot afford.

Water Privatization

In the face of degraded water infrastructure and economic constraints on the development of water resources, local and national governments are turning to privatization as a solution to inadequate water delivery and treatment systems. In many cases, international lending agencies and export credit agencies require privatization of water systems as a condition for loans. Lobbying behind them are private transnational corporations that stand to make huge profits from privatized water systems (Godrej 2003). Although many people have come up with creative ways to regulate, control, and combine private and public sector needs and environmental concerns, past and current experience raises critical questions about whether accountable private water systems can be realized in practice. As Dinyar Godrej points out in an article entitled "Precious Fluid: Challenge Posed by World's Freshwater Crisis," "Transnationals cherry-pick the most profitable sectors. . . . they demand upgrades of existing infrastructure from the public purse and tax cuts, they shed staff, they raise prices and cut off people unable to pay" (2003, 12).

South Africa's experience with the privatization of water services is illustrative of problems that frequently arise from privatization. In South Africa, privatization immediately led to sharp increases in water rates (Polar Institute 2000). "In South Africa, white farmers consume 60 percent of the country's water supplies through large scale irrigation while 15 million black people are denied access to clean water. . . . Households in the poor townships who can not afford to pay the rate hikes find themselves with their water being cut off altogether. As a result, people in Soweto and other townships surrounding Johannesburg, Durban and Capetown have been mobilizing their own resistance by ripping out water meters and 'illegally' reconnecting water services in their neighborhoods" (Polar Institute 2000).

The problem is not limited to developing countries. In Atlanta, Georgia, U.S., privatization of the water system was disastrous as well. As Jane Kelly reports in the *Sacramento Bee* newspaper, "In Atlanta, officials thought they could save money on repairs by contracting with United Water, a French-owned firm, to buy and run Atlanta's system. In the first four years of a 20-year contract, residents complained of rate hikes, brown water and poor service. Operating fees and complaints cost the city tens of millions of dollars, even while United Water was billing the city for work it didn't do. In January, Atlanta pulled the plug on that deal" (Kelly 2003, B7). In an article entitled "Busting the Water Cartel," Holly Wren Spaulding describes how the conveners of the Third World Water Forum held in Kyoto, Japan, in 2003 strongly promoted the idea that there is consensus to support aggressive corporate-backed campaigns to privatize control and distribution of world water supply (2003). But their perspective that water is a valuable commodity to be controlled by the market was rejected by many people attending the forum, who perceive water as a basic human and environmental right which needs to be protected by and for communities and people around the globe (Wren Spaulding 2003). A broad coalition of over thirty organizations from more than twenty-seven countries challenged efforts at the forum to privatize water. In response to a report that strongly advocated water privatization written by a group chaired by Michel Camdessus, former management director of the International Monetary Fund, Bolivian human rights organizer Pablo Solon stated, "We are not against this paragraph or that paragraph of the Camdessus Report. We are against the heart of the Camdessus Report, because the heart of the report is that it does not have a heart" (Wren Spaulding 2003, 3).

Some water experts, such as Peter Gleick, president of the Pacific Institute Studies in Development, Environment and Security, have concluded that, with proper regulation and specific principles in place that support social objectives related to water (including the provision of water for human and ecosystem requirements), public-private partnerships and privatization can work (Gleick et al. 2002). In order to achieve a water system that is responsive to these requirements, Gleick proposes that private systems be accompanied by independent monitoring, enforcement of water quality standards, equitable access, democratic decisionmaking by all affected parties, and the adoption of water-efficient technology. Privatization, according to Gleick, can even remedy problems related to water resources by eliminating inappropriate subsidies, such as those supporting industrial agriculture (Gleick et al. 2002).

But many water experts, such as Dinyar Godrej, are concerned that when water is subject to market forces, profits are transferred outside the community or country and there are no incentives for private companies to conserve water; consequently, instead of promoting ecologically and socially responsible water practices, companies are inclined to exploit as much water as possible so as to sell the maximum amount for maximum profit, ultimately undermining the environment, human beings, and all other species that depend on water for survival (Gleick et al. 2002). Most often, treating water as a commodity from which private sector companies can make profit has led to a situation in which those individuals that can pay have access to water and those that are too poor to pay do not have access to water; inequalities reflect and reinforce existing disparities and social injustices.

An additional problem related to water privatization is that in order for water to be traded it must be treated as a commodity and subject to existing and future trade rules and regulatory bodies such as the General Agreement on Tariffs and Trade (GATT), the international trade agreement that provides the legal structure for trade rules that guide trade between World Trade Organization (WTO) member countries. Many of these rules and bodies explicitly constrain the ability of nations to treat water as a social benefit. Under GATT rules, for example, once interbasin transfers have begun between WTO member countries, national governments involved in the transfer cannot curtail, regulate, or stop the process if it turns out to be detrimental. Companies engaged in water privatization are eager for water commodification to get underway precisely because it would open up larger markets and make it more difficult for national governments to exert control over them.

Conflicts over Water Resources

Competition for scarce water in urban areas has major political impli-cations. As demand for fresh water confronts the limits of finite supply, competition for fresh water has increased between urban, periurban, and rural areas, and between cities, states, and neighboring countries. As the demand for fresh water increases, political conflicts stemming from water stress and water scarcity are escalating throughout the world and emerg-ing within and between nations. Rivers are among the most important sources of fresh water available for human use, and more than 245 river basins are shared by two or more countries. Many conflicts have emerged in areas where rivers are shared by two or more nations; these include the Nile, Zambezi, Niger, and Volta river basins in Africa; the Rhine River, which runs through Germany and Holland; the Rio Grande, which is shared by the United States and Mexico; and the Euphrates River, which is shared by Turkey and Syria and runs into Iraq. Tensions are highest in geographic areas where water supply is severely limited (Postel 1999; Pos-tel 2000). The situation is particularly severe in developing countries where urban residents have considerably less access to water and demand for greater water supply is rising rapidly. A study conducted by the Inter-national Food Policy Research Institute in Washington, D.C., found that annual household and industrial demand for water in developing countries will increase by 590 billion cubic meters (772 billion cubic yards) between 1995 and 2020, equivalent in volume to the annual flow of seven Nile Rivers, with the share of water going to urban activities more than dou-bling from 13 percent to 27 percent of total water use (Postel 2000).

Shifting the Burden of Water Use

Many problems arise when nations and cities try to deal with water stress and water scarcity using strategies that shift the burden of water use to other nations and regions. One water-prioritizing strategy in-volves reducing water use through grain importation based on the as-sumption that if grain is imported, domestic water will not be needed to grow grain, and water can be reallocated for urban uses. As Sandra Pos-tel discusses in "Dividing the Waters," cities and industries that need water are looking to irrigated agriculture as the last big pool of available water (1997). The idea is to significantly reduce freshwater supply needs within a city, region, or nation by relying on other countries to use their water supplies to irrigate grain crops and then sell their yields on the open market. The strategy involves reducing a nation's agricultural production by importing grain rather than growing it, based on the assumption that nations and regions short of fresh water can rely upon nations and regions where water is more abundant to support a significant proportion of their food supply. But as Postel points out, the logic breaks down quickly in the face of the growing number of people living in regions of the world where water is in short supply and grain needs are enormous (1997). In addition to Africa, the Middle East, Near East, and China, countries such as India and the United States would qualify as "water-stressed'" if statistical breakdowns of water supplies and population were available by region (Postel 1997). The strategy of importing grain also reinforces existing social and economic inequalities between nations, regions, and cities by ensuring that wealthier countries have greater access to limited and increasingly expensive world grain supplies to support their population needs.

Inadequate and Poor Management of Water Resources

Inadequate and poor management of water resources threatens the long-term quality and availability of the world's water supply. Inefficient water use and lack of conservation measures are a huge part of the problem of water supply worldwide. Water usage in almost every city in the world is unsustainable for at least seven reasons (Anton 1993; Postel 1997; Biswas 2000). First, too much fresh water of high quality is taken from the ecosystem. Second, the supply of good quality surface and underground water is being contaminated through pollution stemming from human and industrial activities, agricultural chemicals, domestic wastes, and problematic land uses. Third, water resources are not distributed equitably. Fourth, poverty is increased when residents without access to clean water are forced to spend their limited income on purchasing water. Fifth, poor management of water resources threatens the long-term quality and availability of the world's water supply. Sixth, as population demands for fresh water confront the limits of finite supply, competition for fresh water has increased between cities and farms, neighboring states, provinces, cities, and nations. Seventh, humans are rapidly depleting underground freshwater sources.

Moving Toward Sustainable Urban Water Management

The goal of sustainable urban water management is to make certain that adequate supplies of water of good quality are maintained for the entire human population while preserving the hydrological, biological, and chemical functions of ecosystems (Okun 1992; Biswas 2000). Without sustainable freshwater management strategies, severe water shortages and water contamination will negatively affect household activities, crop irrigation, industrial activities, and local ecosystems in many parts of the world.

Planners must turn their attention to the problematic effects of urbanization, industrial processes, and inefficient irrigation on water demands and usage. Water conservation and waste minimization planning and implementation policies and measures must be developed and immediately implemented among the multisectored interests that utilize freshwater resources; these include cities that rely on fresh water for water supply and sanitation, urban and periurban development, industries and small businesses, hydropower generation, inland fisheries, low and flatlands management, agricultural sectors, recreation, and other activities (Haman and Brown 1994).

In an article entitled "The Soft Path for Water: the Biennial Report on Freshwater Resources," Gary Wolff and Peter Gleick call for an approach to water resources that pertains to the nonstructural components of water management and use that include equitable access, proper application of economics, incentives for efficient use, social objectives for water quality, and public participation (1998). The soft approach to water would allocate water according to water needs, not based on projected demand. The path involves community participation and cooperation between neighbors to determine water needs. It is designed to decrease the distancing of water consumers from the water resources on which they depend, taking into account variations in local situations in order to determine water needs in specific locations. The soft path approach strives to build bridges among the various parties involved with water, such as agencies dealing with flood control, water delivery and treatment, private companies, and land-use authorities, in order to improve coordination and integration of decisionmaking related to water development.

The soft path relies on reuse technologies and decentralized piping systems. The soft path complements centralized infrastructure with decentralized facilities. For example, the soft path has multipipe distribution networks that deliver potable water for drinking and lower quality water for uses that do not require potable water, such as flushing toilets and landscape irrigation. In addition, the soft path discourages once-through consumptive use appliances. The soft path also treats instream use of water by fish, other organisms, ecological processes, and recreation as a valid demand and considers such use as part of what it refers to as "natural infrastructure" (Wolff and Gleick 1998).

In sharp contrast, the current *hard path for water*, in which it is the task of engineers to supply water based on projected market demand, ignores the actual needs of local communities, takes power away from water users, and leads to the need to seek endless new sources of water. The hard path "leads to more and more ambitious, intrusive and capital-intensive projects that capture and store water far from where the water is needed, culminating in the massive water facilities that dominate parts of our landscape" (Wolff and Gleick 1998, 1). The hard path discounts water-efficient technologies and depends on centralized infrastructure and planning that function the same way in every situation, regardless of the differences. Centralized infrastructure is a single pipe distribution system that delivers clean water and takes away wastewater.

In order for the soft path to be successful, standards must be developed to integrate the cost and benefits among diverse water users. In response to the limitations of traditional measures such as GDP, Gleick offers new incentives and measures for water use that can be embedded in standards that regulate water use. Examples of such measures include best available technology, maximum practical savings, and maximum cost-effective savings, all of which must be developed to determine sustainable standards of water use; Wolff and Gleick emphasize that democratic decisionmaking is critical in developing these measures.

To reduce inefficiency and overuse of water and increase water supply to urban populations, planners must pursue a range of integrated strategies consistent with the soft water path described above. They include strategies to (1) redesign and augment water infrastructure and delivery systems; (2) reduce inefficiency and overuse of water in households; (3) recapture and reuse water; (4) treat wastewater using ecologically based methods; and (5) recognize the true cost of water. Each of these strategies is discussed below.

Infrastructure Changes

Widespread water scarcity, water contamination, and the gradual destruction of freshwater resources demand an integrated and sustainable approach to water resources planning and management related to surface water and groundwater and to water quality and quantity. Infrastructure development must occur based on a commitment to utilize sustainable water management strategies to deliver adequate water supply whenever feasible. Planners need to utilize both conventional and alternative approaches and technologies to bring water to residents in their jurisdictions.

The negative impacts of urbanization on water quantity and quality can be mitigated through infrastructure changes and redesign. For example, when there is a need to resurface pavement, porous pavement can be installed. Unlike concrete, which is impermeable, porous pavement allows water to infiltrate into the ground and recharge groundwater, lowering the risks of floods while at the same time saving money on the cost of pipes that carry urban runoff to the ocean, reducing the risk of water accumulating pollutants as it flows over the land; it also mitigates the possibility of sewer overflow. Developing nations will need to be supported to redesign and extend their water infrastructure in order to deal with inefficiencies and provide their entire urban population with sufficient clean water supply and wastewater treatment services.

In an article entitled "Water for Urban Areas of the Developing World," Asit Biswas points out that whenever possible, instead of emphasizing new construction related to the water infrastructure, city authorities should focus on reducing water losses from infrastructures already in place (2000). In many existing infrastructures, water losses can be as high as 60 percent. Financing the reduction of losses is significantly more cost-effective than developing infrastructures for new water sources, yet this strategy has received inadequate attention from politicians and urban planners. Biswas attributes this lack of attention to politicians and planners who perceive that new water projects will be more attractive to the public who pay taxes, engineers who find the construction of new projects exciting and who are less attracted to the idea of simply fixing existing systems, and contractors and consulting companies who directly gain from the enormous funding needed to finance new construction projects versus the considerably smaller amounts of funding needed for operating and maintaining existing systems (Biswas 2000).

Reducing Inefficiency and Overuse of Water in Households

Inefficiency and overuse of water are among the most problematic characteristics of water use in industrialized countries. At the household level, industrialized nations must use their considerable resources to immediately implement measures to improve efficiency of water consumption. According to a report by the American WaterWorks Association, consumers in the United States could greatly reduce pressure on water supplies and save as much as $35 billion in water costs by using water-efficient home strategies and practices (2001). A typical U.S. home uses eighty gallons of water per person per day. Most of that water is wasted due to inefficient practices and technologies. American WaterWorks's survey of 3,700 U.S. households revealed that the use of more efficient plumbing fixtures *alone* would reduce the amount of water used by Americans by more than three billion gallons per day. Americans could save a third or more of the water now used in their homes by reducing water consumption for landscaping; using non-leaking low-flush toilets, aerated shower heads, and top-loading washing machines; reusing water in washing machines and dishwashers; decreasing rinsing in washing machines and dishwashers; using water efficiently for personal hygiene uses and washing dishes; and reusing gray water from washing and cooking (with biodegradable products) for activities such as watering lawns and plants and washing cars (Stone and Weiss 1995).

Instead of using public policies and resources to import water from far away, urban planners in industrialized nations must begin to manage their water supply carefully and efficiently. Public policies should function to motivate residential and commercial users, and the municipalities in which they are located, to implement water efficiency and water conservation measures; these would include fixing leaks, installing more efficient water fixtures, replacing thirsty water-dependent lawns with drought resistant groundcovers and native shrubbery, and recycling gray water (Larsen and Gujer 1997).

Water Conservation,
Neighborhood Revitalization, Job Creation

The Mothers of East Los Angeles Water Conservation Program provides low-income community residents with free low-flush toilets and showerheads to reduce water consumption and water bills. Residents are motivated to participate in the program because they can save a minimum of $35 a year on their water bills and participate in a program that employs people in their community. Since 1992, twenty-eight neighborhood residents have been employed through the project, which is funded by selling old toilets back to the city for $25 each. The old toilets are recovered and crushed so that the porcelain can be ground up into gravel and used in the construction and maintenance of city streets. The old toilets require three to seven gallons of water per flush, compared to the new ultra-low flush toilets (ULFT) which use only 1.6 gallons of water per flush. To date, more than 50,000 ULFTs have been installed. The Los Angeles Department of Water estimates that those who use ULFTs will save fourteen gallons of water a day. City staff estimated that if all Los Angeles residents had the ULFTs installed in their homes, the city could potentially conserve about 48 million gallons of water daily.

Source: Steve Lerner, *Eco-Pioneers: Practical Visionaries Solving Today's Environmental Problems*, 1997

Recapture and Reuse Water

Gray Water Systems

Water used by urban households and institutions should be recaptured. Although water supplied for urban use must be adequately disinfected and nontoxic, not all urban uses require that water be of safe drinking water quality. These would include water used for industry, cooling, commercial establishments, construction uses, and household and recreational uses, such as toilet flushing. This logic informs the principle behind separating and utilizing gray water. *Gray water* is a term used to refer to untreated wastewater that has the potential to be recycled and used for secondary uses. The principle supporting gray water is that most urban wastewater does not contain feces, urine, or high concentrations of organic wastes; therefore, it can and should be reused. Using gray water in urban areas could save anywhere from 25 percent to 50 percent of the drinkable water supply.

Since large quantities of gray water will always be produced in urban areas, it is essential to develop strategies to capture, treat, and reuse this high volume of valuable water. Treating gray water in an environmentally responsible manner will also have the radiating effect of reducing health hazards for those living in and around urban areas. After being appropriately treated, this water could serve as a *new* source of water for particular urban uses. Although it may be restricted to specific types of water use because of quality considerations and cultural perceptions, gray water could still be used for many purposes, and the overall effect would be to release high-quality water for those uses that warrant it (Biswas and Arar 1988; Biswas 2000).

Gray water systems range in complexity from a simple drain hose leading to an outdoor landscape to a complex filtering system using septic tanks, settling filters, and microbial filters. Technically, the idea is to create a separate system for gray water sources away from the sewer lines. The goal is to separate water that contains feces, urine, or high concentrations of organic wastes from gray water, sending unclean water to treatment plants and routing gray water to a separate system for reuse purposes.

Municipalities with well-developed water treatment and disposal infrastructures and financial and material resources have the capacity to separate gray water within a household by having separate lines from the kitchen, sink, and bathing drains. Only the line from the toilet would go to the sewer for chemical or optimally biological treatment and release into open water. Implementing this process does depend on behavioral change and environmental awareness, since residents must be attentive to the chemicals they pour down the drain. Solvents, toxic cleaners, paint thinners, drain openers, and so on should be avoided in a gray water system. Biodegradable soaps, shampoos, and cleaners are the most compatible. For optimum results, the line leading to the gray water system needs to have a filter that captures and separates macrodebris such as hair and lint before flowing through a piping system into a septic tank where it settles, with heavy material falling to the bottom and then flowing into one or more filtering systems depending upon water quality and other factors. It is important that gray water be filtered properly in order to avoid contaminating edible plants or groundwater. Municipalities with less developed water treatment and disposal systems and fewer material resources can create gray water processes that require less investment. A leaching pipe can carry gray water from the house to an outside area where it can be put through a series of filtering tanks containing mulch, sand, gravel, and plants. Materials such as gravel can act as a grease and oil trap. It is also important to consider how gray water could be allocated to support the aesthetic needs of an urban population; this would include water to feed fountains, ponds, public parks, green space, and botanical gardens (Larson and Gujer 1997).

Quayside Village Gray Water System

Members of the Quayside Village cohousing community in North Vancouver, Canada, created a gray water recycling system that allows the water recycled from sinks, bathtubs, and laundry machines to be recovered, treated, and redistributed to toilets within the building. In order to do so, they had to work closely with city planners and staff from the city's department of public health in order to get an exception from existing building codes, which prohibit any connections between potable and nonpotable water. Some city staff were resistant to the project, questioning the validity of an urban gray water system when the buildings were already receiving services through the municipal infrastructure. Others doubted whether the system could meet health requirements and were concerned about the liability risks involved in gray water recycling stemming from possible water-related illnesses. Conservative municipal responses to the system resulted in minimal allowances and design problems. Restrictions and limitations on what the system was allowed to do resulted in a system that is "overdesigned" for what it is permitted to accomplish—the group was only able to reuse treated gray water in the toilets, although they had initially wanted to reuse the treated water for toilets, bathtubs, and gardening. To satisfy city staff concerns about safety, the group contracted with a consulting company to monitor the system and sample the water each week to ensure its safety; additionally, they were required to add chlorine to the captured gray water, which was not necessary for toilet use. The case illustrates how important it is for city planners and other urban authorities to be informed about alternative approaches and technologies that can be used to reduce water use, increase efficiency, and reduce the flow of toxic chemicals into the water supply. Working with staff who responded skeptically and conservatively to the proposed system led to minimal allowances, an overbuilt system, and chlorine added to the water when it was almost certainly unnecessary to do so for toilet use only.

Source: www.betterbuildings.ca

Rainwater Catchment Systems

Rainwater catchment systems (also known as *rainwater harvesting systems*) collect rainwater on a catchment surface, usually on the roof of single-family homes or small buildings, and then divert it, usually through pipes, to an impermeable storage container for future use. Rainwater catchment systems provide urban planners with an excellent opportunity to reduce water use and to use water more efficiently by capturing runoff. Though they are not useful in all geographic areas, rainwater catchment systems can save water wherever they are used.

Rainwater harvesting is used in many different ways. In some parts of the world, it is used to capture just enough water during a storm to save a trip or two to the main water source. In this case, only a small storage capacity is required, and a few small pots can be used to store enough water for a day or half day. In more arid areas, storage collection systems are designed to hold larger amounts of rain water. In dry regions with little annual rainfall, rainwater catchment systems can be designed to supplement a municipal water supply. The more water collected and stored locally, the less water diverted from a distant river or lake supply, resulting in less natural habitat destruction and less natural resource depletion. Not only does collecting water conserve water, it also lessens local erosion and flooding caused by runoff from impervious cover such as pavement and roofs. Storm water runoff, the normal consequence of rainfall, becomes captured rainfall, which can fulfill a number of production uses (Texas Water Development Board 2002). In industrialized countries, rainwater can be stored and used for backyard watering. In some urban areas, rainwater can be of higher quality than ground or surface water. When collected from a roof, rain water does not come into contact with soil or rocks, where it dissolves salts and minerals and picks up pollutants discharged from surface waters such as rivers. Rain water is also free from hard water deposits, reducing the need for a water softener and extending the life of water heaters and piping systems. When resources are available, sophisticated rainwater catchment systems can be constructed to incorporate pumping systems and be hooked up to a municipal plumbing network. When resources are lacking, the catchment surface can be as simple as a piece of cloth or plastic sheet tied at its corners to four poles and then pulled tightly over a storage pot.

Large or small, rainwater catchment systems are typically comprised of six basic components: a catchment area, gutters and downspouts, leaf screens and roof-washer systems, cisterns or storage tanks, conveying, and water treatment. The catchment area is the surface on which the rain that will be collected falls. While roofs are most common, channeled gullies along driveways or swales in yards can also be used to catch rain, collecting and then directing the rain to a french drain or bermed detention area. Catchment surfaces along the ground should only be used for non-human consumption, since contact with the ground increases the risk of contamination. The roofs of buildings are ideal for in-home water use collection systems; in rural areas this can include outdoor buildings such as barns and sheds called rain barns. *Rain barns* are typically open-sided sheds designed with a large roof area for catchment and cisterns placed inside the barn along with other farm implements. Gutters and downspouts are used to catch the rain from the roof catchment system and transport it to a cistern or containment system. To minimize bacterial contamination from debris, animal droppings, and insects that enter the tank, gutters and downspouts must be cleaned regularly. To prevent leaves and other debris from cluttering the system, gutters should have a leaf screen, ideally made of quarter-inch wire mesh in a metal frame installed along the entire length of the gutter and a screen or wire basket at the head of the downspout. Some systems incorporate first flush (or roof-washing) systems, which divert dirty water containing roof debris away from the cistern or storage tank. *Roof-washing* refers to the collection and disposal of the first flush of water from a roof when the water is to be used for human consumption; the first flush picks up most of the dirt, debris, and contaminants, such as bird droppings, that have collected on the roof and in the gutters during dry periods. Rather than wasting this first flush, the water can be used for nonpotable uses such as irrigation. Cisterns located close to the water supply and demand points are the most efficient. To facilitate the use of gravity (and lower stress on a pump), the cistern should be placed on the highest level that is workable. A shaded area is best, since direct sunlight will heat the stored water supply and encourage algae and bacterial growth. When resources are available, pumps can be used to take water to more distant areas, including uphill areas. Some type of water treatment is preferable when water is to be used for cooking, drinking, and bathing; this can be accomplished by using a cartridge sediment filter which traps and removes particles of five microns or larger (Texas Water Development Board 2002).

Green roofs are another type of rainwater catchment system that could be employed in urbanized areas to save water and to facilitate sustainable storm water management. *Green roofs* have a soil layer on which vegetation is planted. They reduce urban runoff and preserve the hydrological balance by returning water to the atmosphere through evapotranspiration, and as the excess water percolates through the soil layer, water is directed into a cistern for other uses. When the water percolates through the soil, natural treatment occurs. Green roofs help with stormwater management and improve energy efficiency by prohibiting excessive heat gain or loss. They also enhance urban ecology, prevent pollution and sedimentation of nearby waterways, and provide shade and aesthetic benefits.

Another strategy for capturing and conserving water is the use of *rain gardens*, which are landscaped depressions that retain and treat storm water while recharging groundwater supplies. Rain gardens collect storm water runoff and allow infiltration into soils so that groundwater is replenished, replicating natural conditions. They contribute

Rainwater Catchment Systems

Rainwater technologies are especially appropriate for cities located in regions that have alternating rainy and dry seasons and that experience flooding and/or have restricted local water supply and water shortages. The municipality of Sumida, Japan, introduced rainwater management strategies to address water shortages and problems related to flooding. After conducting a study that showed that rain water was safe for nondrinking purposes and could be used for drinking if sterilized, rainwater utilization was incorporated into the city's operations and also recommended for private institutions. The city encouraged rainwater management measures for both households and government institutions.

Rain water is collected on roofs and then directed to below-ground storage tanks through a net, basket, or precipitation box to prevent dirt and other debris from getting into the tank. To increase pressure, the water is then pumped to a delivery tank located on the roof or on a higher level floor and then directed to a pumping system. Typically, stored rain water is used to supply water for toilets, but the city has also installed community-level rainwater collection systems to provide water for firefighting and drinking in case of emergency. During the dry season, rainwater users are encouraged to connect to the municipal water system. Rainwater catchment technologies are relatively simple, inexpensive, and highly transferable. In Sumida, savings on city water fees allowed households and businesses to recover infrastructure investment costs within ten years. Public education campaigns were necessary to make local residents and businesses aware of the technology and its potential benefits and long-term financial savings.

Source: International Council for Local Environmental Initiatives 1999

aesthetic benefits to cities and perform critical ecological functions such as flood control.

Ecological Wastewater Treatment Strategies

Conventional wastewater treatment utilizes technological, chemical-based processes that treat water with chemicals to kill pathogens and bacteria with little or no recycling of the water. In contrast, *ecological wastewater treatment systems* mimic natural wetland systems, which gradually detoxify and purify wastewater using natural processes and systems to remove sediment, metals, nutrients, pesticides, etc. as the water flows through wetland vegetation. Other pollutants such as nutrients and pesticides are partially extracted as the water percolates through wetland soils" (Waterwise 1995, 1).

Throughout time, natural wetlands have purified water and functioned as natural wastewater treatment systems for pollutants from sources ranging from rainfall runoff in forested areas to intentional discharges of household sewage. Wetland functions include water purification, flood water storage, flooding reduction, erosion control, sediment stabilization, sediment retention, groundwater recharge and discharge, nutrient removal and retention, food chain support, chemical and nutrient absorption, fish and wildlife habitat, migratory waterfowl habitat and usage, recreation, heritage value, and natural water purification. The ability of wetlands to transform and store organic matter and nutrients has resulted in wetlands being described as "the kidneys of the landscape" (Mitsh and Gosselink 1993).

Constructed wetlands treatment systems are ecosystems constructed by humans that are designed to imitate natures processes ranging from the creation of a marsh in a natural setting to the extensive construction of a wetland involving the movement of large amounts of soil and the addition of impermeable barriers (Corbitt and Bowen 1994). Constructed wetlands are designed and engineered to control hydrology, configuration, substrate, and vegetation to utilize the same treatment mechanisms that exist in natural wetlands. The hydraulics and loading rates are managed to maximize naturally occurring physical, chemical, and biological processes to treat wastewater (www.soil.ncsu.edu).

Surface flow wetlands are similar to natural marshes through which water flows at low velocities above and within a substrate of shallow channels and basins. Free water surface systems are the more commonly used systems and are easy to identify as the system consists basically of a shallow basin and means of transporting water to it. This is the closest replica of the natural wetlands system, where water is flowing over vegetation and soil. *Subsurface flow wetlands* are designed to flow underneath the ground through usually rock, sand, gravel, soil, roots, and/or vegetation of one to three feet in depth. Typically wastewater flows horizontally through a substrate of soil, sand, gravel bed, rock, or artificial media which is planted with aquatic plants. Purification occurs during contact with the surface of the media and plant rhizospheres. Subsurface flow wetlands are particularly suited to cold weather applications (Wallace 2001).

Constructed wetlands were developed about forty years ago to take advantage of the biodegradation ability of aquatic plants. They are designed to be both functional and beautiful, as well as provide beneficial habitat for wildlife. In addition to treating wastewater, constructed wetlands can treat urban and highway runoff (Shutes 2001). Although they do not function as efficiently as natural wetlands and can never replace the value of an existing wetland, constructed wetlands have the capacity to function as water treatment systems and are excellent alternatives or complements to conventional wastewater treatment plants that "depend on the use of chemicals and costly mechanical devices to coagulate, skim off, or settle out impurities in the water that subsequently must be disposed of through burial or incineration" (Lerner 1997, 48).

Constructed wetland wastewater treatment systems are relatively easy to operate and maintain and are ecologically friendly, cost-effective systems that have the ability to extract toxic materials from water and have many advantages. When compared to industrial systems, they are extremely energy-efficient. They are appropriate for both small communities and as final stage treatment systems in large municipal systems. They provide a beneficial habitat for a variety of wildlife. Wetland systems provide wastewater treatment by significantly reducing oxygen-demanding substances, suspended substances, nutrients, and other pollutants, such as heavy metals. Wetland plants provide support to algae and bacteria that provide wastewater treatment capability in a created wetland environment. There are more than five hundred constructed wetlands successfully functioning to treat municipal and industrial wastewaters in Denmark, Austria, Saudi Arabia, Italy, Thailand, Hungary, Brazil, Mexico, Finland, the United States, and many other countries (Juwarkar et al. 1995).

Constructed Wetland System Treating Leachate from Landfill

A constructed wetland and prairie in Des Moines, Iowa, U.S., is being used to naturally treat leachate produced from an urban landfill site. Previous to setting up the wetland, the state was treating its landfill's leachate by hauling it to local wastewater treatment plants. The process was environmentally risky and cost the metropolitan waste authority about $250,000 each year. To eliminate offsite hauling and reduce operating costs, urban authorities constructed a wetland that has the capacity to handle approximately 4.4 million gallons of wastewater each year. The project is projected to save the government more than $5 million over thirty years. The constructed wetland uses a piping system that sits under the buried waste in the landfill to collect the leachate and pump it through a series of wetland areas called cells. Each cell contains a combination of plants that have the capacity to naturally remove contaminants in the wastewater. After purification, the effluence is sprayed onto 4.5 acres of constructed prairie, where prairie plants complete the purification process and then return the water back to the environment through a combination of evaporation and transpiration (the release of water vapors by plants). The wetlands facility does not result in any releases of the treated leachate into surface or groundwater.

Source: Rasmussen 2000

Cycling wastewater through ponds and wetlands goes back to ancient Chinese integrated farm systems wherein pond systems were used to detoxify water. Today, intensive indoor technological versions of these ancient systems are being designed to cycle wastewater through a series of natural processes that use constructed food webs to gradually detoxify and purify wastewater (Todd 1997). This ecological technology (frequently referred to as a *living machine*) allows natural systems that use tanks, biofilters, and greenhouses filled with bacteria, algae, plants, and fish to purify contaminated water. After flowing through the food web system, the resulting water is pure enough to discharge directly into rivers or to be recycled (Lerner 1997).

A *living machine* is a human-made biological system consisting of a series of reactors housed in high-density polyethylene tanks (Todd and Josephson 1996). Each reactor has a different ecological environment designed for a specific treatment purpose. The system can be structured to process thousands of gallons of wastewater each day, purifying the water as it flows through a series of tanks and filters. As wastewater moves through tanks and filters, living organisms digest and reduce pathogens in the water (Riggle and Gray 1999). The best plants and organisms for the system have a very rapid growth cycle. After going through a series of tanks, purified water will eventually flow outside of the tanks into a constructed wetland or pond. The ecological diversity in a living machine used to purify wastewater typically includes plants, aquatic insects, snails, aquatic worms, and other flora and fauna (Todd and Josephson 1996).

A living machine operating at a private school in upstate New York processes 6,500 gallons of wastewater per day generated from the dormitories, faculty residences, classroom buildings, and school kitchen (Riggle and Gray 1999). "Wastewater flows into a 12,000 gallon underground anaerobic reactor before being pumped into a greenhouse's closed anaerobic reactor where it is rapidly oxygenated. The effluent then flows through a series of five open-aerated reactors planted with tropical vegetation that thrives in saturated conditions. . . . The liquid then moves into a settling tank where consolidated biosolids drop to the bottom before the water flows through two lava rock tanks and moves through a constructed wetland to a fish pond, where its cleanliness is demonstrated; the water is then returned to the watershed" (Riggle and Gray 1999, 41).

Floating Living Machine

A biotechnology and engineering firm in Budapest, Hungary, created an innovative living machine to treat raw sewage generated by urban residents. Designed as a floating arboretum located on a 176-foot, 500-ton capacity gravel barge, this floating living machine is designed to treat 8,825 cubic feet of raw sewage daily. The floating greenhouse consists of polycarbonate panels set in galvanized steel trusses that hold thousands of plants, bacteria, microorganisms, zooplankton, snails, clams, crabs, and fish in an enclosed, sunlit managed environment designed to break down and digest organic pollutants in municipal and industrial wastewater. Though living machines have the capacity to function as permanent sewage purification systems, at this time, urban authorities in Budapest plan to use the floating living machine only as a backup system when permanent facilities on land are not available.

Source: Kovac 2000

Indoor and Outdoor Living Machine Wastewater Treatment Systems

Indoor: The Adam Joseph Lewis Center is a 14,000-square foot building built to house the Environmental Studies Program at Oberlin College's 2,600-student liberal arts university located in Ohio, U.S. A living machine was created to recycle the building's daily wastewater. The Lewis Center living machine takes waste from the restroom toilets and puts it through an anaerobic digester that settles out fats and solids. Anaerobic bacteria microbes convert wastes into ammonia, methane, and organic acids. Water then flows into a closed aerobic reaction that uses aquarium pumps and diffusers to aerate the wastewater, reducing the remaining amount of organic material by 90 percent. Open aerobic tanks that include plants like papyrus, calla lilies, and willows root provide habitat for protozoan and microinvertebrates that eat the bacteria and pathogens in the wastewater. Sludge formed by bacteria is returned to the closed aerobic tanks, where a spillway sends the purified water into a constructed wetland stocked with plants similar to those found in the open aerobic tanks. Additional protozoan and microinvertebrates in the wetlands further cleanse the water, after which time an ultraviolet disinfection unit eliminates any remaining pathogens, and the water is collected into a pressurized holding tank that recycles the purified water back into the building's toilets and urinals.

Source: Barista 2001

Outdoor: The state of Vermont has installed a wastewater treatment system at its busiest interstate highway rest area that serves over 500,000 people a year. The living machine uses a series of tanks containing plants and other organisms to naturally clean wastewater. The cost of a conventional system would have exceeded over a million dollars, compared to the living machine technology which cost only $250,000 to install. Another advantage is that the living machine can easily be moved and used at another location. Sewage from the rest area is treated in a biological system and then recycled back into the toilets to be used as flush water. The system uses a series of reactors in high-density polyethylene tanks, each of which has a different ecological environment designed for a specific treatment purpose. The system uses plants, aquatic insects, snails, aquatic worms, and other flora and fauna. The first treatment tanks are closed aerobic reactors that function to remove odors from the wastewater and metabolize the organic material as microbes consume the waste in the water. Aerators bubble air through the tanks, keeping their content mixed and providing oxygen for waste-eating microorganisms. After that, the water flows through four open aerobic reactors, where they move through an ecosystem of vegetation and microbes. They then travel to another tank where the microbial communities are separated from the treated water; the remaining biological solids settle and are then pumped back into the septic tank for further digestion. The wastewater is then circulated though different habitats that remove organic material and nutrients. This water is then disinfected with a hypochlorine solution that destroys pathogens. In the final step, the water is dechlorinated and the reclaimed water is pumped into a holding tank to be reused in the rest area's flush toilets. The system can handle visits from up to 4,300 visitors per day.

Source: Farrell et al. 2000

Recognizing the True Cost of Water

In many cities around the world, government water subsidies support agribusiness and manufacturing by keeping water prices artificially low. By artificially lowering the true cost of water, subsidies discourage growers and manufacturers from implementing water conservation measures and using water efficiently. Public policy measures that reduce and eliminate water subsidies must be passed in order to encourage water conservation. Institutionalizing policies that would result in large users paying more of the true cost of water would motivate manufacturers and small businesses to begin to utilize processes and technologies that use water more efficiently.

Agriculture profoundly impacts water supply and quality. The impact of taking water away from agriculture in order to increase water supply to urban populations is not well understood, but it is clear that a two-tiered management strategy needs to be developed. First, strategies must be implemented to reduce inefficient water use in the agricultural sector. Second, measures must be taken to increase water efficiency in urban areas at both the household and industrial levels (Postel 2000).

Farmers in California pay about 1/100th of the price that the state's urban residents pay for water. Consequently, they have little incentive to use water efficiently. A government official in the state noted that because water is so cheap, farmers use primitive irrigation techniques, typically flood irrigation, that often pour so much water on the crop that the evaporation alone makes the air humid (Merline 1993). Additionally, water-logged soil eventually evaporates, which can leave a higher concentration of salts in the soil, diminishing or completely destroying its productivity.

During periods of drought, price distortions stemming from water subsidies lead to overuse of water by growers and shortages of water for urban residents (Okun 1992). Irrigation has become so integral to agricultural sectors throughout the world that it is frequently used to grow crops whose value is considerably less than the value of the water required for the crops' production. This is possible only because irrigation and water use on the whole are heavily subsidized and inefficiently used. Reducing water subsidies would encourage agribusiness to reduce the use of water for low-value, high-water using crops such as cotton, sugar, and rice, making more water available for urban use (Okun 1992). After conducting a study on water allocation in the state, the Bay Area Economic Forum in San Francisco concluded that California's water problem is not a problem of supply but of poor allocation and recommended a move towards greater reliance on market prices for water to solve water allocation problems (Merline 1993).

Reducing water used in agriculture will result in more water available to support growing urban populations. A range of farming practices and agricultural technologies exist to increase irrigation efficiency. In "Re-designing Irrigated Agriculture," Sandra Postel concludes that drip irrigation ranks near the top of measures with substantial untapped potential to reduce water usage (2000). *Drip irrigation* consists of a network of plastic tubing perforated with holes that direct the water as close to the plant as possible that is installed on or below the soil surface, sending water directly to the root of individual plants. In contrast to a flooded field, which allows a large amount of water to evaporate without benefit of a crop, drip irrigation has almost no evaporation losses. When combined with soil moisture monitoring, drip irrigation can achieve efficiencies as high as 95 percent. Because it maintains a nearly ideal moisture environment for the plants, drip irrigation also usually increases crop yield and quality. Studies conducted in India, Israel, Jordan, Spain, and the United States have consistently shown that drip irrigation cuts water use between 30 percent and 70 percent and increases crop yields by 20 percent to 90 percent, often doubling water productivity (Postel 2000). Other farming practices that are suitable to arid environments include dryland farming, hydroponic farming which can use recycled water, and desert greenhouses.

Treadle Pump Irrigation Device

One irrigation technology custom designed for small plots and affordable for small-scale farmers is the treadle pump, an irrigation device used in Bangladesh. This human-powered irrigation machine resembles an exercise Stairmaster and is operated in much the same way. Grasping a horizontal arm on a bamboo frame, the farmer pedals up and down on two long poles (treadles). On the upward stroke, groundwater is sucked up into a pair of cylinders while water from the previous stroke is expelled directly into a field channel. How much water is pumped per hour depends on the distance to the water table, the diameter of the pump cylinders, and the energy expended by the user. Typically, the pump can lift water up to six meters below the surface, irrigating about half an acre. The machine costs about $35 to install, and net returns average more than $100 per pump, so farmers make good on their investment in less than a year.

Source: Postel 2000

Summary

This chapter on urban water management outlines the problems stemming from unsustainable water planning, collection, and management related to urban settlements and to industrial and agricultural processes that place severe strains on existing water resources and environmental protection capacities in urban areas. Current water usage in most cities is unsustainable for many reasons. Too much fresh water of high quality is taken from the ecosystem. The supply of good-quality surface and underground water is being contaminated. Water resources are not distributed equitably, forcing some people to use their already limited incomes to purchase water. Poor management threatens the quality and availability of water supply. Competition for fresh water has increased between cities and farms, neighboring states, provinces, cities, and nations. Underground freshwater sources are rapidly being depleted.

The goal of sustainable water management is to ensure that adequate supplies of water of good quality are maintained for the entire human population while preserving the hydrological, biological, and chemical functions of ecosystems. To move this goal forward will require the integration of water reuse technologies, conservation, waste minimization planning, and the implementation of policies that reduce the use of freshwater resources across all sectors.

Strategies include capturing and reusing gray water, using wetlands and living machines to purify wastewater, recognizing the true cost of water and reducing water subsidies, and reducing inefficient water usage in agricultural irrigation in order to provide more water to increasing populations in urban areas. Inefficiency and overuse of water in wealthy, industrialized countries must be addressed immediately. Developing countries must be assisted to develop an infrastructure that provides clean water for all urban residents but is based on a commitment to utilize sustainable water management strategies to deliver adequate water supply to the entire population. The soft path for water provides a very promising framework for developing and implementing a plan that meets these objectives.

Chapter Questions

The chapter provides readers with information to address seven essential questions related to planning for sustainable urban water quality, supply, and management.

1. What problems arise from unsustainable urban water management?

2. What problems have been identified as a result of the privatization of water?

3. Why is it important for industrial countries to use water more
conservatively and efficiently?

4. How do gray water and rainwater systems function?

5. What water management systems and technologies are available
to deal with wastewater using biological treatment systems?

6. What are the differences between the soft path and hard path
for water?

7. What would a sustainable water management strategy look
like?

Notes

1. In the absence of human intervention, rain precipitation hits the ground as
rainfall, penetrates the soil, flows on soil surface, or evaporates according to natural patterns. Under different ecological conditions, water is absorbed differently.
In forests, water filters directly into the soil, where it may be stored in the soil,
travel to an underground aquifer, be absorbed by plants that later return it to the
atmosphere through transpiration, or be discharged to nearby streams. There is
relatively little runoff in forest ecosystems. In desert areas, where there are fewer
plants to hold water and the soil has less water retention capabilities, there is a lot
of runoff. On flood plains, the amount of water entering aquifers can be great, but
at the same time, evaporation can be significant in closed or semiclosed basin areas. In subhumid grasslands, the hydrological cycle behaves in an intermediate
manner (Anton 1993).

2. An analysis of water stress and water scarcity conducted by Falkenmark
used estimates of a nation's renewable freshwater supplies (not including water
withdrawn from fossil groundwater) to develop an estimate of a minimum need
of one hundred liters per day per person for household use and from five to
twenty times as much for agricultural and industrial uses (1998). These estimates

are widely accepted and used by hydrologists, international lending associations, and other organizations. A nation is facing *water stress* when annual water supplies drop below 1,700 cubic meters per person. Periodic water shortages are expected when levels are between 1,700 and 1,000 cubic meters per person. When annual water supplies drop below 1,000 cubic meters per person, a nation is experiencing *water scarcity*. Chronic shortages of fresh water limit food production, industrial activities, and urban infrastructure management and damage ecosystems. As of 1995, thirty-one nations, with a combined population of 458 million, faced either water stress or water scarcity. United Nations calculations project severe increases in both water stress and water scarcity around the world; by 2025 more than 2.8 billion people living in forty-eight nations will face water stress or water scarcity (Falkenmark 1998).

CHAPTER TWO

URBAN SOLID WASTE DISPOSAL, COLLECTION, AND MANAGEMENT

The challenge is to redesign the materials economy so that it is compatible with the ecosystem. This initiative has several components. It includes designing products so that they can be easily disassembled and recycled, redesigning industrial processes to eliminate waste generation, banning the use of throw-away beverage containers, using government purchases to expand the market for recycled materials, developing and using technologies that require less materials, banning gold mining or at least its use of cyanide solution and mercury, adopting a landfill tax, and eliminating subsidies for environmentally destructive activities.

—Lester Brown, *Eco-Economy: Building an Economy for the Earth*,
Earth Policy Institute, 2001

Solid Waste

W *aste* is an inherent and inevitable feature of human society, part of the cycle of eating, producing, working, playing, and consuming. Waste is the unwanted material intentionally thrown away for disposal (World Bank 1999). Substitute words for *waste* include squander, fritter away, throw away, litter, and misuse. This last word, *misuse*, provides an important insight about waste—what is considered waste in one context may not be viewed as waste in a different context. I view the vegetable castings thrown into the garbage by my neighbor as valuable contributors to my compost pile. In Metro Manila, the Philippine Business for the Environment runs a program in which shrimp heads generated as waste by shrimp exporters are being used as raw materials by animal feed milling companies. A program in Italy utilizes urban agricultural food industry wastes, in this case the leftovers from citrus fruits and the residuals of sugar-beet processing and abundant seaweed, to make ecological, recyclable, and biodegradable paper. In each of these examples, what is viewed as waste in one context becomes a *material resource* in another. As the saying goes, one person's trash is another person's treasure.

Solid waste is a category of waste that includes all the materials that get thrown away by people, businesses, industries, institutions, and governments. It includes *organic* waste materials, composed primarily of biodegradable materials (i.e., food, human and animal matter, paper, and wood) and *inorganic* waste materials, composed largely or completely of nonbiodegradable material.

For centuries, people threw their waste into the streets for animals to eat or dumped it into areas in close proximity to where it was produced—in streams, ravines, abandoned quarry sites, natural depressions, open pits, streets, rivers, oceans, and vacant land use areas. This waste disposal system functioned for three reasons: (1) local populations were small; (2) most products were reused, which meant little waste was produced overall; and (3) the vast majority of waste generated was composed of organic matter that decomposed rapidly in the open air. Over time, social changes, technological advances, and business practices have increasingly promoted development strategies and economies based on the extraction, processing, consumption, and disposal of tremendous quantities of materials (Gardner and Sampat 1999). Fundamental processes associated with urbanization and industrialization have been developed with little concern for their environmental effects, resulting in governments, industries, businesses, and consumers generating greater amounts of waste, increasing amounts of which are inorganic and toxic. As these changes occurred, new products were developed that generated more waste and changed the composition of the solid waste stream. Currently, the solid waste stream includes huge amounts of inorganic materials— plastics, metals, glass, synthetic materials, large "white" goods like refrigerators and stoves and computers, "brown goods" like tires and batteries, and immense quantities of toxic materials that are harmful to humans and the environment.

The type and quantity of waste generated in a particular urban area is determined by many factors, including population density, economic prosperity, differences in fuel sources, variations in diet, climatic differences, cultural practices, and differences in manufacturing production and processing activities. Among these factors, economic prosperity (typically measured by per capita income) is among the most salient. One of the negative characteristics of increased affluence is that it almost always brings more waste (World Bank 1999). As nations and cities become wealthier and more urbanized, and people become more affluent and consumption-oriented, more solid waste is produced and thrown away, the composition of the solid waste stream increases and changes, and waste becomes more toxic. Wealthy communities create throwaway cultures as utilization of paper, paper packaging, plastics, rubber, metals, multimaterial items, consumer products, and related packaging materials accumulate due to increased use of newspapers, magazines, fast-service restaurants, single-serving beverages, disposable diapers, packaged foods, electronics, and thousands of other mass-produced products. The waste stream becomes larger and increasingly composed of materials that are harmful to human health and the environment and take centuries to break down.

An analysis of the quantity and composition of municipal solid waste in Canada, Denmark, Germany, Netherlands, Sweden, United States, and Japan reveals that the waste stream in wealthy industrialized countries is composed primarily of paper, packaging, metals, plastics, glass, and organic materials (Sakai et al. 1996). Although prosperous, industrialized countries contain only 16 percent of the world's population, they consume about 75 percent of the world's paper supply. In 2001 people in the United States, who make up less than five percent of world population, threw out 232 millions tons of paper, glass, plastic, wood, food, metal, clothing, electronics, and other rubbish, equivalent to about 4.5 pounds of waste per person each day (Rogers and Parenti 2002).

Quantity of Solid Waste Produced in the United States

- About 2.5 million plastic bottles are used every hour; only a small percentage are recycled.

- Enough iron and steel is thrown away to continuously supply all the nation's automakers.

- Every week more than 500,000 trees are used to produce newspapers in the U.S.; two thirds of these newspapers are never recycled.

- Enough office and writing paper is discarded annually to build a wall twelve feet high stretching from Los Angeles to New York City.

- At least half of all the paper circulating each day ends up in a landfill.

- About 95 percent of solid waste is disposed in almost bursting landfills; one out of every two of these landfills is leaching.

- Every year, households dispose about 24 million tons of leaves and grass clippings which could be used in composting, thereby conserving precious landfill space and contributing to soil fertility.

- In the 1990s, more than thirteen times more virgin plastic packaging was produced than was recycled.

Source: Black Rhinoceros 2002

Low-income countries have less to throw away and are more likely to reuse, recycle, and refurbish goods that wealthier nations and communities would discard. In resource-scarce cities, all kinds of "wastes" are utilized by small and large businesses and industries and by low-income residents (Furedy 1992). Developing countries utilize far less paper and plastics related to packaging materials than industrialized nations, and those that exist are much more likely to be reused (Blight and Mbande 1996). India, Indonesia, and China are three of the world's four most populous countries but among the lowest consumers of paper per capita (Blight and Mbande 1996). Wastes that are not utilized by the people or institutions that generate them are collected by waste pickers, waste buyers, small waste shops, second-hand markets, waste dealers, waste transporters, and recycling industries who sell them to those who find them useful (Furedy 1992).

Yet despite the fact that people in developing countries generate less waste, cities in developing nations face severe waste accumulation problems due to rapid increases in population, urban density, and changes in consumer behavior. Managing and disposing solid waste has become one of the most serious problems facing municipal authorities in developing nations. The scale of urbanization does not seem to make that much difference; small cities are suffering from waste accumulation just as much as large cities (Drakakis-Smith 1995). The problem is primarily the result of two factors: first, immense amounts of solid waste are accumulating in urban areas, and second, the solid waste stream increasingly includes toxic materials, which contribute to environmental and public health problems when they leach into ground and surface water or are released into the atmosphere.

Environmental and Social Impacts of Conventional Solid Waste Disposal Approaches

Despite the fact that cities throughout the world differ in the number of resources they have available for waste management, urban authorities throughout the world confront the growing municipal solid waste problem in their jurisdictions using an identical waste management paradigm composed of two components: bury and burn. The paradigm is focused around five waste management approaches: open pit dumping, landfill dumping, open pit burning, landfill burning, and incineration. Planners promote all five approaches as waste reduction solutions, but in fact each of these approaches creates severe environmental and social problems. In every country around the world, the municipal solid waste stream increasingly includes inorganic and toxic materials. These include household waste; street litter; commercial refuse (including food waste); abandoned vehicle parts; synthetic materials such as plastics, papers, inks, fabrics, dyes, cellulose materials, tires, metals, glass; and many other organic and inorganic solid materials. When buried or burned, these materials release toxins into the air, ground, and water and create problems for the communities located closest to them as well as those more distant. Problems include millions of tons of garbage being transported each year to distant landfills (spreading pollution far outside the areas where it originates, raising health concerns, costing tax payers billions of dollars, and increasing environmental degradation related to transport); water, soil, and air contamination production of greenhouse gases which contribute to global warming; billions of public dollars spent to build bury-and-burn facilities that do not adequately resolve waste accumulation problems; discouraging and stifling planning and policy efforts to reduce waste at the source of production; and decreasing the amount of waste that could be diverted through reuse and recycling strategies and programs.

Open Pit Dumping and Burning

In a book entitled *The Waste Crisis: Landfills, Incinerators, and the Search for a Sustainable Future,* H. Tammemagi writes about early waste management systems: "The first recorded regulations to control municipal waste were implemented during the Minoan civilization, which flourished in Crete from 3000 to 1000 B.C. Solid wastes from the capital, Knossos, were placed in large pits and covered with layers of earth at intervals. This basic method . . . has remained relatively unchanged right up to the present day. The first garbage collection service was established during the period of the Roman Empire. Householders tossed their refuse into the streets, and then it was shoveled onto horse-drawn carts and transported to an open pit, often located within the community" (Tammemagi 1999, 19–20).

Open pits are small or large authorized or illegal spatial areas where residents, businesses, and institutions regularly dump their waste. Most open pits are initially formed by spontaneous, haphazard dumping that takes place without the permission of local authorities as garbage begins to accumulate in neighborhood and business districts. Consequently, open pits are typically located in close proximity to where waste is produced. As urban populations grow in size, increase in population, and become more affluent, waste problems increase and planners respond by more formally regulating the areas that can be used for open pit dumping. While open pits function to remove waste from its source and store it for long periods of time at a specific site, there are many social and environmental problems associated with open pit dumping. Open pits quickly become home to rodents and insects that carry public health diseases. As waste decomposes, open pits generate bad odors. When the wind blows, waste in an open pit is carried into outlying areas. As waste runoff leaches into the ground, it contaminates local water supplies.

In order to reduce the volume of waste that accumulates in open pits, the garbage is frequently set on fire, resulting in air emissions that contribute

Burn and Bury: The Story of Tires

In 1988 the United States sold 320 million tires to Japan, France, West Germany, and the U.K. and produced 209.5 million new car tires, 42.7 million new truck tires, and 19 million new off-road tires. Of these, only 30 percent will be retreaded; the rest will be sent to dumps or landfills, used to make asphalt for roads, or chipped and burned as boiler fuel, a practice which produces huge quantities of carcinogenic air emissions (i.e., dioxins, furans, and benzene). When heated in the absence of oxygen, as happens in a tire dump fire, tires produce vast quantities of oil (more than a gallon per tire), accompanied by huge volumes of thick black smoke. Tire dump fires are extremely polluting, affecting both air and water quality. A licensed dump of ten million tires burned for several months in Wales, U.K. A 1990 fire in Ontario, Canada, resulted in flames seventy meters high rising from a dump of 14 million tires. Serious tire fires are common in the United States.

Source: Greenpeace 1995

to serious environmental and public health problems. The authors of a 1997 U.S. Environmental Protection Agency study on the burning of household waste in the open air (in this case, in barrels) concluded that burning the residential waste of 1.5 families in barrels releases an equal amount of dioxins into the environment as a municipal solid waste incinerator burning 200 tons per day (Hassig 2002). In addition to dioxin, the study documented substantial releases of polychlorinated biphenyls (PCBs) and other toxins harmful to human health. In many developing countries, impoverished families living near or in open pits use open pit sites to collect scraps to eat, use, and sell in order to survive; while this contributes to their daily survival, open pits are unhealthy and dangerous environments for children and adults.

Landfills

As cities increase in population and become more industrialized, the composition of the waste stream increases and becomes more toxic. If resources permit, municipalities will transition from open pit dumping and burning to specified landfill sites. *Landfills* are huge, legal dumping areas that provide formal, authorized places to dispose of solid waste. Unlike open pits, landfills are constructed in ways that allow small and large trucks to bring waste into the landfill site as well as allowing for entry of large machinery that is used to compact the waste down over time. The preferred site for a landfill is in a natural depression like a ravine or a quarry. When these cannot be found, a hole is dug into the soil using bulldozers and other machinery. Typically, garbage is dumped into the landfill in sections; as old sections fill up with garbage, new sections are added until the landfill site reaches its holding capacity (Tammemagi 1999).

In areas where land in and near cities is cheap and readily available, most local governments and industries view landfills as the ideal waste management system because they conveniently store solid waste at one large site for long periods of time. The working assumption underlying a landfill is that over time organic (biodegradable) components will break down and inorganic materials will be crushed down by machines, thus reducing volume and, theoretically, allowing for continual use of the landfill site. Based on this (false) assumption, urban authorities in cities throughout the world are dumping billions of tons of waste into a growing number of huge landfill sites located within and on the periphery of their jurisdictions. The Fresh Kill landfill in New York City occupies 2,500 acres (1,000 hectares) and can easily be seen from space.[1]

Though landfills function to remove waste from the source and store it for long periods of time, they are fraught with problems. Landfills take up valuable urban and periurban land areas, and purchasing land and maintaining a landfill drains public coffers of much needed funds to finance urban infrastructure. Throughout the world landfills are becoming filled with increasing amounts of synthetics, including plastics, white goods, and brown goods, most of which are composed of highly toxic materials. Landfills are filled with solid materials, many of which may seem impermeable, but over time these solid materials become saturated with water from rainfall and the toxic materials in them (i.e., heavy metals discarded from batteries) begin to leach into the ground, gradually turning into a contaminated, toxic liquid soup that percolates downward into the ground, polluting underlying soil and groundwater and harming human health (Eighmy and Kosson 1996).

Off-gassing from landfills contributes to atmospheric pollution. As waste decomposes, gases such as methane, carbon dioxide, vinyl chloride, and hydrogen sulfide are created. Over time, these gases gradually make their way into the air surrounding the landfill, contributing to the greenhouse effect and global warming (Tammemagi 1999). The problem of off-gassing stems largely from the release of methane gas, which has a twenty-one times greater impact on global warming than carbon dioxide; landfill methane accounts for about four percent of all greenhouse emissions measured in terms of global warming potential and related climate change.[2] Further, since decomposing waste generates explosive methane gas, it becomes both difficult and expensive for the land on which landfills are located to be reused for future urban development.

Public officials prefer to site landfills away from residential areas and on the periphery of an urban area, but in many cities, landfills are located in close proximity to residential communities, where they are increasingly contaminating local water supplies. Contaminated groundwater typically includes heavy metals including arsenic, chromium, and lead. Some municipalities have tried to deal with this problem by enacting legislation that bans the disposal of hazardous household waste, but in the vast majority of cases, landfills continue to be filled with huge amounts of toxic materials, including mercury and nickel-cadmium batteries, scrap metal, non-biodegradable plastics, inks from printing paper, and so on.

CHAPTER TWO

Public opposition to landfill dumping has increased substantially over the past two decades. Like open pits, landfills are breeding grounds for rats and other rodents, and they smell bad. Although most landfills compact waste, when the wind blows, garbage and litter can be carried into outlying areas in close proximity. Residents become even more opposed as they learn more about landfill leaching contaminating local air and water supply.

In addition to needing landfills to hold solid waste from household and commercial sites, governments and private corporations around the world are increasingly searching for locations in which to dump and store hazardous waste, a signigicant proportion of which is radioactive. In this case, public opposition to waste siting is particularly strong. The case of nuclear waste, generated in uranium mines, nuclear power plants, and research reactors, is illustrative. Like many governments around the world, the government of India needed a new site to store nuclear wastes generated by its vast establishment of nuclear power plants. The government had been dumping the waste into a pond near its main processing facility in Hyderabad until it contaminated nearby wells and residents protested. When confronted with this opposition, the government selected an abandoned gold mine in Karnataka, one of the deepest mines in the world, to store the nuclear waste, but was forced to abandon its plans to store waste there due to the presence of groundwater below the site. The government then chose the desert village of Sanawada, Rajasthan, as an alternative site because the village is located on vast quantities of granite rock that have the heat resistance and hydrological characteristics necessary to withstand the high temperatures of radioactive waste and because there is no identified groundwater source that can be contaminated by hazardous waste. But to the government's dismay, Sanawada residents organized to prevent the opening of what would be India's first official nuclear waste dumping site. So far no country in the world has found a way to safely store deadly radioactive waste. Over time, radioactive waste leaks from the canisters that are designed to hold it, dumping sites are difficult to monitor over long periods of time, and there is no guarantee that the radioactive material will not inadvertently or purposefully harm humans at some future date (Mahapatra 2000).

Sanitary Landfills

In order to deal with increasing public opposition to landfills, engineers designed the sanitary landfill. Defined as "an engineered method of disposing of solid wastes on land," *sanitary landfills* spread waste in thin layers, compact it into the smallest practical volume, and cover it over with soil or ash at the end of each working day to alleviate problems related to rodents, wind-blown refuse, and uncontrolled fires (Tammemagi 1999). Although sanitary landfills reduce landfill problems, they do not eliminate problems related to groundwater or surface water contamination, gas emissions, or unpleasant odors. Although waste management planners claim that landfills prevent leaching due to their being lined with bottom liners, research has shown that liners have service lives of only a few decades (Lechner et al. 2002). New sanitary landfill technologies (such as bottom liners made of clays and liners and caps made of synthetic materials like high-density polyethylene designed to capture leachate and gases) are stronger and can reduce some of these problems, but they do not eliminate them. Significant amounts of toxic and nonbiodegradable synthetic organic substances (i.e., PCBs, pesticides, degreasers, and paint removers) dumped into modern sanitary landfills continue to generate unpleasant odors, look awful, and contaminate local soil and groundwater as they break down and toxins seep through supposedly protective clay and plastic liners into the ground and waterways.

Incineration

As waste accumulates and urban areas run out of open pit and landfill space to bury and burn the millions of tons of garbage their jurisdictions generate each year, and governments are forced to confront the environmental and public health problems stemming from landfills, municipal authorities around the world are facing a waste crisis of huge proportions. In countries like the United States (the country that produces more garbage than any other nation in the world), thousands of landfills are closed each year as they reach capacity or become environmentally harmful. In many areas, new sites cannot be found due to environmental concerns and public opposition (Newsday 1989).

As urban authorities confront the problem of public opposition to landfills, as landfill space becomes increasingly difficult to find as a result of the increasing value and cost of land located within and on the periphery of urban areas, and as garbage continues to accumulate, waste planners and managers are increasingly proposing *solid waste incinerators* as clean, efficient waste disposal systems that reduce municipal solid waste accumulation and are an alternative to unattractive, overflowing landfills that poison water supplies and are increasingly unpopular with local residents. Most waste management planners have become convinced that incinerators should be an important part of their city's waste disposal infrastructure. In jurisdictions that have the resources to build and maintain incinerators, waste planners are increasingly adopting incineration as a primary urban waste management and disposal strategy.

Solid waste incinerators are designed to burn and sterilize waste and reduce the volume of material requiring final disposal. Conventional municipal incinerators can reduce waste volume as much as 80 percent to 95 percent (Tammemagi 1999). Using a technology called *mass burn incineration*, incineration facilities burn unsorted municipal solid waste in high temperature furnaces that produce steam or energy. Although incineration does destroy some toxins, as toxic products burn, toxins are released through the incineration process which produces *fly ash*, fine particles of ash in flue gases produced by burning garbage. Incinerators are a major source of at least 210 different dioxin compounds, plus mercury, cadmium, nitrous oxide, hydrogen chloride, sulfuric acid, fluorides, and particulate matter small enough to lodge permanently in the lungs. Approximately 30 percent of the waste burned in incinerators is converted into toxic fly ash, which typically contains dangerous levels of dioxin, nitrogen oxides, cadmium, lead, and other highly toxic chemicals (Ibanez et al. 2000). The more efficiently the incinerator reduces air emissions, the more toxic the fly ash (Newsday 1989).

A 2001 study of the health impacts of living near incinerators in the Netherlands, published in the international medical journal *The Lancet*, reported that teenagers living near waste incinerators have high levels of toxic chemicals linked to cancer, heart disease, and breathing illnesses in their bodies and, "are bound to have smaller testicles among males, smaller breasts among females and delayed sexual maturation among both sexes than those living in the rural areas" (Health Alert 2001, 1).

In mass burn incineration systems, nothing is sorted; everything goes into the fire and is burned. Materials like glass, aluminum, and iron, which can easily be diverted through recycling and reuse programs, are put into the incinerator even though they do not burn, their presence in incinerators lowers the burning temperature and reduces technological efficiency, and they contribute more toxic materials to the leftover fly ash.

Incinerators do not eliminate waste; they change the form of solid waste into toxic ash and hazardous air emissions, spreading hazardous contamination worldwide, contaminating air, soil, and water, and adding fly ash to a solid waste accumulation problem that has already reached crisis proportions (Africano 2003). After municipal waste is burned, fly ash is hauled away to be buried as solid waste or, increasingly, used as landfill cover in permanent toxic landfill sites. In their desperate attempt to reduce landfill volume, some local governments are allowing toxic incineration ash to be used as landfill cover and in construction materials. Public officials in some parts of the United States allow tons of toxic incinerator ash to be spread under newly surfaced roads and parking lots (Newsday 1989; Africano 2003).

Municipalities are increasingly incinerating medical waste produced by hospitals and other medical and dental facilities. Medical waste is any solid waste generated in the diagnosis, treatment, or immunization of human beings or animals, in related research or in the production or testing of related biological materials and chemicals. Medical waste includes laboratory and pharmaceutical products and chemicals (i.e., alcohols and disinfectants); infectious wastes like contaminated needles and other sharps; human blood, blood products, tissues, body parts, and cultures; paper, plastic, and styrofoam plates, cups, and utensils; and laboratory refuse (Ibanez et al. 2000). Hospitals in countries like the United States routinely burn 75 percent to 100 percent of their waste (Health Care without Harm).

Incinerating medical wastes releases emissions containing atmospheric pollutants and toxic chemicals and often produces extremely unpleasant odors associated with the burning of plastics. The unnecessary burning of polyvinyl chloride plastic, paper, batteries, discarded equipment, and other noninfectious materials leads to emissions of dioxins and mercury, as well as furans, arsenic, lead, cadmium, and the generation of toxic ash. Medical waste incinerators are a leading source of dioxin and mercury pollution in our environment and food supply (Health Care without Harm). In fact, waste incineration (which includes medical waste incineration) is the predominate source of dioxin release, accounting for 60 percent to 90 percent of total dioxin releases worldwide.

The country of Taiwan provides an important example. In Taiwan incineration is becoming a dominant municipal waste treatment method. In addition to 150 small waste incinerators, there are currently nine major waste incinerators operating in Taiwan, with another twelve major waste incinerators scheduled to be constructed. It is estimated that by 2003, more than 90 percent of municipal waste (over nine million metric tons) will be treated through incineration (Hwong-wen et al. 2002). Scientists in the Institute of Environmental Engineering, the Institute for Occupational Medicine, and the College of Public Health in Taiwan studied the anticipated impact of Taiwanese residents consuming food contaminated by dioxin releases from the incinerators. Using various risk exposure methodologies, ranging from eating only food contaminated with dioxin to eating only some food contaminated with dioxin, they concluded that the incinerators would significantly increase cancer risks for the population even when the proportion of food eaten that was contaminated with dioxin was as low as ten percent.

In terms of cost, an investigative report of landfills in the United States revealed that incineration facilities are built by private firms but frequently subsidized by utility ratepayers whose garbage may never even go to the facilities (Newsday 1989). The authors revealed that incinerators are built with little regard for the financial consequences and are opened and operated even though environmental and public health questions related to air emissions and fly ash remain unresolved. Among their most important findings was that energy-generating incinerators strongly discourage waste reduction, recycling, and reuse in local areas. When incineration facilities are designed to generate energy, energy sales become a money-making enterprise for incinerators, and managers are under great pressure from investors to increase profits by burning as much as they can. In these cases, incinerators compete with local and regional recycling efforts because incinerator operators want guarantees that they will get enough garbage (especially paper and plastic, which burn well and provide a lot of energy) to keep their plants operating and producing energy. In some areas, energy-generating incinerators are sold as the *only* solution to waste accumulation, stifling efforts to encourage reduce, recycle, and reuse initiatives and programs (Newsday 1989).

Sustainable Solid Waste Planning and Management

Although bury-and-burn waste management systems and technologies have become more efficient over time, none of the technological advancements associated with bury-and-burn waste management approaches re-solve the environmental, social, economic, and public health problems caused by huge amounts of inorganic and toxic solid waste entering the solid waste stream. Although improving waste collection services and building waste embankments and landfills with sanitary and leaching con-trols reduce some waste problems and would definitely improve the im-mediate situation in many developing countries where these services are badly lacking, fundamentally, bury-and-burn approaches contribute to, rather than resolve, the environmental and social problems associated with urban solid waste accumulation. Although bury-and-burn strategies re-move waste from its source, they are not sufficient or desirable long-term responses to the growing problem of solid waste accumulation in urban ar-eas, especially as the waste stream becomes increasingly composed of in-organic and toxic solid waste. This has been proven in industrialized countries, where despite an extensive and highly technological waste man-agement and disposal infrastructure, the volume of waste generated is too high, the spaces to dispose of it too scarce, and the air and water contam-ination and public health problems stemming from open pit burning, landfills, and incineration too severe (Tammemagi 1999).

Urban authorities must face the fact that there are limits to the num-ber of resources human beings can extract and process in relation to the rate at which the natural environment can absorb the increasingly large amounts of waste being generated by humans, especially in cities. Munic-ipalities must confront the environmental and social problems associated with bury-and-burn waste management strategies and move away from a *waste disposal* mentality, in which waste is buried and burned, and toward a *materials management* mentality, in which waste is reduced, reused, and recycled (Furedy 1992). To do so will require a huge paradigmatic shift for urban planners and for the waste management industry, requiring a flexi-ble and strategically driven waste reduction approach at the household, local authority, business, industry, and government levels (Aspinwall and Cain 1997).

In an article entitled "Garbage: Exploring Non-conventional Options in Asian Cities," Christine Furedy describes this required philosophical shift as moving away from "resource management" and toward "resource recognition" (1992). Sustainable waste management (resource recogni-tion) requires the reduction of waste in production and distribution processes and the enhancement of waste through reuse and recycling based on two fundamental and complementary goals (Furedy 1992). The first goal is to reduce the amount of waste being generated at the source of production and consumption. This goal requires changing the production and consumption patterns of goods and services in order to lower the volume and type of waste generated. Accomplishing this will require deep economic, social, and cultural transformations (Pereira et al. 2000). Reducing the amount of solid wastes entering the waste stream will be accomplished by diverting it through recycle and reuse strategies.

The second goal is to create new uses for waste generated in cities (and other areas) by highlighting particular benefits and uses and reducing the volume of waste to be disposed through recycling and reuse strategies. This second goal will require municipalities and businesses to view waste materials as unused resources. Whereas waste is typically seen as having negative value because it is costly to dispose of, the reuse and recycling of waste products inverts this perception by adding social and economic value to waste through the identification of new markets and the creation of jobs (Pereira et al. 2000). The more waste reused and recycled, the less waste buried and burned. Sustainable waste management approaches and strategies aim to reduce, recycle, and reuse as large a proportion of the solid waste stream as possible.

Creating a Sustainable Materials Economy

In *Eco-Economy: Building an Economy for the Earth*, Lester Brown, president of Earth Policy Institute, describes what it would take to design a *new materials economy*, by which he means an economy that is compatible with the earth's ecosystem (2001). Brown begins by discussing how the concepts of "planned obsolescence" and "throwaway products" were introduced after World War II as a way of promoting economic growth and employment: "The faster things wore out and the sooner they could be thrown away, the faster the economy would grow. For numerous consumer products, year-to-year changes in design became a key to stimulating sales. . . . Throwaway products, facilitated by the appeal to convenience and the artificially low cost of energy, account for much of the garbage we produce each day and an even larger share of the material that ends up in landfill" (Brown 2001, 123–24). As Brown notes, a huge number of contemporary products are explicitly designed to be fully disposable, as in the case with disposable diapers, cups, plates, forks, spoons, knives, beverage and food containers, and cameras. Many more products, such as newspapers, could easily be reused but are designed to be thrown away; tossing newspapers into the garbage essentially functions to convert forests into landfill. According to Brown, designing a new materials economy would require the following core components:

- Redesigning industrial products to eliminate waste generation.

- Designing products to be easily dissembled and recycled.

- Banning one-way beverage containers to reduce materials use in many different sectors including raw materials, energy, transportation, and dramatic reductions in waste going to land-fills.

- Developing and using technologies that require fewer materials and integrating these technologies in developing countries.

- Redesigning urban transport systems to better achieve the so-cial goals of increased individual mobility, clean air, less traffic congestion, and creation of more opportunities for exercise.

- Redesigning manufacturing processes to eliminate the discharge of pollutants.

- Clustering production facilities so that waste from one process can be used as the raw material for another.

- Eliminating subsidies that encourage the use of raw materials.

- Providing market subsidies for recycling.

- Taxing the burning of fossil fuels.

The overarching goal is to shift material economies around the world away from a throwaway mentality and towards a closed loop/recycle mindset. Brown describes how people in many different sectors and locations are getting together to figure out new models of economic activities and infra-structure development and management (2001). One very interesting group organized in France under the name Factor 10 Institute. Factor 10's goal is to increase resource productivity by a factor of ten. They believe this goal is well within the reach of existing technology and management if policy incentives can be put into place to encourage natural resource and waste reductions. Their goal is to reduce materials use by 90 percent, dramatically challenging the traditional assumption that a healthy economy is one that uses increasing amounts of energy, materials, and resources to produce more goods, jobs, and income. To move this goal forward, Factor 10 Institute members developed three recommendations for measures which could be easily implemented by urban authorities: (1) Replace automobiles with bicycles; this would increase mobility in congested cities and lower materials use by more than 90 percent. (2) Ban the use of one-way beverage containers; this would dramatically reduce the flow of garbage to landfills and reduce energy inputs. (3) Increase the longevity of buildings; this would greatly reduce the use of materials and of the energy used in their manufacture.

Materials Management and Resource Recognition

To shift the field of waste management away from the existing waste disposal and resource management paradigm and toward a new materials management and resource recognition paradigm will require urban authorities to work with businesses and industries in their localities to reduce waste by adopting more efficient manufacturing and disposal processes. Incentives to move toward materials management and resource recognition include making more land available for other uses, reducing greenhouse gases, increasing efficiency, improving public health, reducing costs related to the disposal of toxic and hazardous waste, improving environmental quality, and saving money from byproduct opportunities.

Some cities are attempting to change production and consumption patterns and create new utilities for waste by adopting a waste management hierarchy to manage the flow of solid waste; the hierarchy includes prevention/minimization at the top, materials recovery in the middle, and incineration and landfill at the bottom. The overarching goal is to minimize raw material requirements (thus generating less waste) and facilitate the reuse and recycling of materials and products. Planning and policy approaches and strategies to accomplish this goal include (1) pollution prevention/producer responsibility; (2) tax incentives; (3) refund deposit strategies; (4) subsidies and incentives; (5) materials exchange/reprocessing strategies; and (6) reducing household and small business waste output. Each of these approaches is discussed in more detail in the following sections.

Pollution Prevention/Producer Responsibility

The term *pollution prevention* has been introduced within the industrial sector to refer to source reduction strategies and in-process recycling of materials. *Source reduction* refers to waste minimization via input substitution, production reformulation, production process redesign, or modernization. A number of incentives and requirements can be used to promote waste reduction and recycling at the industrial production, manufacturing, and distribution levels. A powerful economic incentive is to require waste generators to pay directly for the full costs of collection, treatment, and disposal of the waste they generate in proportion to the quantity.

The idea of *producer responsibility* has been introduced in the policy arena to encourage pollution prevention approaches. Producer responsibility requires the manufacturers, importers, distributors, and retailers of goods who are responsible for producing the waste to take responsibility for those wastes rather than simply expecting society to pay for waste collection, disposal, and storage.

Germany was the first country in the world to require mandatory recycling for packaging and is widely recognized as the leader in the field of waste management recycling programs. The German Packaging Ordinance, the toughest packaging law in the world, was passed in 1991 in order to reduce the amount of waste going to landfill and incineration. The program sets targets for recycling of packaging waste. The ordinance requires 80 percent of all packaging waste to be collected by product manufacturers. Of these collected materials, 90 percent of glass and metals and 80 percent of paper, cardboard, plastics, and laminates must be recycled. Germany's program encourages retailers to sell products in less packaging and rewards consumers for returning reusable beverage bottles, which are then collected, washed, refilled, and resold by manufacturers. Between 1991 and 1996, individual recycling of paper and plastics had increased to

50 percent and 70 percent for metals and glass (Ueta and Koizumi 2001). Most consumers in Germany now use reusable bags when they purchase food and goods. Over ten years, recycling of beverage cans *alone* has led to reductions in energy by 37 percent and potential greenhouse gases by 48 percent (Ratingen 2001). One of the important dimensions of the German Packing Ordinance program is that it has had a radiating effect on manufacturers and nations worldwide. In order to continue operating in Germany, Hewlett-Packard, an American computer company, redesigned its packaging by switching from plastic to cardboard, altered some of its products to make them less vulnerable to being bumped around, and surveyed German customers to see if they would accept products in reused boxes, which they reported they would (Anonymous 1991). Other European Union nations are following Germany's lead; Holland, France, and Austria are implementing package recycling requirements.

Waste Disposal Taxes and Refund Deposit Strategies

Tax incentives can be used to motivate industries and businesses to reduce waste output. Many governments, including those of Austria, Australia, Belgium, Denmark, and Holland, now charge industries a waste disposal tax as a means of raising revenues, some of which are used to support environmentally responsible waste management programs (i.e., clean up of contaminated sites, waste reduction education programs, market development for recycled materials, and so on).

Denmark's waste management taxation program demonstrates how national taxes can be a very effective incentive to reduce waste, increase recycling, and reuse waste materials, and can create a materials market for products previously deemed as waste (Hufnagel 1999). In response to high outputs of waste and severely limited new landfill space, Denmark implemented a waste tax that places charges on the disposal (dumping, landfilling, and incineration) of nonhazardous waste according to weight. The purpose of the tax is to reduce waste generation at the source and increase recycling and reuse of household, industrial, and construction materials. To increase effectiveness, the tax has consistently been increased and expanded. Since it went into effect in 1987, the tax has resulted in a significant decrease in the amount of waste delivered to both public and private sites throughout Denmark. Between 1987 and 1997, total waste collected decreased by 26 percent; a study done in 1993 revealed that household waste was reduced by 16 percent, construction waste by 64 percent, and mixed waste by 22 percent (Hufnagel 1999). These decreases were accompanied by a significant increase in the recycling and reuse of varying types of household, construction, and industrial waste. Recycling and reuse of construction materials increased over 100 percent; recycling of paper and cardboard expanded by 77 percent; recycling of glass increased over 50 percent. Since the implementation of the tax, there has been a growing market for used construction materials, which makes it possible to sell them before they are defined as waste (Hufnagel 1999).

Refund deposit strategies also function as incentives for industries to reduce waste at the source. Rather than being taxed on waste generated, refund schemes return money to companies that produce less waste over time. The government of South Korea requires industries that produce disposable or nonrecyclable goods to pay a deposit to the government for the quantity of waste generated; the deposit is refunded if the company collects and recycles or otherwise treats the product itself after consumer use (Wilson 1996).

Subsidies and Incentives

Subsidies and other reward-focused incentives encourage industries to promote waste reduction. Possible approaches include supporting waste prevention programs, research and development for new appropriate waste management technologies, in-house recycling and waste treatment schemes, new treatment facilities, educational programs designed to increase demand for recycled materials, and rebate schemes to encourage individual recycling efforts. In the early 1990s, authorities in Malaysia estimated that out of 230 waste disposal sites available, 80 percent of them had a remaining operating lifetime of fewer than two years (Hassan et al. 2000). This situation motivated authorities to consider alternative ideas and technologies that would conserve disposal space and resources. In 1992, less than two percent of solid waste in Malaysia was being separated at the source or by scavengers for recycling purposes. A policy introduced in 1994 focused on reduction of municipal solid waste generation (waste minimization), especially those of packaging wastes and household wastes. Strategies were introduced to increase public awareness, create economic incentives and tax exemptions for investors who use recycled materials, ecolabel specific "green" products, establish separation and deposit systems for recyclables, fund research and development in the manufacturing of products from recycled materials, and support separation at source and reduction of wastes. Together, these waste reduction incentives function to considerably reduce waste accumulation in Malaysian cities (Hassan et al. 2000).

Reprocessing/Materials Exchange

Reprocessing (also referred to as *materials exchange*) approaches, strategies, and programs allow companies to trade, sell, or give away unwanted materials to one another, in order to use them as raw materials for manufacturing or reuse them in their existing form (Covey and Shew 2000). The idea behind reprocessing is to create an open loop system that utilizes used materials to manufacture a different "new" product (i.e., manufacturing clothing from plastic soft drink bottles or insulation from waste paper). Using recycled materials can be cost-effective for several reasons: (a) it saves hauling and disposing costs; (b) it can lower the energy input needed to produce the end product; and (c) used materials can be purchased at low cost or received for free in exchange for hauling recyclables away. At the same time, it is important to note that reprocessing schemes that attempt to turn waste into new products sometimes consume significant additional material and energy resources, and by not dealing with the problem of ultimate disposal, must be recognized as ultimately a precursor to disposal and not necessarily reducing waste or energy inputs.

The government of Taiwan has established an information service center to provide information to waste reuse demanders and waste suppliers (Wei and Huang 2001). Waste generators provide the center with an accounting of the wastes they generate. People interested in reusing waste provide the center with information about the wastes they seek and their planned reuse purpose. The idea is to use the waste outputs of one manufacturer as inputs (resources) for another. The match-ups are considered and discussed until a deal for waste exchange is agreed upon. The center holds participants to strict confidentiality. The function of the center was considered so important that the Taiwan Environmental Protection Agency incorporated the exchange and reuse mechanism into the legal system by drafting the General Industrial Waste Items Exchange and

Reuse Review Work Guidelines, which encourage organizations to handle their wastes through exchange and reuse rather than through disposal or processing (Wei and Huang 2001). To support the government's commitment to implement sustainable resource use, waste reduction, waste recycling, and reuse approaches, Taiwan introduced strict regulatory controls and policies that require manufacturers to reduce resource use and generation of toxic substances, reduce waste, and increase their use of recycled materials. Manufactures are also required to record their use of virgin resources and recycled resources for government review and inspection (Wei and Huang 2001).

A collaborative statewide program in Ohio, U.S., promotes the exchange of materials among manufacturers, commercial businesses, and nonprofit organizations. In "Building Partnerships: The Ohio Materials Exchange," Covey and Shew describe how the Ohio Materials Exchange (OMEX) program supports companies and nonprofits in the state of Ohio to trade, sell, or give away unwanted materials to one another, use them as raw material for manufacturing, or reuse them in existing form (2000). The program is promoted in workshops, presentations, exhibit halls, and other exchanges throughout the state. Materials available for reuse and the materials wanted for reuse are collected into lists. Trading partners fill out forms that give their contact information; these forms are then made available to trading partners who contact one another and make the arrangements. In 1998 OMEX materials included acids, solvents, oils and waxes, plastics, textiles and leather, paper, metals, construction materials, shipping materials, computers and electronics, glass, paints, agriculture byproducts, durable furniture, rubber, sand, and wood. In the two years between 1997 and 1999, the OMEX program resulted in 720 metric tons of materials successfully exchanged and 416 listings of materials wanted or available on file (Covey and Shew 2000).

The city of Beijing, China, was able to reduce waste output by using municipal solid waste as an input to produce fertilizer and construction bricks (Yeung 1986). Most cities in China either dump their municipal solid waste in open spaces or bury it underground. Satellite pictures show that Beijing's garbage is gradually surrounding the entire city. In addition to taking up valuable land space, municipal solid waste pollutes the urban environment and poses significant health problems for the poorest populations. Recognizing the environmental problems stemming from burying and burning municipal solid waste in urban areas, authorities in Beijing are experimenting with a process designed to treat 250 tons of municipal solid waste a day and use it to produce 50,000 tons of fertilizer annually. Municipal solid waste is collected by city workers who transport it to a facility where it is put into a fermenting room together with a certain quantity of bacterium. The fermented waste is then put through a sieve. Material that stays in the sieve is burnt and made into brick shapes. The finer material that goes through the sieve is combined with trace elements, natural minerals, and microbes good for the growth of crops, after which time it is adjusted for nutrient content, baked, grounded, and turned into organic compound fertilizer to be used by farmers (Yeung 1986).

Household and Small Business Waste Reduction and Recycling

The term *waste reduction* refers to reductions in the amount of waste generated at the source. The term *waste recycling* refers to recycling waste that has already been produced and generated (Ueta and Koizumi 2001). The terms *reuse* and *recycle* refer to the use of a waste material as raw material for the manufacture of a different material or product. Recycling metals, paper, glass, plastic, textiles, and organic waste and reusing water have been shown to reduce the demand for energy, raw materials, fertilizers, and freshwater sources. Reducing electric power also helps to reduce the negative externalities related to the environmental impacts of mining and transforming primary energy resources into electric power whatever the process (nuclear, hydro, thermal, or other), including air, water and land pollution, acid rain, and global warming and its associated climate change impacts. A World Bank study of recycling and recuperation activities in Bogotá and Medillín, Columbia, revealed that recycling practices led to energy savings equivalent to 19 percent of the country's oil imports at the time (Pacheco 1992). Benefits of reuse and recycle approaches include:

- Reduced pressure on urban space and more space for habitation and recreation.

- Decreased air contamination outputs.

- Social benefits and cost savings stemming from improvements in public health related to reductions in ground, water, and air contamination resulting from bury-and-burn waste management processes.

- Financial gains stemming from the sale of recycled materials such as paper, plastic, glass, and metals, using organic materials to generate fertilizer for crop production.

- Money saved due to the nonextraction or nonproduction of primary raw materials such as wood and chemical products used to make paper, bauxite for aluminum, resins, feldspar and calcium for glass, resins for plastics, and iron for steel.

- Reducing the huge amount of funding allocated to mainstream waste collection and management practices.

- Energy savings stemming from savings in electric power used in the production stages of a product.

Reduce, reuse, and recycle campaigns are based on the recognition that shifting from a "waste management" to a "waste reduction" paradigm will require changes in the behavior of people, both individually (as householders and employees) and institutionally (as businesses and institutions). At the household level, curbside collection of residential and business waste is essential to this change in behavior. Curbside collection is designed to make it easy for individuals to prepare waste products for recycling. Implementing curbside collection requires that an infrastructure be put into place for this specific purpose. Ideally, street grids that allow trucks and carts easy access to homes and buildings need to be in place. The city or company responsible for pickup must supply the household with a system for trash collection and waste separation. If the city or company is dependent on waste recycling to support the waste collection system through the sales of recycled products, officials need to ensure that there is not a competitive informal waste collection system in place which will function to remove needed recycled material before city or private company workers can get to it. There needs to be harmony between waste collection, separation, and pickup; if these components are implemented jointly, the volume and quality of recyclable materials will grow, reducing costs over time. In addition to an efficient waste collection and separation system, policy measures must be introduced to make waste reduction easier, and there should be coordinated information campaigns to help people understand what needs to be done and persuade them to do it (Wilson 1996). Public information campaigns aimed at consumers can be focused in schools and neighborhoods. Information campaigns aimed at employees and businesses need to be supported by companies and industries. Requiring businesses, industries, and public institutions to prepare waste management and waste reduction recycling plans for employee recycling of waste and waste management audits is also important (Wilson 1996).

In Brazil, the city of Curitiba's highly successful *Lixo Que Nao E Lixo* (*Garbage That Is Not Garbage)* waste collection and management system is among the most successful household level urban recycling and reuse waste management programs in the world. The system, which was implemented in 1989, relies on three integrated waste collection system components: household, small business, and industrial. The city takes responsibility for collecting all waste produced by households and small businesses. To encourage recycling, the city utilizes ongoing public education campaigns in newspapers, radio, television, and other media to teach residents about the value of recycling (i.e., how recycled paper goods can be transformed into new paper and recycled plastics can be transformed into new products). The city's public information campaign is reinforced by a highly accessible, well-organized waste collection system consisting of green pickup trucks and strictly enforced mandatory recycling requirements.

Residents are required to separate household waste into two categories— organic and inorganic. The organic household waste stream consists almost exclusively of food waste. Green matter related to garden and property maintenance is collected separately; beginning in 1991, the city began composting household green waste in one of Curitiba's many city parks. Food waste is deposited into small plastic bags within the kitchen area. Garbage pickup by large trucks occurs regularly and consistently on specific days and during specific hours, typically every two or three days to prevent garbage accumulation in front of residences. Residents are alerted to the truck when they hear the sound of a bell ringing, calling them to bring out their garbage for pickup. If residents are not home when the truck comes, they deposit their garbage bags into small metal garbage bins which are positioned on the street in front of each house. The metal bins are typically constructed on stilts about four feet high so that animals cannot get into the garbage bags. After pickup, organic household waste is taken to a large landfill site located about twenty kilometers outside the city center. The plant is itself built out of recycled materials.

Curitiba's inorganic household waste stream includes all household waste that is not food or green matter—aluminum, paper, iron, plastics, glass, and small white goods. Although paper is an organic product, it is picked up as part of the inorganic waste stream so that it can enter the recycling market. Residents deposit inorganic garbage into larger plastic bags, which are brought to people's residences and left outside their home when the truck comes by for pickup. Small white items can be left alongside the bags. Inorganic waste is also collected by a garbage truck, which takes it to a recycling center located several kilometers outside the city center where it is carefully separated by employees. Materials then considered reusable are separated and stored in large containers in the hope that they will be purchased and reused by local businesses and industries. Materials that are considered nonreusable are taken to the same landfill site that holds organic waste; these would include, for example, paper boxes coated with plastic that are used to hold milk.

One of the important features of the program is that the recycling center functions as an employment training facility for recent migrants to the city with limited job skills, people with disabilities, and people recovering from alcoholism and drug abuse. Some recycled materials are specifically separated out and used to help low-income residents; for example, shredded styrofoam is used to make quilts for low-income residents. Between 1991 and 2000, the *Lixo Que Nao E Lixo* program quadrupled its annual collection of food waste and almost tripled its annual collection of recyclables (Secretaria Municipal de Meio Ambiente 2000). By 2002 Curitiba was recycling more than two thirds of its garbage—one of the highest rates of any city in the world.

Household Waste Collection in Informal Settlements

While some public officials have the luxury of contemplating what kind of changes they would like to introduce into their waste management system to reduce waste and encourage recycling, many city governments in developing countries do not have the financial resources necessary to develop even a basic infrastructure for waste disposal and collection in some areas of their cities. At least 400 million urban residents in developing countries lack sanitation services; between 30 percent and 50 percent of urban solid waste in developing countries is left uncollected (United Nations Centre for Human Settlements 1994). One of the most difficult household waste collection challenges exists in cities that have informal settlements (i.e., squatter camps and shantytowns) in their jurisdiction. Informal settlements exist in most developing countries; in 2000 informal settlements made up about 32 percent of Sao Paulo, 33 percent of Lima, 34 percent of Caracas, 59 percent of Bogotá, 60 percent of Dar es Salaam, 70 percent of Luanda, and 85 percent of Addis Ababa (Choguill 1996).

Most informal settlements located within and on the outskirts of many cities in developing countries have a haphazard settlement and road design that becomes even more haphazard as the population increases and informal settlements spread, typically causing the street grid to become more random and narrow. Lack of a formally developed street grid and infrastructure makes it difficult, and sometimes impossible, for trucks to enter the settlement area to pick up garbage. In many informal settlements, the street grid is so narrow and/or unpaved that even small carts cannot easily access them. This condition poses major structural challenges for waste collection vehicles and systems, especially when it rains. The situation is made worse when public officials do not acknowledge informal settlements as neighborhoods and consequently deny these areas critical infrastructure and public services, a combination that results in no formal waste collection system whatsoever in many informal settlement areas. Under these conditions, garbage goes uncollected and builds up in the immediate area surrounding homes and/or accumulates in unauthorized open pit dumping areas located close to people's homes. Within a short time, these garbage dumping areas become homes to disease-carrying rodents and insects; they also smell awful and contribute to urban blight. Inadequate collection and disposal of waste is a major factor in the spread of insect-borne diseases and social despair. When residents take matters into their own hands and illegally burn waste that has collected in an open pit, local air contamination and health problems are increased.

To avoid waste accumulation and the problems associated with it, public authorities working in urban areas that include informal settlements with difficult road access for collection trucks and/or from which they cannot easily collect garbage need to create incentives that encourage individual households to physically collect their garbage and carry it to designated sites where collection trucks and workers can receive it on designated pickup days. The best programs motivate households to separate the waste before they bring it to the pickup site or at the specific collection site in preparation for recycling and reuse.

One of the most successful household waste collection programs operating in an informal settlement context is also located in Curitiba, Brazil. The city's *Cambio Verde* (*Green Exchange*) program grew out of its *Lixo Que Nao E Lixo* (*Garbage That Is Not Garbage)* program. Implemented in 1991, the *Cambio Verde* program builds directly on the waste collection system city planners designed to collect household/small business waste. The most significant difference is that, in order to motivate low-income residents living in squatter communities with irregular land-use patterns to carry their recyclables by hand to garbage collection trucks waiting on the street, the municipality offers residents fresh seasonal vegetables and bus tickets in exchange for garbage. Collection trucks come to several different locations: neighborhood streets close to informal settlements, supermarkets, and certain city agencies. On specified days, residents bring their garbage to the collection site of their choice in whatever container systems and small carts they can find. Container systems include paper and plastic bags and boxes, pails, garbage cans, wheelbarrows, even baby strollers. In exchange for their recyclables, people receive bus tickets, vegetables, fruits, eggs, and milk bought from local periurban farms.

Cambio Verde has four main objectives: (1) to establish a waste collection system for informal and hard to reach housing settlements; (2) to motivate low-income residents in the informal settlements to separate organic from inorganic waste in order to support recycling in order to keep the city clean of waste and reuse valuable products; (3) to increase low-income resident's intake of fresh vegetables, leading to public health and educational benefits; (4) to instill a commitment to recycling among Curitiban children and youth; and (5) to support small-scale local farmers. This last objective emerged when city planners realized that the *Cambio Verde* program could provide city officials with an opportunity to purchase seasonal produce from local farmers whose consumer markets were declining as they competed with global food corporations that were selling produce at lower prices.

Individual Recycled Material Collectors

In many developing countries, municipal authorities that lack the resources to develop a local waste management system throughout their jurisdiction rely on individuals who function to collect recyclable materials in their city. Traveling on foot, these adults and children spend their days collecting reusable waste from households and small businesses. They do this work because they need the meager income they can generate from selling recyclables to wastebrokers or to the city directly.[3]

Individual waste collectors typically gather waste in small, handheld wooden carts. Collectors visit households and small businesses regularly to collect easily transportable solid waste that has economic value (i.e., paper, glass, cans, tin, and scrap metal). The collection system focuses almost exclusively on reusable/recyclable materials, not on organic waste. Materials most typically collected are cardboard and other paper, glass, plastics, metals, and wood. Sometimes individual collectors work formally with officials who sanction their activities, but most often they work without official permission. In either case, this informal collection system is accepted by public officials because it functions to remove rapidly accumulating waste generated by households and businesses in residential and public street areas which would otherwise cause major environmental and social problems. The materials they gather are either used by the people who collect them or sold to buyers who then sell them to individuals and businesses that can utilize them.

Although many municipalities in developing countries depend informally upon individual waste collectors to assist them with waste management in their city and many people depend on the income they earn selling recycled materials, there are many disadvantages to this informal waste collection system. It is hard work physically; workers use their bare hands to collect garbage and haul heavy, poorly balanced carts on streets that are often unpaved and bumpy. Most workers earn almost nothing for a long, hard day's work. Most workers are exploited since they are performing an important function for the city and are not being paid for the service they provide, they are often harassed by officials, and their work is socially considered to be of very low status even though it contributes to society. Finally, in most countries the system relies heavily on children and youth, who are not attending school and are, instead, spending their days collecting garbage.

If the system could be changed so that adults were hired by the state, given well-made carts and protective equipment, and paid a living wage to collect recyclables, the system might function well. It could employ adults who need and want to work, but have few skills valued in their local labor market. It could be cost-effective since conventional waste management systems require significant initial and ongoing capital infusions for a depot center, trucks, insurance, uniforms, employees, loading centers, fuel for the trucks, truck maintenance, and so on. It could generate income for the city through the sale of recyclables to businesses. It would make it easier to separate waste materials for recycling and reuse.

A Cautionary Word about Recycling

Recycling is clearly an important component of a sustainable waste management system. Recycling is an economically attractive alternative to increasing landfill costs; if conducted properly, it can greatly reduce ecosystem damage. But when recycling becomes a strategy for wealthy, industrial countries to export hazardous waste to developing countries, it ceases to be a sustainable solution to waste accumulation. Many wealthy, industrialized countries are exporting waste products that include known toxic ingredients such as lead, beryllium, mercury, cadmium, brominated-flame retardants, polychlorinated biphenyls (PCBs), polyvinyl chloride (PVC), and plastics to low-income developing countries under the banner of "recycling." This legal trafficking of international hazardous waste exports poses a direct threat to public and environmental health in lower-income nations and also results in moving toxic and hazardous materials into secondary products that eventually will have to be disposed of. Under these conditions, "recycling" becomes an affront to the principles of producer responsibility, clean production, pollution prevention, and sustainability (Puckett et al. 2002).

International hazardous waste exports are motivated by several factors, of which cheaper labor costs, lower environmental standards, weaker enforcement of environmental regulations, and legislation which allows countries to export toxic waste are the most salient. As long as manufacturers can evade the social and environmental costs of their hazardous processes and products by exporting end-of-life wastes, they can avoid or delay having to use their creativity and ingenuity to make their production processes and consumer products less toxic and harmful to human health and the planet (Puckett et al. 2002).

The electronics industry, the world's largest and fastest growing manufacturing industry, is a case in point. Electronics waste products include large household appliances such as refrigerators, air conditioners, handheld cellular phones, personal stereos, consumer electronics, and computers. Electronics waste has two primary characteristics: (1) it contains over one thousand different substances, most of which are toxic and hazardous to human and environmental health; and (2) it is generating and accumulating rapidly due to extreme rates of obsolescence. Data from single-day recycling collection in the United States revealed that more than 50 percent of turned-in computers are in good working order but are discarded to make way for new technology. In 1998 the overall electronics waste generated was estimated as being between five and seven million tons; approximately six thousand computers in the state of California, U.S., become obsolete each day (Puckett et al. 2002).

Industry growth, combined with product obsolescence and discarded electronics products, has created the fastest growing waste stream in the industrialized world. A growing accumulation of electronics waste has reached disastrous proportions. European studies estimate that electronics waste is increasing more than three times faster than the general municipal waste stream (Puckett et al. 2002). Approximately 70 percent of heavy metals found in landfills come from electronic discards. These heavy metals (including mercury and cadmium) contaminate groundwater and pose a direct threat to public health. A study conducted by the U.S. Environmental Protection Agency estimated that it was ten times cheaper to ship computer monitors to China than it was to recycle them within the United States (USEPA 1998).

An international investigative report entitled *Exporting Harm* documents what happens to "recycled" electronics waste exported by the U.S. high-tech industry to countries in Asia (Puckett et al. 2002). The findings reveal that between 50 percent and 80 percent of electronic wastes explicitly collected under the banner of "recycling" are not recycled domestically; instead they are placed on container ships bound for destinations in China, India, and Pakistan, where vast amounts of electronic waste, most of it hazardous, is burned or dumped in rice fields, rivers, and wetlands, along riverbanks, irrigation canals, and waterways. Electronic waste recycling and disposal operations in these countries include waste separation conducted by children and adults who use hammers, chisels, screwdrivers, and other instruments held in their bare hands to separate computer parts in order to recycle the aluminum, steel, copper, plastic, and circuit boards that contain valuable minerals. Most of these materials expose the workers to toxins, and much of the work is done by adults and children wearing no health-protective equipment. Landfilled electronics waste leaches toxins into groundwater and local water supplies. Burning of wires and other parts to recover metals such as steel and copper releases highly toxic pollutants into the air. Large-scale burning and acid baths release substantial quantities of harmful heavy metals, dioxins, beryllium, and other toxic chemicals into the air and water. Parts that are not reusable are burned or incinerated; river dumping of acids is common, as is widespread dumping of solid electronic waste (Puckett et al. 2002).

Countering the unsustainable and unjust effects of legally sanctioned international trade in toxic wastes will require policies that make it difficult and even illegal for rich countries to dump hazardous wastes in poorer countries. One such policy is the Basel Convention. Conceived in 1989, the Basel Convention is designed to prevent the economically motivated dumping of hazardous wastes from rich to poorer countries by mandating a total ban on the export of all hazardous wastes from rich to poor countries for *any* reason, including for recycling. The convention calls on all countries to reduce their exports of hazardous wastes to a minimum and, to the extent possible, deal with their waste problems within national borders. This is obligatory, regardless of the level of waste management technology in the importing country, because even with state-of-the-art waste management technologies, and the resources and infrastructure to ensure that such technologies work optimally, it is inappropriate and unjust for wealthy nations to export toxic waste and pollution to particular regions of the world simply because they are poorer. Fifteen European Union countries have implemented the Basel Convention and banned the export of all hazardous wastes to developing countries for any reason. These national governments have also prepared legislation to ensure that manufacturers in their countries are responsible for the entire life cycle (cradle-to-grave) of their computer products; for example, they are required to take computers and appliances back (with the costs borne by the producers) and agree to specific phase-out dates for toxic inputs. Japan has mandated upstream design criteria and manufacturer take-back programs. The United States is the only industrialized county in the world that has not ratified the Basel Convention.

Preventing International Trafficking of Hazardous Waste

International experts concerned about the accumulation and international trafficking of hazardous waste products have developed the following eight recommendations to prevent international waste trafficking:

1. Ban all exports of hazardous wastes from wealthy, industrialized to poor, developing nations.

2. Produce less quantity of waste and less hazardous waste.

3. Clearly label all products to identify social and environmental hazards and proper materials management.

4. Develop and implement strict protocols for testing all new chemicals and mixtures before they are introduced into the market.

5. Assert the principle of extended producer responsibility (EPR), which requires continuing accountability on producers over the entire life cycle of their products. The goal is to encourage producers to prevent pollution and reduce resource and energy use in each stage of the product life cycle through changes in product design and process technology.

6. Require producers to adhere to a take-back agreement, wherein a producer takes back a product at the end of its useful life (i.e., when discarded) either directly or through a third party. Implied in the take-back requirement is that manufacturers be required to assume full responsibility for life cycle costs and to take their products back and devise and implement environmentally sound and ethical recycling and reuse solutions.

7. Design for longevity, upgradeability, repair, and reuse rather than for obsolescence.

8. Design to ensure clear, safe, and efficient mechanisms for recovering raw materials through recycling. The product must be made for rapid and easy dismantling or reduction to a usable form. Input materials must be suitable for safe reconstitution and recycling, and there must be preidentifiable recycling markets and mechanisms established for the input materials.

Source: Puckett et al. 2002

Reducing Organic Waste Accumulation: Composting

An important step toward a sustainable waste management system is to complement and augment the waste reduction, reuse, and recycling paradigm with processes that actually reduce solid waste accumulation. One of the most compelling processes in this category is composting. *Compost* is the stabilized and sanitized product obtained from the composting of organic substances derived from urban and agroindustrial biodegradable solid wastes, free from heavy metals, glass pieces, plastic, and sometimes cellulose materials with pH value around eight and subjected to partial microbial fermentation (Sharma et al. 1997). *Composting* is a process wherein organic residues (i.e., agricultural wastes and food wastes from industries, small businesses, and households) are converted into biofertilizers that are then used to enhance soil health. It involves "the biological oxidative decomposition of organic constituents in wastes of almost any nature under controlled conditions" (Sharma et al. 1997, 456).

Compost plays a critical role in soil health and enrichment. Produced both ecologically and economically, composting helps to restore the basic elements consumed during plant cultivation. Through its neutral pH value, it helps arable land to have quick decomposition of organic substances. Through absorbent action, it minimizes the migration of contaminants into the environment. It has been scientifically established that all crops benefit from compost, which provides soil with essential nutrients and improves the physical, biological, and physiochemical properties of the soil.

In urban areas, organic materials can be obtained from five main sources: (a) household organic waste (i.e., food and garden waste); (b) organic waste from local hotels and restaurants; (c) schools that serve food to their students each week; (d) parks; and (e) green wastes available from commercial food establishments such as wholesale fruit and vegetable markets, agroindustries that process fruit and vegetable matter, supermarkets, and food stores (Sharma et al. 1997). The compost that is created from urban waste can be made available for soil used in municipal facilities (i.e., parks and schools) and in individual household gardens. If produced in large enough quantities, compost can also be taken to periurban and rural farmland to support agricultural activities. There are three popular methods of composting: (1) composting in waste piles turned periodically; (2) composting in static but ventilated waste piles; and (3) composting using bioreactors which involve

Small Scale Composting in Southern India: Lessons Learned

The vast quantity and rapid accumulation of organic waste materials in Indian cities with weak waste management infrastructures motivated public interest litigation filed in the Supreme Court of India. The litigation resulted in the formation of a committee charged with (a) investigating all aspects of solid waste management in India's largest cities and (b) submitting recommendations for improvements. One section of the legal ruling required local governments to segregate wet waste (the biodegradable organic fraction) and treat it in an appropriate manner. From this ruling, four models of decentralized community level composting schemes emerged:

1. Neighborhood initiatives and community-based waste collection and composting schemes;

2. Initiatives of companies and institutions composting on their premises;

3. Medium-scale private sector composting enterprises; and

4. Public-private partnerships in larger-scale composting schemes.

All of the programs that resulted from this requirement were small-scale, neighborhood-based composting schemes that have multiple benefits, including:

• Creating employment in local communities;

• Enhancing environmental awareness;

• Increasing flexibility in operation and management;

• Promoting labor-intensive technologies that are better adapted to specific socioeconomic conditions in India;

• Reducing waste management cost for the municipality as organic waste was diverted from the municipal waste stream, thus reducing transportation and disposal costs; and

• Combined with strengthening primary municipal collection services, decreasing dependency on poor functioning municipal services.

Source: Zurbrugg 2002

different combinations of different techniques for material handling and forced air ventilation in the system (Sharma et al. 1997).

Summary

This chapter outlines the problems stemming from mainstream bury-and-burn approaches, which are at the core of the contemporary urban waste management paradigm and its associated approaches and technologies. The chapter describes the huge paradigmatic shift that will need to take place in order for the waste management industry to move from a *waste disposal* mentality (in which waste is buried and burned) and toward a *materials management* mentality (in which waste is reduced and reused). New socially and ecologically responsible approaches will have to be adopted; these approaches must be flexible and strategically driven at the household, local authority, business, industry, and government levels.

This philosophical shift will require a move toward *resource recognition,* which involves the reduction of waste in production and distribution processes and the enhancement of waste through reuse and recycling. Aside from its ecological benefits, the recycling of metals, paper, glass, plastic, textiles, and organic solid waste has been shown to reduce the demand for energy, raw materials, and fertilizers. Incentives to move toward resource recognition include financial savings from byproduct opportunities, more land becoming available for other uses, reducing greenhouse gases, increasing efficiency and reducing costs related to the disposal of toxic and hazardous waste, improving public health, enhancing soil fertility, and improving environmental quality.

Two complementary goals must be pursued to move forward the goal of sustainable waste management. The first is to reduce the amount of waste being generated at the source of production and consumption; this requires changing the production and consumption patterns of goods and services in order to lower the volume and type of waste generated. The second is to create new uses for waste generated in cities by highlighting its benefits and reducing the volume of waste to be disposed through recycling or reusing it directly; this requires municipalities and businesses to view waste materials as unused resources.

Urban authorities must work with industries in their localities to reduce waste by adopting more efficient manufacturing and disposal methods.

These include minimizing raw material requirements (thus generating less waste), minimizing the weight and volume of packaging used for shipping and sales, and encouraging the reuse or recycling of materials and products. Changing production and consumption patterns and creating new utilities for waste must be based on a waste management hierarchy, which includes (1) prevention/minimization, (2) materials recovery, and (3) incineration and landfill.

The ultimate goal is to create a *new materials economy,* an economy and markets that will promote and support redesigning industrial products to eliminate waste generation, developing and using technologies that require fewer materials, eliminating subsidies for environmentally destructive activities, providing market subsidies for recycling, redesigning manufacturing processes to eliminate the discharge of pollutants, and clustering production facilities so that waste from one process can be used as the raw material for another. Planning and policy measures should promote comprehensive pollution prevention practices, resource recognition programs, separate recycling approaches and systems for organic and inorganic wastes, and reprocessing when environmentally beneficial and cost-effective. Governments and foundations should support the development and use of environmentally safe materials, technologies, and products. Planners and others should be trained and prepared to educate and inform those working in the public, private, and nonprofit sectors about the following four waste management issues: (1) the social, environmental, and public health impacts caused by mainstream approaches to solid waste accumulation; (2) the urgent need to significantly reduce packaging across industries and sales; (3) the urgent need to reduce bury-and-burn waste management programs and to increase reuse and recycle programs; and (4) the need to ensure that hazardous materials are not exported from high-income to low-income nations by complying with the Basel Convention and developing producer-responsibility legislation and incentives.

Chapter Questions

This chapter provides readers with information to address seven essential questions related to planning for sustainable urban waste disposal, collection, and management:

1. What are the core components of the conventional waste management paradigm?

2. What are the essential elements of bury-and-burn waste management approaches?

3. What social, environmental, and public health problems are created by bury-and-burn approaches?

4. What other types of waste management paradigms, approaches, and technologies exist?

5. How viable are these alternatives to existing waste management bury-and-burn approaches and systems?

6. What is required to move from a waste disposal mentality to a materials management mentality?

7. What can we learn from existing examples of sustainable waste management?

Notes

1. Ironically, Fresh Kill had been used well beyond its full capacity when it was closed in the late 1990s, but was, nevertheless, reopened after September 11, 2001, to accept the huge amount of solid waste generated by the destruction to the World Trade Center and surrounding area.

2. Most or all of the organic waste in landfills decays anaerobically, wherein most of the carbon is gradually released into the atmosphere, about half of it as carbon dioxide and half as methane (Ackerman 2000).

3. It is important to note that waste collectors also exist in wealthy, industrialized countries, but in these countries, the collectors do not substitute for a nonexisting or inadequate waste collection system.

CHAPTER THREE

URBAN ENERGY SUPPLY
AND MANAGEMENT

Since the nineteenth century, with the industrial revolution, the human population and its economic activities have grown to such an extent as to interfere seriously with natural phenomena by complex feedback mechanisms we do not wholly understand—mechanisms that could accelerate and intensify climate changes. . . . Urbanization, industrialization, the development of over-intensive agriculture, deforestation, and, perhaps most important, consumption of ever growing amounts of energy in the form of fossil fuels (first coal, then increasingly, oil and gas) with the release of huge quantities of carbon dioxide in the atmosphere: all of these anthropogenic processes are making us finally reflect on the fact that we have begun playing with the climate on a planetary scale, leading to the irreversible global problems of the depletion of the ozone layer, acid rain, and, most important of all, greenhouse warming which could induce climatic changes of geological proportions even before the end of the twenty-first century.

—Umberto Columbo, "Development and
the Global Environment," 1992

Energy

In *Energy and the Ecological Economics of Sustainability*, author John Peet defines *energy* as the ability to do work (1992). "Energy has the ability to cause changes in the physical or chemical nature, structure, or location of matter or things. . . . Energy is not a thing that can be seen or touched, it is a concept used to explain changes in the state of matter under certain circumstances. Heating, cooling, chemical change, motion, and so on result from changes in the nature or location of the energetic state of matter. . . . Some changes alter the structure of matter, as when dough (chemically) is converted into bread by baking (heat energy) or when elevated water is used to turn turbines into hydroelectric power to generate electricity" (1992, 26–27).

During the nineteenth century, sociopolitical and technological processes allowed cheap and abundant access to fossil fuel to become the main facilitator of development and economic growth. Harnessing energy from coal, oil, and gas allowed humans to manufacture the tools and factories that make and shape the cement, bricks, steel, and timber that make up the structures and products associated with modern life (Peet 1992). Urbanization, industrialization, and economic growth were fueled by intense exploitation of fossil fuel-based energy sources, mineral resources, and human labor. By the mid-nineteenth century, the environment was already significantly stressed as a result of the massive exploitation and degradation of local and global resources in the name of development and economic growth. As Jack Hollander notes in *The Energy-Environment Connection*, for industrializing societies the basic presumption about the environment was that the earth, with its vast untapped resources and lands, could support human development essentially without limit, its resources abundant enough to supply all material needs, its winds and waters robust enough to cleanse the earth of all of industry's effluents (1992). A century later, the processes associated with Western-style urban industrial development were being replicated throughout the world as international lending associations like the World Bank and the International Monetary Fund provided governments in Africa, Asia, and Latin America with funds to put Western-style infrastructures systems into place to support economic growth and development activities.

The oil and gas industry quickly became the world's largest industry, fueling the industrial revolution, transportation sector, land uses, rapid urbanization, the rise in consumerism, and the modern global economy (Rain Forest Action Network 1998).[1] Nations in every region of the world became dependent on energy generated from fossil fuels for economic growth and development. Cheap, abundant access to fossil fuel allowed political leaders, manufacturers, developers, planners, and policymakers to conveniently ignore three critical issues: (1) environmental problems caused by burning fossil fuels, (2) issues related to energy efficiency, and (3) the social implications of the inequitable distribution of energy resources.

World Energy Mix

By the 1980s, fossil fuels were supplying almost 90 percent of total commercial energy demand worldwide; consumption of fossil fuels have increased from 500 million tons a year at the beginning of the twentieth century to seven billion tons a year by the 1980s; in 1989 oil contributed 43 percent to the total worldwide supply of fossil fuels (Columbo 1992).

By 1997 the world energy mix was overwhelmingly produced from nonrenewable resources. Total energy consumption on earth was over 9.5 billion TOE (tons of oil equivalent). The overwhelming majority of that energy (86 percent) came from nonrenewable resources and about a quarter of that total came from nonrenewable solid fuel, primarily coal. Coal, the dirtiest of all energy sources (emitting the most carbon dioxide and other air pollutants), fueled the industrial revolution and still provides about a quarter of the world's commercial energy; coal generates about two fifths of world electricity (Lean 2002). The largest portion (36 percent) came from nonrenewable liquid fuels (including oil, gas, and diesel), and another 20 percent came from nonrenewable gases (primarily natural gas). Oil and gas currently account for about two thirds of the world's commercial energy and provide fuel for almost all of the world's vehicles (Lean 2002). A much smaller, but significant, six percent of total world energy comes from nuclear fuels. Globally, 435 nuclear reactors produce about six percent of world commercial energy, generating about 16 percent of electricity (Lean 2002). Only 14 percent of the world's energy mix comes from renewable sources, including biomass fuels (World Resources Institute 2001). Biomass is the primary fuel source for two billion people worldwide, almost all of whom live in developing countries. Biomass fuels include wood, crop wastes, and dung. Collecting biomass fuels is time-consuming, back-breaking work; burning biomass fuels releases harmful air pollutants (Lean 2002). Omitting biomass sources, renewable energy provided only four percent of world commercial energy in 2002, and although wind and solar energy are the fastest growing renewable energy sources, half of that total came from hydropower (Lean 2002).

Globally, energy resources are distributed extremely unevenly. "In 1997, slightly more than one billion people living in industrialized countries consumed about 54 percent of the world's total energy supply, while around five billion people in developing and transition economies consumed the remaining 46 per cent" (Clini 2002, 19). Energy consumption in developing countries is 0.8 tons of oil equivalent per capita, compared to 4.8 in industrial countries (Roussely 2002).

In 2003 the United States, which includes less than five percent of the world's population, was consuming about one third of the world's oil—equivalent to 20 millions barrels of oil per day, compared to the entire rest of the world, consuming 65 barrels of oil per day. Two billion people around the world were collecting wood or cow dung to heat their homes and cook in inefficient stoves that emit fumes harmful to public health and the environment (Adam 2002). According to Corrado Clini, cochair of the G8 Task Force on Renewable Energy, "a business as usual scenario—based on energy policies in place in mid-2000 and consistent with the *World Energy Outlook 2000* reference scenario—suggests that during the period 1997–2020, dependency on fossil fuels will grow, and carbon dioxide emissions from energy use will increase by a projected 60 percent, over two thirds of this in developing countries . . . and nearly two billion people—up to 30 percent of the world's population, and all in developing countries—will continue to have no access to electricity" (Clini 2002, 19). These bleak projections must be prevented—carbon emissions must be dramatically reduced, particularly in industrialized countries; poverty cannot be alleviated without adequate energy supplies in developing countries. Both problems can be addressed by increasing reliance on renewable energy sources—solar energy, wind power, geothermal energy, small-scale hydro, and, to a lesser extent, more efficient biomass systems. The principal finding of the G8 Task Force on Renewable Energy was that "renewable energy resources can now sharply reduce local, regional, and global environmental impacts as well as energy security risks, and they can, in some circumstances, lower costs for consumers" (Clini 2002, 20).

Environmental and Social Impacts of Fossil Fuel Dependency

Greenhouse gases are a natural part of our atmosphere and are essential to most life on earth. When the sun shines on the planet, some of its energy warms the surface of the earth and some is reflected back out to space. Some of this reflected heat is caught by greenhouse gases high in the earth's atmosphere and returned to earth; greenhouse gases act as a blanket, returning heat that would otherwise be lost in space back to earth. If the atmosphere didn't have these gases, or had too little, then too much heat would escape and the planet would be much colder. Ironically, humans have produced the opposite effect by burning fossil fuels, which introduce massive quantities of greenhouse gases into the atmosphere and increase the heat-retention capabilities of the green-house gas blanket. The main greenhouse gases (nitrogen oxides, carbon dioxide, and methane) result from electricity generation and use, transport, coal mining, and manufacturing production (Gibbs 1996). As world markets have increased, so too have consumption of oil and gas and the impacts of greenhouse gas emissions on climate change have become even more severe.

Since the 1970s, scientists and others have become increasingly concerned about increasing reliance on fossil fuels related to massive emissions of carbon dioxide from the combustion of fossil fuels for both energy generation and use in the internal combustion engine, which have produced environmental changes on a global scale. Climate change due to global warming caused by greenhouse gases (including carbon dioxide, methane, and nitrogen oxides) is perhaps the most significant environmental threat on earth.

Globally, burning fossil fuels currently results in the release of more than six billion tons of carbon into the atmosphere each year. The problem is worsened by deforestation, which removes trees that act as carbon sinks by absorbing carbon from the air and using it to construct their tissue (as trees grow they absorb and store carbon). As a result of the increased presence of greenhouse gases in the stratosphere, our planet is warming. Climate change is reflected in increasing average global temperatures, and its effects are far reaching. Some of the known environmental effects of global warming include changing precipitation levels (either higher or lower than usual), which can drastically affect land use (especially agricultural land), increase storm and flood activity, disrupt weather patterns, and cause a rise in sea levels due to the melting of the polar ice caps. All of these changes affect biodiversity. As ecosystems change, millions of people living in or near human settlements located close to rising sea waters or in areas with changing precipitation will be affected. This will result in increased threat of damage and destruction to built areas and natural systems due to storms and floods. If present trends of fossil fuel consumption continue, many scientists predict that the earth's temperature will increase by two to four degrees centigrade (Brown 2001). If this happens, sea level will rise between thirty to sixty centimeters, resulting in the displacement of fertile zones for agriculture and food production, decreasing availability of fresh water for essential uses, and causing land mass changes that will affect millions of people living in coastal cities around the world (Columbo 1992).

Coal

The process of mining for coal to use in power plants involves removing entire mountaintops and then dumping the dirt, vegetation, rocks, and soil accumulated as "overburden" into nearby valleys and waterways. In one year, a typical 500-megawatt coal plant:

- Burns 1.4 million tons of coal

- Uses 2.2 billion gallons of water

- Generates 10,000 tons of sulfur dioxide, 10,200 tons of nitrogen oxide, 3.7 million tons of carbon dioxide, 500 tons of small particles, 220 tons of hydrocarbons, 720 tons of carbon monoxide, 125,000 tons of ash, 193,000 tons of sludge, 170 pounds of mercury, 225 pounds of arsenic, 114 pounds of lead, and four pounds of cadmium.

Source: Union of Concerned Scientists 1999

Despite the fact that the world's top climate scientists agree that burning new petroleum reserves will lead to devastating global climate change, oil, coal, and natural gas continue to be viewed as resources that should be exploited as efficiently and rapidly as possible. Since 1998, when nations around the world acknowledged the threat of climate change and committed themselves to reducing the factors that cause climate change, the petroleum industry has drilled 113,466 new exploration wells out of a total number of more than a half a million wells. The industry has awarded 4,040 contracts for new exploration that covers an area equal to both the United States and Europe together and cut 15 million kilometers (9,320,568 miles) of new seismic lines equal to more than twice the distance of the entire United States road network. These activities threaten frontier forests in twenty-two countries, coral reefs in thirty-two countries, mangroves in forty-six countries, indigenous peoples on six continents, and global climatic stability worldwide (Rain Forest Action Network 1998).

In a report on the impacts of oil mining, entitled *Drilling to the Ends of the Earth,* the authors conclude that "global expansion of petroleum exploration not only threatens to irrevocably commit us all to the worst impacts of climate change, it is endangering fragile ecosystems and threatens indigenous people worldwide" (Rain Forest Action Network 1998, 5). Throughout the world, indigenous people are struggling in defense of their rights and their homelands in response to existing and proposed oil and gas projects on native lands. "The *Gwich'in* people in Alaska, the *Achual* people in Peru, the *U'wa* people in Colombia and the *Khant-Matsy* people in Siberia all seek an end to oil and gas projects imposed on their lives and their lands" (Rain Forest Action Network 1998, 38).

The industrial processes used by oil refineries are toxic to human health, particularly for those living closest to the sources of production and processing. In Richmond, California, local industries dominated by chemical manufacturers and petrochemical processors routinely generate large amounts of toxic pollution that are harmful to the health and well-being of local residents. They also store vast quantities of extremely hazardous chemicals that could cause immediate danger to life and health if accidentally released into Richmond neighborhoods through catastrophic chemical accidents. Each year chemical manufacturers and petrochemical processors in Richmond generate about 800,000 pounds of toxic air contaminants, nearly 18,000 pounds of toxic pollutants in waste water, and about 179,000 tons of hazardous waste (Citizens for a Better Environment 1989). Many of the toxic air pollutants released are known or suspected cancer-causing agents. Others form particulates or ground-level ozone (smog) that can irritate the respiratory system and cause lung disease. A review of Census Bureau data shows that the people who live closest to industrial sources of toxic hazards in Richmond are primarily lower-income, minority residents. In 1990 African-American residents made up over 70 percent of the population living closest to the heavy industrial zone; many of these families were living in poverty. This form of institutional discrimination, wherein low-income communities of color are disproportionately impacted by environmental hazards, has been called *environmental racism.*

Indigenous Perspectives on Drilling for Oil on Native Land

At the same time as our resources are being exploited, our culture is scorned. Our wealth of traditional knowledge is deteriorating, new illnesses are being introduced, new needs are continuously being imposed and poverty not previously known in the region has become widespread. And when we defend ourselves, we are threatened and imprisoned. In the midst of the process to protect our rights . . . three million acres of Madre de Dios were handed over for oil exploration to Mobil, Exxon and Elf.

—Antonio Iviche Quicque, Harakmbut, Peru

We have to be honest with you; we will welcome you as a friend to our community but if you still wish to come with bulldozers, long pipes, and dynamite to put into our mountains, we will fight until each of us is dead. Our land is ourselves and if you put a gas pipeline in our mother the Yungas Forest, you put a pipeline in our bodies. We cannot tolerate this feeling much longer.

—Spokesperson for the Kolla people, Argentina

Twenty years ago, PEMEX arrived and invaded our lands. My father owned about 20 acres of land. Today, this land is invaded by PEMEX pipelines, and two highways run through it. We are left with nothing. Money cannot cover the loss of communal lands, of a house, of a life. We arrived before PEMEX. Our documents prove it.

—Statement from Platano y Cacao community, Mexico

We do not understand how the judicial system of the white people is not capable of defining our rights—which have been recognized for millennia and are recognized by the Constitution—as a priority in relation to economic interests.

—Statement from Cabildo Mayor U'wa community, Columbia

Sources: Rain Forest Action Network, 1998, 38

The Fossil Fuel Regime

Even if strenuous efforts are made to increase the efficiency of energy use, energy demand is going to increase as a result of worldwide increases in urbanization, population, and economic activities (Johansson et al. 1992). Recall the predictions of the G8 Task Force on Renewable

Energy—between 1997–2020, dependency on fossil fuels will grow and carbon dioxide emissions from energy use will increase by a projected 60 percent, over two thirds of this increase will be in developing countries (Clini 2002). The realities of global warming, ozone depletion, climatic change, depletion of nonrenewable energy resources, destruction of indigenous communities, and health problems associated with air pollutants and living near petrochemical and other fossil fuels refineries compel urban authorities to face the fact that the associated costs related to high levels of energy use and dependency on fossil fuels must be decreased.

No one is seriously considering eliminating fossil fuels and replacing them with renewable energy sources; we will continue to rely on fossil fuels, but energy efficiency and renewable energy technologies must be aggressively pursued. "Technologies already available make it possible to cut energy consumption by half in existing industrial installations . . . and by 90 percent in new ones. Studies have suggested that developed countries could reduce their energy consumption by two thirds without penalizing economic growth" (Lean 2002, 17). Renewable sources currently provide less than five percent of the world's commercial energy. In the United States, one of the most technologically advantaged societies in the world, only six percent of energy consumed comes from renewable sources (World Resource Institute 2003). It will not be possible to provide the energy needed to bring a decent standard of living to the world's poor or to sustain the economic well-being of the industrial countries in environmentally acceptable ways if the present energy course continues.

Green Building and Design

Energy efficiency is one of the most critical steps on the path to changes in the world's energy system and toward sustainable urban development. The negative social and environmental impacts of increasing dependence on fossil fuels compel planners and other urban authorities to completely rethink energy systems and patterns of energy use as they relate to the lighting, heating, and cooling of all buildings—public, residential, commercial, and industrial (White 1992).

In *Greening the Built Environment*, authors Smith, Whitelegg, and Williams (1988) describe how the vast majority of modern buildings worldwide are built without regard to working in tandem with nature; consequently, they neglect the importance of climate and light and do not take advantage of appropriate technologies such as solar heating and cooling, natural ventilation, lighting, gray water systems, and so on. Rather than taking advantage of southern exposures and natural lighting and heating, conventional architects design the windows of modern urban offices and factories to face north in order to minimize changes in brightness inside the work area. Instead of relying on natural lighting and heating, designers and builders prefer the security of expensive, energy-guzzling lighting, heating, cooling, and insulation technologies and choose to create sterile built environments that greatly increase dependency on fossil fuel-based energy sources (Devencenzi 2002).

Planners working in the field of green design consider these building designs and technologies as *inappropriate*, making the point that just because they rely on modern technology does not make them more sophisticated or appropriate (1995). Inappropriate technologies allow urban planners, architects, builders, engineers, and others to create built environments that have huge energy and water costs resulting from dependency on fossil fuel, as well as having negative health impacts on building users. As a result of inappropriate building and design practices, the U.S. Green Building Council reports that buildings in the United States use 65 percent of total U.S. electricity consumption, account for more than 36 percent of total U.S. primary energy use, and produce 30 percent of total U.S. greenhouse gas emissions. Each day 136 million tons of building construction and demolition waste are produced in the United States (approximately 2.8 pounds per person per day). Buildings in the United States use 12 percent of total potable water and account for 40 percent (three billion tons annually) of raw materials used globally. The term *green building and design* refers to a synthesis of many different sustainable design techniques and technologies that are used to create structures that intentionally reduce the consumption and waste that buildings generate (Devencenzi 2002). The goal is to reduce dependence on the wider environment for resources and reduce the pollution of the wider environment by waste products (Barton and Bruder 1995). To achieve this goal, planners, contractors, architects, designers, and engineers need to research and utilize the latest (and sometimes the oldest) systems and technologies designed to reduce the consumption and waste that buildings generate. Each green building project is unique in its scope and design, but all green building and design structures are designed to (1) reduce input of natural resources, (2) reduce energy and water consumption, (3) reduce air, water, heat, and light pollution, (4) improve storm water management, (5) reduce waste output (solid and liquid), and (6) reduce the impact of externalities through the intensive use of green products. Good planning and design can substantially reduce resource and energy inputs and pollution outputs (Barton and Bruder 1995).

The design of a given building depends upon several factors including (1) environmental and climate related influences, (2) availability and applicability of different technologies, (3) regulatory restrictions, and (4) financial input. Green building and design projects focus primarily on aspects of site planning, construction, conservation of materials and resources, efficiency of a building's operational processes (primarily energy and water usage), disposal and reuse of building materials, indoor environmental quality, and reduction or elimination of waste and pollution produced during all of the above. To achieve the highest environmental standards possible, designers must use the most current and appropriate technologies and techniques available as they relate to energy, water, building materials, and waste.

Appropriate Technologies

A wide range of appropriate technologies are available to be used in green building and design. Appropriate green building and design technologies are critical to the pursuit of energy reduction and energy efficiency in industrialized nations, related to the critical global pursuit of reducing greenhouse gases and slowing down the problems of the depletion of the ozone layer, acid rain, global warming, and destruction of local communities and habitats (Devencenzi 2002). The appropriate technologies described below are most suitable for existing and new buildings located in prosperous, industrialized nations where material resources are abundant and the technology infrastructure is strong. But if support is provided, as it should be, these appropriate technologies could be utilized in countries with fewer material resources. Below, appropriate technologies in six categories: (1) energy efficiency, (2) heating and ventilation, (3) solar, (4) water, (5) landscaping, and (6) reduce, reuse, recycle are described (Devencenzi 2002).

Energy Efficiency

Energy-efficient lighting uses the minimal amount of electricity to produce the optimal amount of interior light.

Energy-efficient appliances can greatly reduce the amount of energy used by refrigerators, washing machines, clothing dryers, dishwashers, and so on.

Occupancy sensors use technology that senses the occupancy of a room and adjusts the lighting and heating accordingly, reducing energy use when rooms are unoccupied.

Heat efficiency is based on the idea that the less distance that hot water or air needs to travel, the less energy is lost during the transportation.

Daylighting maximizes the use of direct and indirect daylight to illuminate the indoor area of structures through basic structural design and windows, often eliminating the need for electrical lighting during the daytime.

Heating and Ventilation

Insulation, when done properly, helps maintain appropriate indoor temperature, reducing the need for heating/air conditioning; recycled materials can meet or exceed the efficiency of conventional (synthetic) insulation materials.

Programmable thermostats control air temperatures and reduce unnecessary heating/cooling of buildings.

Proper ventilation is achieved through controlled and operable windows that use passive air pressure to allow for natural building ventilation.

Solar

Solar hot water heating systems pump water through a solar heat collection system, usually on the roof of a unit. This water can then be stored and used for the hot water needs of the building, reducing electrical and gas usage.

Photovoltaic systems are systems in which photovoltaic (PV) cells convert sunlight into electricity, reducing the total amount of energy used from exterior sources.

Passive solar heating uses the architecture of the structure to reflect heat from sunlight in the summer and absorb it during the winter. Effective use of this technique combined with proper ventilation can remove the need for any heating or cooling system in a building.

Water

Rainwater catchment systems harvest and store rainwater runoff for use on commercial and residential properties.

Gray water recovery systems use wastewater from baths, showers, lavatories, washing machines, and other sources that can be recovered, filtered, and used for heating, cooling, irrigation, and many other nonpotable water needs.

Indoor water conservation involves using water-saving devices on all plumbing fixtures, faucets, toilets, and showers; large amounts of water can be saved by reducing the flow to the minimal amount necessary for operation.

Landscaping

Xeriscaping involves landscape planning and planting using the minimal amount of water necessary in irrigation; when used in conjunction with rainwater and gray water systems for irrigation, this method can be very efficient.

Landscaping for energy conservation is achieved by using carefully planned landscaping (primarily trees and shrubs) to control wind and sunlight around a building.

Pervious material can be used to replace solid ground cover such as concrete and asphalt with porous materials. This allows water to enter the ground due to its porous nature or through open spaces in the material and to be absorbed into the ground instead of being flushed into sewers or storm drainage systems.

Reduce, Reuse, Recycle

Composting toilets use little to no water and can produce fertilizer as an end product.

Recycled materials include a wide variety of items, including recycled newspaper used for insulation, recycled plastics used for tiling, insulation, decking, and benches, and recycled carpet and carpet padding.

Reused materials are created through a range of reuse strategies, including using concrete as aggregate and fill, reusing ceramics such as toilets and sink basins, and using materials salvaged in the demolition of buildings.

Lumber is an important component in reuse strategies; *dimensional lumber*, which is precut to size, greatly reduces waste at the construction end; *certified wood* which comes from certifying organizations that guarantee that the lumber used in construction was harvested in a sustainable manner; *used lumber* and other related materials such as nails can be used in many processes.

Recycling wastes involves the source separation of recyclable materials, which can reduce waste by 50–75 percent; building design can most effectively encourage recycling through specific recycling areas near workstations, kitchen areas, and outdoor waste collection areas; construction material recycling can greatly reduce the waste generated during the creation of new buildings; packaging, new material, scraps, and old materials and debris all constitute potentially recoverable materials.

Local manufacturing includes buying local, which not only supports the regional economy but also reduces energy usage in the shipping and packaging requirements for building materials.

Compost systems remove organic materials from the waste stream and create valuable fertilizer that can be used for landscaping.

The public health, social, and environmental benefits of integrating appropriate energy technologies in building and design will be realized immediately. Economic benefits will come through energy savings, new market opportunities, and job creation. Social benefits will come through improved indoor environmental quality, improved air quality, improved lighting, reduction of materials emitting toxic substances (paints, sealants, carpet, and so on), less strain on local infrastructure, buildings that are more people-friendly, maximization of open space, and environmentally responsible site planning that will encourage other sustainable design approaches and behaviors, such as recycling, mass transit, bike use, and carpooling. Optimally, green building and design integrates as many appropriate technologies and techniques as possible, but it is important to note that application of some technologies is not feasible in all instances for a range of different reasons. First, some technologies are not suited for particular geographic areas (i.e., solar technologies are not applicable in areas with poor sunlight availability). Second, in many cities, administrative barriers (i.e., stemming from existing planning codes) prevent appropriate technologies such as gray water and/or rainwater catchment systems from being installed due to building code restrictions.[2] Third, some appropriate technologies will not be readily available from distributors and/or the cost of materials and/or installation may not be economically feasible until they are used on a large scale.

Improving Household Biomass Systems

In stark contrast to the green building energy efficiency strategies discussed above, which are designed to be used in buildings that are built by developers and others who have access to immense material resources, millions of low-income families living in cities in developing countries throughout the world live in housing conditions and human settlements that rely exclusively or almost exclusively on traditional biomass resources to supply their energy needs—fuel wood, charcoal, various forms of agricultural residues, and animal wastes.

Sixty percent of the world's population relies on biomass resources as their primary source of energy. Biomass fuel sources provide about half of the energy used in developing countries (Pasztor and Kristoferson 1992). In some countries (such as Burkina Faso, Ethiopia, Malawi, Tanzania, and Uganda), the proportion of traditional biomass resources for fuel is as high as 90 percent. Most traditional biomass fuels are collected by the users or come from informal, noncommercial markets. They are either free or purchased at low costs, although they may still be too costly for many very poor families to purchase (Pasztor and Kristoferson 1992).

The indoor combustion of biomass fuels (particularly fuel wood and dung) in traditional settings, such as typically unvented cooking spaces, releases toxic gases, which cause considerable health problems to the principal users, mainly women and children. "Hundreds of millions of people in developing countries are thus exposed to high concentrations of carbon monoxide, nitrous oxide, and hydrocarbons, and other organics, which are risk factors for several of the leading causes of illness and death in developing countries" (Pasztor and Kristoferson 1992, 181). Cow dung, which is a principal source of fuel in many parts of India, has been linked to a high rate of heart failure caused by chronic lung disease in northern and central India. Other health problems include the risks of burns and the scarcity of biomass fuels in many places, resulting in cutting down on cooking times or failing to boil water for drinking. Charcoal burns more cleanly, but it takes more than twice as much wood to make an amount of charcoal that delivers the same final energy as using fuel wood, and it is very costly since most coal is sold by vendors. Charcoal also contributes directly to deforestation since commercial producers in urban and industrial areas typically cut down whole trees specifically to produce charcoal.[3]

At the same time, as Janos Pasztor, senior officer at the United Nations Conference on the Environment and Development, and Lars Kristoferson, vice director of the Stockholm Environment Institute, point out, it is important to recognize the benefits that come from open indoor combustion: fire provides lighting, and smoke both repels insects and preserves thatched roofs. Thus, it is critical for those involved in designing strategies and appropriate technologies to reduce the use of indoor combustion with traditional biomass fuels to consider an integrated approach that evaluates the entire system of cooking and kitchen management, rather than simply focusing on increasing stove efficiency or reducing smoke emissions (Pasztor and Kristoferson 1992).

Fortunately, scientists in many developing countries have developed modern biomass systems that are quite different from traditional systems and which can play an important role in green building and design for the urban (as well as periurban and rural) poor in developing countries. Most modern systems convert wet biomass into a combustible gas through anaerobic digestion in a biogas digester. Biogas digesters include small-family units, small biogas plants, and large industrial-scale facilities. The process involves collecting animal or human wastes or wet plant material, mixing it with water, and feeding it into an airtight container; the gas that is produced is collected through a piping system and the resulting waste (sludge) is often used as fertilizer (Pasztor and Kristoferson 1992). The advantages that modern systems have over traditional systems are that (a) they lower environmental impacts, (b) the digestion process destroys certain harmful bacteria and pathogens found in animal wastes, (c) they use biofuels more efficiently, and (d) they potentially have wide applicability.

Renewable Energy

Integrating renewable energy approaches and technologies into economic and social activities is the most important component of sustainable energy planning. The good news is that it should be relatively easy and cost-effective to integrate renewable energy into the global energy mix. In 1990 the United Nations General Assembly mandated the United Nations Solar Energy Group for Environment and Development (UNSEGED) to prepare a comprehensive and analytical study on new and renewable sources of energy aimed at providing significant input to the United Nations Conference on Environment and Development held in Rio, Brazil, in 1992. According to the authors of the UNSEGED report, entitled *Renewable Energy: Sources for Fuels and Electricity*, "given adequate support, renewable energy technologies can meet much of the growing demand at prices lower than those usually forecast for conventional energy. . . . By the middle of the twenty-first century, renewable sources of energy could account for three-fifths of the world's electricity market and two-fifths of the market for fuels used directly" (Johansson et al. 1992, 1). The report describes an energy future making intensive use of renewable resources as likely to have the following characteristics (Johansson et al. 1992, 5–7):

- There would be a diversity of energy sources, the relative abundance of which would vary from region to region. Electricity could be provided by various combinations of hydro-electric power, intermittent renewable power sources (wind, solar-thermal electric, and photovoltaic power), biomass power, and geothermal power. Fuels could be provided by methanol, ethanol, hydrogen, and methane (biogas) derived

Biogas Digesters

Biogas digesters are providing an economically viable and sustainable means of fuel in China, India, and Nepal, where over 37,000 biogas digesters were installed from 1992 to 1998. The use of biogas digesters extends throughout the entire developing world, where millions of families rely on biogas sources. Aside from providing households with fuel for cooking, biogas digesters have many benefits, including:

- Improved air quality (less smoke)

- Improved health and reduced respiratory ailments

- Better management of animal dung and human excrement since they produce a better, higher-quality fuel and the manure is better as a fertilizer for crops

- Reduced ground water pollution

- Reduced deforestation and soil erosion

- Reduced greenhouse gas emissions

- Production of an excellent fertilizer that increases crop production or can be sold to generate income

Components of a biogas plant include:

- A digester in which the slurry (dung mixed with water) is fermented

- An inlet tank used to mix the feed and let it into the digester

- A gas holder/dome in which the generated gas is collected

- An outlet tank to remove the spent slurry

- Distribution pipeline(s) to take the gas to the kitchen

- A manure pit where the spent slurry is stored

Source: www.solarengineering.com

from biomass, supplemented by hydrogen derived electrolytically from intermittent renewable energy sources.

- Emphasis would be given to the efficient use of both renewable and conventional energy supplies in all sectors.

- Biomass, grown using sustainable farming methods and processes, and converted efficiently to electricity and liquid and gaseous fuels using modern technology, would be widely used.

- Intermittent renewable energy sources would provide as much as one third of total electricity requirements cost-effectively in most regions, without the need for new electrical storage technologies.

- Natural gas would play a major role in supporting the growth of a renewable energy industry. Natural gas-fired turbines, which have low capital costs and can quickly adjust their electrical output, can provide excellent back-up for intermittent renewable energy sources on electric power grids.

- A renewable energy sources-intensive energy future would introduce new choices and competition into energy markets and reduce the likelihood of rapid price fluctuations and supply disruptions. It could also lead eventually to a stabilization of world energy prices as well as new opportunities being created for energy suppliers.

- Most electricity produced from renewable sources would be fed into large electrical grids and marketed by electric utilities.

- Liquid and gaseous fuels would be marketed much as oil and natural gas are today (Johansson et al. 1992, 5–7).

Industrialized and developing nations should take the lead on moving away from a fossil fuel regime and toward the integration of renewable energy sources in every sphere of life since industrialized nations have the technical, material, and financial resources needed to accelerate the development of renewable technologies and to convert technical concepts into practical products. Industrialized countries should be at the forefront of encouraging and supporting the development and implementation of worldwide efforts to promote energy efficiency and renewable energy both in their own countries and around the world. "Renewable energy technologies are not likely to be rapidly and widely adopted without a global commitment to support the research, development, and demonstrations needed to stimulate early market interest in renewable energy technologies, to eliminate or neutralize market biases embedded in current policies, to provide incentives to promote the risk-taking involved in launching new industries, and to ensure that renewable energy technologies are rapidly transferred to developing countries" (Johansson et al. 1992, 43).

Fundamentally, because industrialized nations use the bulk of the world's global energy resources and represent only a small proportion (26 percent) of total world population, people in industrialized nations will need to significantly *reduce* their consumption of fossil fuel-based energy sources in order to provide the energy resources that are needed to increase the standard of living for the majority of people living in developing countries. According to Svend Auken, who served as Denmark's Minister for the Environment, "climate change means that industrialized countries have to move vigorously towards cutting their emissions of greenhouse gases. We need very substantial cuts over the next few decades to make room for the aspirations of developing countries, which will inevitably lead to their emissions rising in coming years" (Auken 2002, 24).

Developing countries are in the opposite position; in order to meet social and economic demands, developing countries will need to substantially *increase* their use of energy in the coming decades. The question is, how? Most developing countries are characterized by widespread lack of access to energy and very little prospect of providing it in the future (Auken 2002). As noted in an Overseas Development Council report, most developing countries are now way over their heads in debt as a result of borrowing heavily to expand power supplies focused on traditional large-scale hydropower, fossil-fuel-based, and nuclear energy sources (Petesch 1992). The report confirms that traditional energy-generating approaches have exacted a high economic, social, public health, and environmental toll in developing nations because they increase foreign debt burden, are capital intensive, rely on foreign expertise and technologies, lead to the forced location of people and the degradation of their lands, and contribute to air and water pollution, the spread of hazardous nuclear materials, and climate change (Petesch 1992).

Approximately 40 percent of the foreign debt burden of the developing world is linked to conventional (mostly large-scale) power projects. In this context, alternative energy strategies could be particularly beneficial to low-income countries. Alternative energy strategies cost less than traditional supply expansion investments, decrease dependence on oil imports, have the potential to make industries more competitive (if energy efficiency lowers production costs, then savings provide resources to spend on other infrastructure needs), and significantly reduce emissions that cause air contamination and acid rain, and many have zero emissions. A series of studies on energy in developing countries suggests that the rapidly growing demand for energy in developing countries can be significantly met by alternative energy strategies and approaches that emphasize greater efficiency by energy users and in the actual provision of electricity (Petesch 1992). Unfortunately, as confirmed by the Overseas Development Council report, multilateral development banks (the leading source of external financing for energy projects in developing countries) rarely include energy-saving approaches or renewable systems in their portfolios. This will have to change. Significant increases in the flow of resources from international lending institutions and from industrialized countries to developing countries will be essential to support developing countries to implement strategies and technologies that control the buildup of greenhouse gases, safeguard biodiversity, protect forests, advance economic prosperity, and alleviate poverty. "The rich countries also have a special obligation to help because the same processes that have produced such unprecedented levels of wealth and power for them have given rise to the majority of the risks that the planet faces" (Petesch 1992, viii).

To encourage the introduction of small, dispersed, and diverse energy strategies that can meet the need for cleaner, less costly, and more equitable energy development, international banks and wealthy industrialized nations will need to shift their policies and begin to provide developing countries with significant support for energy efficiency strategies and appropriate technologies such as photovoltaics, solar hydrogen power, biogas, and wind energy. Planning and policy measures which could support investments in renewable energy include price increases and energy taxes, load management, time-of-day tariffs, performance standards, building codes, labeling and efficiency ratings, public education, and more efficient motors, construction materials, lighting systems, and refrigeration technologies. Low-cost strategies for supplying unmet energy needs include solar energy, wind power, small-scale hydroelectricity, and biomass fuels from wood, rice husks, or *bagass* from sugar cane, which creates ethanol. Existing inefficiencies in the power, industrial, and transportation sectors, and in the construction of buildings, represent great opportunities for expanding economic activities without corresponding increases in energy inputs (Petesch 1992).

Wind Energy

Wind energy is one of several renewable energy technologies that should be rapidly and widely adopted. Wind energy is produced by a wind turbine. A windmill's rotors work as a moveable obstacle to the wind. When the wind pushes past, it moves the rotors, generating *torque* (turning energy), which is caught by the turbine and converted into electricity. There are three major factors that determine the amount of energy produced: (1) the density of the air—heavier or more dense air will put more torque on the rotors, more humid or wetter air adds density, as do lower altitudes and lower temperatures; (2) the width of the rotor—larger rotors catch more wind, which is why rotors sizes have doubled and tripled over the last decade; today, rotors are built with diameters of over 200 feet; and (3) the speed of the wind—faster wind produces more torque.

Windmills have been used for centuries (Cavallo et al. 1992). As early as 400 B.C., simple windmills were being used to pump water in China. By 200 B.C., vertical-axis windmills were being used to grind grain in Persia and the Middle East. Europeans began using windmills in the eleventh century. In eighteenth-century pre-industrial Europe, there were more than ten thousand windmills being used in the Netherlands alone, primarily to grind grain, pump water, and saw wood. Windmills were used in the United States in the mid-nineteenth century to supply water for the railroads and for cattle in areas remote from streams and springs. They were also used by farmers to obtain water for small-scale irrigation, and as stand-alone systems to generate electricity for isolated homesteads in the American West and Great Plains areas. Although windmills provided valuable energy resources in many parts of the world, by the nineteenth century windmills were unable to compete with the low-cost, convenience, and reliability of fossil fuels and were quickly replaced by steam engines (Cavallo et al. 1992).

Wind energy systems of the twenty-first century are quite different from early stand-alone wind systems; today's wind energy technologies are based on large arrays of wind turbines joined to a utility grid. Over the past two decades, outstanding progress has been made in the technology used to convert wind energy to electrical energy. Thousands of wind turbines operating in California, U.S., and Denmark have been integrated into existing utility grids and are routinely operated in conjunction with conventional energy sources (Cavallo et al. 1992). The cost of wind-generated electricity has decreased, turbines have been improved, and an increasing number of wind resource locations have been identified. In an average location, the energy produced by a wind turbine throughout its twenty-year lifetime is eighty times larger than the amount of energy used to build, maintain, operate, dismantle, and scrap it again. Wind turbines use little space; turbines and access roads occupy less than one percent of the area in a typical wind park (the remaining 99 percent of the land can be used for farming or grazing, as usual). The only drawback of wind energy systems is their visual impact, particularly when turbines and their towers and rotors are built on a large scale, which significantly increases the efficiency of the system but creates a larger impact on the visual landscape.

Wind turbines are less intrusive if they are placed in the ocean, and there are major advantages to building offshore-located wind turbines and farms. The four primary advantages are (1) fewer obstacles compared to land, where there frequently are large buildings and trees which may cause "wind shade" or block the direct push of the wind; and (2) less wind shear, which is important, as even smaller obstacles like bushes or rough ground can slow wind down. Because obstacles and roughness cause the wind to slow down closer to the earth, turbines often have to be built high off the ground. Turbines at sea don't have to be built as high to avoid wind shear; this means turbines can be built using shorter masts, thereby saving building material and capital; (3) lower turbulence because the temperature difference between the air and the surface of the sea is almost always smaller than the difference between the air and the surface of the earth. Higher temperature differences cause turbulence, so offshore windmills experience less extraneous movement or turbulence in the air. A lower level of turbulence leads to less wear and tear on the turbine and rotors, saving time and capital needed for replacement; and (4) ocean placements often have higher wind potential than land placements.

In terms of capacity, wind turbines should be able to be a part of the utility grid of most, if not all, countries. According to Grubb and Meyer, scientists affiliated with London's Royal Institute of International Affairs and Denmark's Technical University respectively, "wind power is already cost competitive with conventional modes of electricity generation under certain conditions and could, if widely exploited, meet 20 percent or more of the world's electricity needs within the next four to five decades" (1992, 157). North America, the former USSR, Africa, and, to a lesser extent, South America, Australia, southern Asia, and parts of Western Europe (particularly England, Ireland, Greece, and Denmark) have the greatest wind potential. Grubb and Meyer predict that only 0.6 percent of land area in the United States (primarily in North Dakota, Wyoming, and Montana) could generate about one fourth total U.S. electricity generation. As wind technology advances, more than 13 percent of U.S. land areas could prove economically viable for wind energy and the corresponding electricity potential would exceed, by four times, total U.S. electricity generation (1992).

By emphasizing savings and improvements in efficiency, Denmark has been able to keep the use of energy stable over the last thirty years while increasing its economy by 75 percent (Auken 2002). Wind energy has been a critical component of curbing and reducing air emissions in Denmark. In 2003 wind energy was providing 13 percent of Danish electricity consumption, with plans to increase capacity to 20 percent by 2005 (Auken 2002). Denmark is at the forefront of wind energy technology; between 1994 and 2000, Denmark's wind industry grew by 40 percent a year, accounting for about 16,000 jobs in wind turbine manufacturing, maintenance, installation, and consulting services (Auken 2002).

The world's largest wind park is located in Denmark, a country with some of the highest levels of wind resources in Europe. The wind park is situated just offshore of downtown Copenhagen in a small, polluted shoal called Middelgrunden. The site had previously been used as an industrial dump for the harbor. The turbines are arranged into a slight curve, 180 meters apart from each other, 3.4 kilometers in length total. To enhance visual impact, the curve was designed as a continuation of already occurring lines within the city (major streets and medieval defenses) with the center being the capital building. Middelgrunden was designed, constructed, and now operates as a 50–50 partnership between the municipality of Copenhagen and a cooperative of Danish citizens (Bale and Hoffman 2002). More than 100,000 families in Denmark are members of the cooperative in Middelgrunden. The cooperative's first purpose is to produce electricity by establishment and management of wind turbines on the Middelgrunden shoal. The second purpose is to contribute to a sustainable energy supply in Denmark.

Middelgrunden uses a composite gravitational foundation design. Turbines are anchored by a steel plate surrounded by concrete placed at the sea bottom. The weight of the plate holds the rest of the turbine erect. In this particular geographic area, the weight of the foundations has to be great enough to withstand currents and ice. A special ice-breaking cone shape was adopted for the hull of the foundation. The use of steel reinforcement allowed the foundations to be light enough for transport to their sites by ship, where they were then laid down onto special beds of compacted stone.

The wind energy system uses a two megawatt turbine on a 60-meter tower; the rotor diameter comes to 72 meters. The system uses a Danish design that has three rotors. The rotors use what is called *active stall* and *active pitch control*; this means that the rotors themselves can shift on the housing to adjust to different wind speeds and directions. When wind strikes the rotors, the shape of the blade causes the wind to lift the blades, making the rotors spin. Sometimes the angle of the wind changes and instead of sticking to the rotor blade, the wind tumbles off; this is called *stall*. In this case, the lift is dramatically reduced (and thus so is the torque or power). The turbines use both lift and stall to their advantage. When there is too little lift, the rotors adjust to gain the best "angle of attack" or position for most lift. When there is too much lift and the system might become overloaded, the rotors shift to allow the wind to tumble off the back of the blades, thereby reducing torque and associated system problems.

A report on wind energy in Middelgrunden concludes that the wind park is working well (Bale and Hoffman 2002). The costs of operation are low enough per kWh that Middelgrunden should be profitable for both its public and private investors for some time to come. The turbines have outperformed their guaranteed levels of efficiency and production of electricity has steadily outpaced the budget. The public/private partnership between the municipality and the cooperative is one of the most important dimensions of the project; it allows the wind park to function with the resources, capital, and infrastructure of a state-run project while keeping the efficiency and knowledge of the private sector and public awareness of the shareholders. Middelgrunden also illustrates the value and importance of fully studying the potential impacts of a development project before construction; the substantial number of public hearings held and studies released before the start of construction facilitated a greater dialogue with the public and led to a greater level of acceptance for the park. Middelgrunden, which currently produces about three percent of the electricity of Copenhagen, demonstrates how wind power can be used to complement conventional energy systems, providing the benefits of a clean (generating no pollution of any kind), safe, efficient, profitable, and attractive alternative energy system.

Wind energy must be supported through incentives, opportunities, and a sustained effort to develop new technologies and bring them to the market at affordable prices. The challenge is to create long-term national and international policy frameworks for energy, which will reduce reliance on fossil fuels, reduce greenhouse emissions, and increase reliance on renewable energy sources, of which wind is a central component.

Solar Energy: Photovoltaic

Solar energy is generated by harnessing the energy of the sun. Most solar energy systems use a photovoltaic cell (*photo* means light, *voltaic* refers to electricity). These cells are just like those used in small devices like calculators and are the central location where solar rays are converted into electricity (Africano et al. 2002). A group of photovoltaic cells are known as a *module*; a group of modules is referred to as an *array*. A photovoltaic (PV) cell is constructed using pieces of silicon doped (a process used to add impurities to the silicon) with either phosphorous or boron (Scott 2000). The phosphorus-coated silicon is negatively charged, the boron-coated silicon is positively charged, and when these silicon pieces are pushed together, the movement of electrons from one to the other creates an electric field. When exposed to the sun, photons from the sun's rays carry enough energy to knock electrons free from the positive side, and they come into contact with a conductive metallic grid that is placed over the top of the cell and flow through the grid, creating an electric current. Because silicon is a very shiny material, an antireflective coating is

119

applied directly above the metallic grid to promote maximum absorption of the sun's rays by the cell. A metallic black contact plate is used on the bottom of the cell to improve conduction and allow electrons to flow back into the cell more freely. A weather-proof glass panel is then installed to cover the entire unit and protect it from moisture. (Scott 2000; Africano et al. 2002).

Nonrenewable resources are used to manufacture PV cells and systems, and waste is generated as part of the production process. However, after manufacture, PV energy generation is a zero-emissions process, which generates no pollution or noise. Since the sun is the source of energy, it is a completely renewable and sustainable energy source. PV cell systems can be used in either large scale applications in place of a fossil fuel-powered electricity plant, or they can be used in smaller applications. Large or small commercial or residential buildings in urban or rural areas can use PV arrays, commonly on their rooftops. Individual buildings that use PV electricity reduce the need to use conventional sources of energy from the grid. On sunny days during full sun hours, PV systems typically produce more energy than is required, and this can either be stored in battery banks or, more commonly, be sent into the grid, adding renewable energy to the urban power mix. PV systems contain no moving parts, so there is nothing to break down or wear out; they are virtually maintenance-free systems which have twenty-to thirty-year warranties, with some forty-year-plus design life expectancy.

A report by the European Photovoltaic Industry Association and Greenpeace, entitled *The Solar Generation*, concluded that the global solar PV industry could experience an unprecedented boom in both industrialized and developing nations. According to their calculations, solar PV could easily supply electricity for over one billion people, including 30 percent of the entire continent of Africa, and provide 2.3 million jobs by 2020; by 2040 the industry could provide 26 percent of total projected global energy needs (Leggett 2002). Innovative solar technologies are already providing high-tech, durable, emission-free energy in many parts of the world. Jeremy Leggett, chief executive officer of Solar Century, reports that the "two billion people who now lack electricity could have their needs met by micropower technologies, avoiding the need for new, polluting, costly, and centralized grid infrastructures" (Leggett 2002, 28).

SolarHost

Beginning in year 2000, a worldwide web host company called SolarHost has powered its servers and company offices with an array of photovoltaic cells that convert sunlight into electricity. SolarHost uses panels to collect solar energy, which is converted into an alternating current and stored in batteries that provide electricity when the sun isn't shining. The solar collectors, which take about five hours per day of peak sunlight to charge, provide about 140 percent of the energy needed to run computer servers and keep the lights on in one of SolarHost's buildings. Excess electricity is transferred to the regional power grid, and SolarHost can draw electricity from the grid at its other sites. From 2000 through 2003, an increasing number of environmental groups and small businesses moved their websites to SolarHost's server. Since going live in March 2000, SolarHost was down for only eleven minutes, primarily for service upgrades. The system SolarHost uses cost about $40,000 to build and is expected to last at least twenty years.

Source: Whipple 2001

Solar Energy: Thermal

An older and technically simpler form of solar energy is solar thermal energy. In its simplest form, solar thermal energy is used to heat things, typically water. A solar thermal hot water system can be as simple as a dark tank or barrel sitting in the sun. More advanced systems for solar thermal water heating are relatively cheap and simple. About 1.5 million homes and 250 thousand commercial and industrial buildings in the United States use solar thermal hot water heaters; homes using solar thermal water heaters in the United States recovered the cost of the new systems in five to ten years from energy savings (Philip 2001).

The country of Yemen, among the poorest nations in the world, provides an interesting example of how national and local officials have become interested in the possibility of using solar water heaters in major cities. Yemen is characterized by tropical, hot, sunny weather in the coastal, southern, and eastern regions. Despite these ideal solar conditions, almost all of the hot water users in Yemen, both commercial and domestic, use electricity or gas to heat the water. Using solar heaters would conserve energy and money needed for other infrastructure development. As of 2003, several domestic solar water heaters had been installed in Yemen's major cities, including Sana and Dhamar. The results generated from an analysis of these solar water heaters revealed that while there were problems stemming from improper installation and usage, as well as high initial cost per unit, the potential of using solar water heaters is good (Bin Gadhi and Mukbel 1998).

A more technically advanced and expensive form of solar thermal energy, called *solar thermal electricity*, can be used to produce electricity. The system includes mirrors and lenses that reflect and concentrate the sun's energy to a central location where a heat transfer fluid (usually water) is heated to produce steam which is then used to turn a turbine, producing electricity. A solar thermal electricity generation plant in southern California produced enough energy in 2003 to power ten thousand homes. Projects of between thirty and one hundred megawatts are in the planning stages for locations in Spain and Nevada, U.S. (Philip 2001).

Summary

This chapter outlines the social and environmental problems stemming from overwhelming dependency on fossil fuels in cities throughout the world. Globally, the principal environmental problem associated with fossil fuels stems from the gases emitted when fossil fuels are burned, which cause a greenhouse effect resulting from the emission of heat-trapping gases, principally CO_2, in the atmosphere. Rising temperatures lead to extreme climatic events, including heat waves, the melting of ice, rising sea levels, and destructive storms. Global expansion of oil exploration endangers fragile ecosystems, locks countries in a spiral of debt and dependency, and devastates indigenous people and communities. Oil refineries are harmful to human and environmental health and, when linked to wars for control of oil resources, fossil fuel dependency threatens people worldwide.

Achieving the complimentary goals of energy efficiency and expanding markets for renewable energy technologies will require the passage of new planning and policy initiatives that would be specifically developed to encourage and support innovation and investment in renewable technologies. Excessive energy consumption needs to be curbed. This can largely be accomplished through energy efficiency and renewable energy sources.

Planning and policy must be focused on supporting energy-efficient buildings and appliances, energy-efficient industrial processes, energy-efficient vehicles, tax incentives and subsidies for innovations, and cost reductions in wind and solar energy. Funding must be provided to strengthen the energy supply and management infrastructures in developing nations, but based on a commitment to reducing reliance on fossil fuels and increasing reliance on renewable energy sources. In their article "Renewable Fuels and Electricity for a Growing World Economy: Defining and Achieving the Potential," Johansson et al. suggest the following policy initiatives (1992):

- Remove subsidies that artificially reduce the price of fuels that compete with renewables; if these subsidies cannot be removed, renewable energy technologies should be given equivalent incentives.

- Introduce taxes, regulations, and other policy instruments that ensure that consumer decisions are based on the full cost of energy, including environmental and other external costs not reflected in market prices.

- Increase government support for research, development, and demonstration of renewable energy technologies (in close cooperation with the private sector).

- Review government regulations of electric utilities to ensure that investments in new generating equipment are consistent with a renewable-intensive future and that these utilities are involved in programs to demonstrate new renewable energy technologies in their service areas.

- Encourage the development of a biofuels industry, working in close coordination with both national agricultural development programs and efforts to restore degraded lands.

- Create and/or strengthen national institutions to implement renewable energy programs.

- Direct available international development funds for the energy sector increasingly toward renewables.

- Create a strong international institution that would assist and coordinate national and regional programs for increased use of renewable energy sources, support the assessment of energy options, and support centers of excellence in specialized areas of renewable energy research (Johansson et al. 1992, 8–9).

The chapter describes ways in which sustainable urban energy production and use must progress. Because energy demand is projected to increase globally, even if conservation efforts are successful in industrialized countries, a combination of energy conservation and increasing reliance on renewable energy sources must be employed. Green building design strategies and technologies, which reduce dependence on natural resources and reduce the pollution of the environment by waste products, are also essential. Wind energy, photovoltaic (PV) solar energy, and thermal solar energy systems are described with examples of their use in cities around the world. Planning and policy approaches must be introduced to reduce our dependency on fossil fuels by supporting an energy future based on a system that supports energy efficiency and makes intensive use of renewable resources. Achieving the complementary goals of energy efficiency and expanding markets for renewable energy technologies will require the passage of new policy initiatives that would be specifically developed and supported to encourage innovation and investment in renewable technologies.

Chapter Questions

The chapter provides readers with information to address six essential questions related to planning for sustainable urban energy supply and management:

1. What are the principal problems stemming from the burning of fossil fuels?

2. What do we mean by the concept *renewable energy*?

3. What energy systems and technologies are considered renewable? Why are they considered renewable?

4. What problems are caused by burning traditional biomass fuels in unvented rooms? How do modern systems resolve these problems?

5. What are the benefits of wind and solar energy systems?

6. What economic and social policies would need to be implemented to promote the widespread use of renewable energy?

Notes

1. The oil and gas industry divides itself into three integrated areas: upstream, midstream, and downstream. Upstream activities revolve around the exploration for new reserves of oil and gas and the production of known, proven reserves. Midstream activities revolve around the processes by which crude oil and gas are transported to refineries via tankers and pipelines, often distant from their point of extraction. Downstream activities revolve around refining, marketing, and distribution (Rain Forest Action Network 1998, 8). As existing identified oil reserves begin to diminish, the petroleum industry (a global industry that involves more than six thousand companies) is spending about $156 billion a year searching for new oil and gas reserves around the globe. The issue is not how much oil we can find and extract; the issue is that oil extraction is increasingly more expensive and, more importantly, that its associated activities are destroying our climate, endangering indigenous cultures, threatening the last pristine places on the planet, and perpetuating a cycle of debt and dependency for developing countries (Rain Forest Action Network 1998, 8–9).

2. It is critical for city planners and other urban authorities to become informed about alternative approaches and technologies. As was seen in the example of the attempt to implement gray water systems in the Quayside Village co-housing community in North Vancouver, Canada (chapter 1), working with staff who responded skeptically and conservatively to the proposed gray water system led to minimal allowances, an overbuilt system, and avoidable water contamination.

3. In addition to these biofuel sources, families in periurban areas may also rely on agricultural residues (various wood and green crop residues, cereal remains, and residues as their main cooking fuel) (Hughart 1979). The two principal problems associated with this biomass fuel source are that removing agricultural residues in large quantities contributes to soil erosion (resulting in the loss of soil nutrients, water-holding capacity, soil organic matter, and soil biota) and significantly increases the rate of water runoff.

Photograph by Raquel Pinderhughes

CHAPTER FOUR

URBAN TRANSPORTATION PLANNING AND MANAGEMENT

If people continue to exercise their choices as they are at present and there are no other significant changes, the resulting traffic growth would have unacceptable consequences for both the environment and the economy .. . and could be very difficult to reconcile with overall sustainable development goals. . . . When it comes to effective policies the air is thick with ideas such as road pricing, fuel tax rises, improving public transport, encouraging land use change, greater use of computer telecommunications and so on. But the commitment to any fundamental change is timid. The notion of balance remains at the heart of policy making. A transport policy that is compatible with sustainable development objectives is one which strikes the right balance between serving economic development and protecting the environment and the future ability to sustain quality of life. . . . The changes necessary in transport will have profound effects on all aspects of life and illustrate clearly why we cannot go on as we are.

—Andrew Blowers, "We Can't Go On As We Are:
Social Impact of Trends" in *Urban Transport*, 1995

Transportation

Transportation is an indispensable component of urban infrastructure and development. Transport is essential to the operation of cities and to the economic and social base of urban areas because it functions to bring raw materials together to create products and services, connect goods and services to markets, and bring workers and others to and from their places of work, school, consumption, and recreation. A functional transportation system is critical to the efficient movement of people, products, and services, an effective commerce and trade system, and the long-term socioeconomic development and vitality of a city (Akinbami and Fadare 1997).

Transportation plays a critical role in urban design and form. Transportation infrastructures and the characteristics of transportation supply and performance impact the physical structure and spatial arrangements of a city and its surrounding area, influence personal and employment-related travel patterns, generate economic opportunities, increase or decrease people's sense of community, and have the potential to improve the quality of living and efficiency in an urban area (DeCorla-Souza 1992; Agarwal 1996; Rabinovitch 1996; Crane 1999).

Transit systems are critical to the economy of every nation. The economic investments required to construct and maintain a transportation infrastructure (i.e., roads, bridges, tunnels, freeways, streets, curbs, rail systems, traffic control systems, parking areas, bikeways, and so on) are huge. Economic activities related to the degree of success with which the transit system moves workers to and from employment opportunities and other services and to the number of jobs transportation generates contribute enormously to a city's economic and social vitality.

People travel through urban areas for many reasons and use different transportation modalities to do so. Today's global transportation mix includes walking, cycling, animal- and hand-pulled vehicles, boats, ships, rail, buses, minivans, trolleys, trucks, automobiles, motorcycles, helicopters, airplanes, and paratransit vehicles.[1] Urban planners have long recognized that development patterns influence travel demand and patterns, mode of travel, congestion levels, cost of travel, and choices about how to travel.

Transportation Patterns in Developing Countries

The vast majority of people living in developing countries travel short distances, typically to and from work and school; in 1990 journeys to and from work accounted for between 40 percent to 50 percent of all urban trips; trips to and from school accounted for another 20 percent to 35 percent of travel (Armstrong-Wright 1997). Transport patterns in developing countries continue to be based primarily around public transit, walking, and nonmotorized transit modes such as cycle rickshaws and bicycles (Evans et al. 2001). People living in developing countries rely on a diverse transit mix for their daily transit needs; this mix includes walking, bicycles, animal-powered vehicles, paratransit, buses, rail, motorcycles, and increasingly cars. The amount of bicycle use in some regions is extraordinary. In Asia the amount of people and cargo moved by bicycles outweighs the amount of people and cargo moved by motor vehicles in all of Europe combined (Workbike Research 2001). Mass transit remains the most critical component of transport systems throughout Asia, Latin America, and Africa. According to a World Bank study, the motorized modal split in developing countries typically falls into the following ranges: buses and minibuses 50 percent to 70 percent; paratransit 5 percent to 20 percent; rail (where available) 10 percent to 20 percent; and private cars and taxis 15 percent to 30 percent (Armstrong-Wright 1997). In Bombay, India, rail use is over 30 percent; in Manila, Philippines, paratransit transport is well over 50 percent; in cities throughout China, the overall share of buses is well above 80 percent, with very little use of private cars (Armstrong-Wright 1997).

Shared taxis are very popular and frequently utilized in most developing countries, despite the fact that they cost more than most buses. Santiago, Chile, has over 40,000 shared and conventional taxis which, despite their higher cost, carry about 500,000 passengers per day. In some small cities, like Jos, Nigeria, taxis are the *only* means of public transport available to and from the area (Armstrong-Wright 1997).

Bicycle- and scooter-pedaled cycle rickshaws remain among the most popular, affordable, and convenient transport modalities throughout India and in many other cities in southeast Asia. However, urban authorities and transportation planners are increasingly viewing cycle rickshaws as hazardous and undisciplined modes of transport which cause considerable traffic congestions. This issue will be discussed later in this chapter.

These trends demonstrate how people living in cities in the developing world rely heavily on mass transit and the bicycle, but it is clear that the increasing spread of urban areas, increased commercial and industrial activity, population growth, and a greater propensity to travel as incomes rise is changing transportation patterns in many developing nations (Armstrong-Wright 1997). Although the bicycle is still an essential component of the transport system in many developing countries, urban authorities are increasingly viewing bicycles as a nuisance, and planners are giving right of way to taxis, buses, and the private car and discouraging bicycles and bicycle-powered vehicles (Kahn 2002).

Shifting transit patterns in many developing countries clearly indicate that the number of people who drive private cars is rapidly increasing in most cities throughout the world. This trend is not exclusively attributed to increases in personal income and national prosperity. Cities like Bangkok, Thailand, which have *lower* levels of wealth than their neighbors in Singapore, Tokyo, or Hong Kong, have *higher* levels of car use and its associated air contamination (Kenworthy and Laube 1999). This is explained by planning and policy initiatives that favor private automobiles over mass transit, specifically, the absence of economic restraints on car ownership and use, poor mass transit options, and an emphasis on large-scale road building to solve congestion problems (Kenworthy and Laube 1999).

China is a case in point. China is now one of the largest producers of automobiles, and the Chinese government is providing people with many different kinds of incentives to purchase and drive private cars. China has some of the worst air pollution in the world, yet despite this fact, urban planners and policymakers are developing policies that discourage bicycle use and encourage automobile use. Use of the bicycle, so fundamental to China's transport system, is declining largely due to public policies that support car use over bicycle use. To encourage car and motorcycle ownership, Chinese officials have banned bicycles from some of the busiest urban roads (Hook and Replogle 1996). In Shanghai, the city has banned bicycles on more than fifty major roads and made no provisions for workers to ride or carry their bikes over the Huangpu River to Pudong, where the city's new financial and industrial center is located (Kahn 2002). "Cycle lanes (in Shanghai) are getting narrower in most of the newly built or rebuilt roads. . . . In some streets, an extra line for sedans is even drawn within the bicycle lane" (Anonymous 2002). Although China still produces more bicycles than any other nation, the government's commitment to bicycles is clearly decreasing. Official preference for the automobile has left bikers at a strong disadvantage on crowded shared roads; between 1990 and 2000, traffic fatalities in China doubled and 35 percent of these deaths were cyclists (Vital Signs 2001).

Transportation Patterns in Industrialized Countries

In contrast to the vast range of transport modalities used in developing countries, people in industrialized countries use fewer transportation modalities to get around because (a) they have the largest share of the world's private automobile use and (b) very little, if any, of the human- and animal-powered mass transit options that are available to people in developing nations (Kenworthy and Laube 1999). At the same time, people in industrialized countries have much more varied transportation patterns; they are much more likely to travel long distances; and they travel for a much wider range of activities. In industrialized countries, work trips account for fewer than one third of all trips; more than two thirds of trips are related to school, household, social, and recreational travel (Ingram 1998).

People in the United States exemplify the problems associated with almost total reliance on the private automobile to meet transport needs.

Although it accounts for less than five percent of the world's population and less than one fourth of its combined gross product, the United States consumes more than one third of the world's transportation energy (Advocacy Institute 1996). Americans use five times as much energy for transportation than the average Japanese resident and nearly three times as much energy as the average citizen in Western Europe; Canadians are five times more likely than Americans to choose public transit over driving (National Resources Defense Council 2002). In 2000 there were more car owners in the United States than registered voters, and nine out of every ten Americans over the age of sixteen had a driver's license and owned or leased at least one vehicle (Curtis 1996; O'Meara Sheehan 2001; Spowers 2001). In 2002 the average adult in the United States took 86 percent of their travel trips by automobile, traveled 13,500 miles per person/per year, and owned the most light vehicles in the world (National Resources Defense Council 2002). Suburban households in the U.S. typically own 2.2 cars per household, generate twelve auto trips per day, and drive 31,300 miles per year (National Resources Defense Council 2002).

Europeans travel about half as much as Americans, and when they do travel, Europeans have a much higher tendency to choose alternative transport modes such as bus, rail, and bicycle. Auto use in European nations accounts for between 11 percent and 26 percent of travel; walking and biking account for between 33 percent and 50 percent of total travel modes in Europe (National Resources Defense Council 2002). Nevertheless, although Europeans use their cars considerably less than people in the United States, between 1970 and 1995, passenger car traffic in Western Europe more than doubled; between 1971 and 1992, the number of private cars in the United Kingdom alone increased by 93 percent (Blowers 1995). Denmark is the only industrial country in Europe that is shifting away from automobile use and toward buses and rail. Eastern European nations are still currently less automobile-oriented than their Western European counterparts, but national governments throughout Eastern Europe are supporting policies designed to encourage car ownership and use (Pucher 1990). Between 1995 and 1996, new car sales in Poland rose by 40 percent; in 1996 Warsaw had about four hundred cars per one thousand inhabitants, and motor traffic had become the most significant source of air and noise pollution, producing 50 percent to 80 percent of the city's air contamination (International Bicycle Fund 2001b).[2]

Environmental and Social Impacts of Automobile Dependency

State of the World's 2001 analysis of current transit trends around the world reveals that despite the wide range of problems associated with increased automobile dependency, global trends are *not* favoring diverse transit systems and modalities (O'Meara Sheehan 2001). Throughout the world, cars, trucks, motorcycles, scooters, and airplanes are increasingly moving more people and goods, while rails, bicycles, many forms of paratransit, and other less environmentally damaging transport modes are rapidly declining. As road transport increases and the infrastructure to support it expands, nonmotorized vehicles and rail are becoming less important. As air travel is an increasingly important part of the transit mix, rail and shipping are becoming less important.

Despite differences in national and regional transport modalities and patterns between industrialized and developing nations, the automobile is rapidly increasing its presence throughout the entire world, and household activity patterns in urban areas are increasingly becoming centered on access to private cars or motorcycles. People increasingly desire automobiles, motorcycles, and scooters based on the perception that they provide riders with efficiency, speed, unprecedented freedom, privacy, convenience, location control, security, and status (Sperling 1995). Individual users are attracted to the door-to-door flexibility, twenty-four-hour availability, and passenger and goods transport capacity that the automobile provides (Sperling 1995). In an article entitled "Sustainable Transportation: The Key to Sustainable Cities," civil and environmental engineer L. C. Wadhwa describes the increasing growth in vehicle ownership levels and the increase in auto miles traveled each year as providing travelers with a sense of hypermobility that creates the false perception that the automobile is convenient, safe, comfortable, fast, dependable, affordable, obtainable, and, finally, essential to a high quality of life. In developing countries, the drive to increase road infrastructure and automobile ownership is tremendous; most federal and local governments are strongly promoting policies that encourage automobile purchase and use (Wadhwa 2000). People are buying cars and motorcycles as soon as they can. The vast majority of these purchases are made on credit, moving households further into debt. This trend is particularly worrisome because the negative impacts of automobile dependency are likely to be even harsher in cities where urban populations are largest and major problems related to air pollution and public health already exist as a result of weak urban infrastructure and inadequate industrial and transportation policies, standards, and enforcement (Wadhwa 2000).

Although some planners are skeptical about the role of the private car in urban life, the vast majority of planners believe that the car is a positive force in the emergence of a new urban structure (Clark and Kuijpers-Linde 1994). But independent of where individual planners stand, the benefits of fossil fuel-dependent private light vehicles (i.e., automobiles, vans, motorcycles, and scooters) to the individual must be weighed against the costs of these vehicles to society as a whole. It is now widely acknowledged that, among transportation modalities, the car is the most damaging vehicle to the environment (Greenpeace 1995).

The environmental and social problems related to automobile dependency are numerous. They include dependency on fossil fuel energy sources, which create greenhouse gas emissions related to climate change; problems related to oil exploration, which endangers fragile ecosystems and devastates indigenous people and communities; air contamination and its associated public health and environmental problems; local and regional environmental degradation; accidents resulting in injuries, deaths, and illnesses; and a range of socioeconomic problems that exacerbate existing social inequalities.

How the Transportation Infrastructure Promotes and Supports Automobile Use

Although much of the variation in transport systems and patterns can be attributed to differences in levels of development, per capita income, and resource availability between countries and cities, most of the variation in transport options is due to the planning and design of the transportation infrastructure. Research on policies and travel behavior in cities around the world reveals that governments in virtually every nation in the world express their preferences in urban transportation by differentially subsidizing and taxing various modes of transportation and by promoting or discouraging the types of transit modalities, land uses, and urban developments that depend on or foster alternative transportation systems (Pucher 1990).

Planners view the automobile and the expansion of a national road transport network as critical to development outcomes, most importantly to increased economic development and wealth creation. The more market oriented a country's economy, the more likely it is to neglect public transit in favor of subsidizing highway construction, auto use, and suburban development (Pucher 1990). The primary function of large interstate and intrastate transportation systems in countries like the United States is to provide access to land; the underlying assumption having always been that transportation functions to supply the capacity to carry people from existing distribution centers to where developers are choosing to build (Dittmar 1995). Public capital (through publicly funded freeway construction and in the form of gas taxes paid by current users of the system) is utilized to provide free access to cheap developable land and increase its value to those who have enough means to exploit it. The goal of planning and design approaches are to develop uniform standards with one overarching objective—to move as many vehicles as possible as quickly as possible and with minimum conflict between vehicles (Pucher 1990). The idea is to apply these uniform standards, not to design for a particular community or natural context; issues related to setting, context, or community are treated as exceptions or anomalies.

Transportation planners continue to assert that the popularity of the automobile is due to individual preferences and lifestyle choices, but in fact, the most salient factors determining automobile dependency are linked to urban planning and policy decisionmaking (Dittmar 1995). Decisionmaking includes land use decisions which promote sprawl and the increased spatial separation of homes and workplaces; shops and schools in the absence of efficient, affordable public transit systems; ever-expanding beltways and highways that make automobile travel appealing; insufficient investment in public transit modalities; the relatively low price of owning and maintaining an automobile; unsafe roads for nonmotorized vehicles and pedestrians; and a lack of safe bicycle parking (Dittmar 1995).

In an article entitled "A Broader Context for Transportation Policy," Hank Dittmar describes the dominant approach to planning and delivering transportation services in the United States (1995). Transportation policy in the United States focuses most heavily on the role of the automobile, with transportation officials asserting that Americans love their cars and cherish driving and that any effort to decrease the centrality of the automobile is doomed. Planners support this tendency by claiming that Americans vote with their gas pedals when they choose to live in suburbs and that building more roadways gives residents what they want. But research on transportation preferences and concerns reveals that Americans may not be as attached to the automobile as planners and transportation officials perceive them to be. Recent studies show that traffic jams, nonproductive time, expense, and increased understanding about the negative environmental and public health impacts of greenhouse gases and polluting emissions are making many Americans deeply conflicted about the automobile and their reliance upon it (Dittmar 1995). As Dittmar points out, what appears on the surface to be a deep attachment to the car is in fact an unconscious response to the signals and relatively limited transportation options that planners give the public by building ring roads and beltways and subsidizing free or low-cost parking and suburban development through the utility infrastructure and tax incentives that favor car use and suburban home ownership (1995). Transportation infrastructures continue to be planned, expanded, and managed within the logic of "predict and provide," with very low priority given to the environmental and social consequences of increasing infrastructure support for the automobile (Guy and Marvin 1999).

Problems with Automobile Dependency

The transportation sector is one of the fastest growing sectors producing greenhouse gas emissions from human activity. Globally, transport contributes more than 30 percent of the world's carbon dioxide emissions. Automobiles are the most significant contributor to climate change and global warming, responsible for more than a quarter of the world's carbon dioxide emissions from fossil fuel use. The global fleet of 532 million gasoline-burning automobiles, combined with thousands of coal-fired power plants, is the engine driving climate change (Brown et al. 2001).

Although there have been significant improvements in the fuel efficiency and design elements of automobiles, these improvements have failed to stem an increase in worldwide consumption of fossil fuels for transportation. This is due to five main factors. First, growing reliance on automobiles and driving alone. Second, average new car fuel economy has fallen since 1987; this is happening for at least two different reasons. In some parts of the world, like China, less fuel-efficient cars are being produced and sold in large numbers. In other parts of the world, like the United States, sales of larger, more powerful, and fuel-inefficient light vehicles, including light trucks and sport utility vehicles, are increasingly rapidly. Third, the increasing spread of urban areas (urban sprawl) within the context of a lack of safe, convenient, and reliable public transportation options to conduct daily activities. Fourth, lack of government support for the development and integration of renewable energy technologies such as electric and hydrogen-fueled cars. Fifth, as much as 20 percent of all the energy consumed throughout the life of a vehicle goes into its manufacture.

The negative environmental impacts of the automobile stem from the *entire* life cycle of the vehicle and all related infrastructure support systems, including extraction of raw materials, construction and maintenance related to road infrastructure, vehicle production, operation, maintenance, and disposal. Vehicle life cycle also includes everything related to the production and processing required to provide automobiles with energy and fuel for varied uses. Although we tend to think of the exhaust pipe as the primary source of an automobile's negative environmental and social impacts, in fact, the manufacturing process generates more pollution per car than ten years of average driving (Spowers 2001). The automobile manufacturing process requires huge amounts of raw materials including steel, iron, rubber, lead, plastics, and aluminum, massive quantities of energy, and large quantities of chemicals that deplete the ozone layer and contribute to global warming (Greenpeace 1995). Despite decades of research and development to increase fuel efficiency and improve vehicle design, the typical car requires 680kg of steel, 230kg of iron, 90kg of plastics, 45kg of rubber, and 45kg of aluminum. Somewhere between 8,000 to 28,000 kilowatt hours of energy are needed to produce a single motor vehicle, equivalent to the energy contained in between 520 and 780 gallons of gasoline or to the amount of fuel consumed by 10,000 to 16,000 km of driving (Greenpeace 1995; National Resources Defense Council 2002). Automobile air conditioners are the single largest source of chlorofluorocarbons (CFC) emissions in the United States, with additional CFCs and other ozone-depleting chemicals released during the auto production process. CFCs are a contributing factor to stratospheric ozone depletion. Despite tighter vehicle-emission regulations in some countries, ground-level ozone and particulates in cities are increasing because of increases in the number of vehicles, average size of vehicles, and the increased distances cars are being driven. In the decade between 1990 and 2000, each car unit produced in Germany involved the assembly of some 15,000 parts by an industry that uses more resources than any others—20 percent of the world's steel, 50 percent of the lead, and 60 percent of the world's rubber; and 29 tons of waste was generated for every one ton of car produced (Spowers 2001). Disposal of old cars and car components has also become a major environmental problem; this is especially true for items like tires, batteries, and used oil.

In many developing nations, problems stemming from automobile emissions are made worse by the fact that the fuel used is of poor quality, predominantly leaded, and often adulterated. Many vehicles are poorly maintained due to lack of income for maintenance and breaches of vehicle pollution laws. Traffic congestion is severe, and one of the most significant sources of health damage is air pollution. Noise is also a problem, and levels on any of the main roads and intersections render human speech unintelligible. Seventy percent of eighteen cities tested in China had noise levels related to transit that exceeded acceptable standards; about 30 percent of the in-use cars had noise levels higher than acceptable levels (Anonymous 2002). In almost every major city in the world, ever-increasing levels of congestion and air contamination are associated with deteriorating quality of urban life.

The economic costs of maintaining the automobile infrastructure are massive. New urban expressways cost up to $60 million per kilometer compared to rail and bike facilities, which cost on average $9 million and $50,000 respectively (Center for Sustainable Transportation 1998). Economic impacts are also felt at the local level. Although automobile use creates jobs, money spent on gas tends to leave local communities and regions. Traffic congestion can stifle local economic development and limit job growth. Although governments and planners promote automobile transit because of the presupposed economic gains stemming from extra mobility, these gains are not guaranteed. Road construction is justified as being essential for the overall economy through aiding the movement of goods and services as well as people. But research on transportation reveals that road construction and increasing levels of road haulage are just as likely to harm as well as stimulate the economy because road infrastructure also provides the means for outside firms to extend their activities into new areas and potentially put local firms out of business (White-legg 2000). New roads increase pressure on surrounding land, produce greater traffic levels, and often increase traffic congestion and the demand for new and wider roads. Road building is expansive because it is heavily subsidized by government; aside from taking huge amounts of money from the public coffers which could be used on other infrastructure needs, building more roads supports an insatiable supply-and-demand model (Smith et al. 1988). The costs of goods traveling further are significant, including those associated with increased fuel consumption and its associated negative environmental and public health impacts.

Construction of highways, roads, parking lots, garages, and so on destroys huge amounts of habitat for both people and wildlife. Road building involves the loss or irreparable degradation of wetlands and other delicate ecosystems all over the world due to the actual construction of roads as well as the large-scale extraction of rock, sand, gravel and other construction materials. Road building requires the large-scale extraction and movement of rock, sand, gravel, and other construction materials and is related to the loss or irreparable degradation of wetlands and other fragile ecosystems all over the world.

Employment impacts related to the automobile industry are tremendous. Workers in more than one hundred nations make parts and components for automobiles. In addition to millions of workers employed in auto manufacturing, supplier industries provide even more jobs than those provided by manufacturing cars. Millions more workers are employed in related businesses, such as gas and service stations, repair shops, car sales and rental agencies, and taxicab companies. In addition to employment impacts and moving workers to and from their workplaces, automobile transit produces the need for road construction and maintenance (Center for Sustainable Transportation 1998).

Worldwide, a quarter of a million people die on the roads every year, and ten million are injured. Of the nearly one million people killed on the world's roads each year, the vast majority of those who die are pedestrians. Exhaust fumes from automobiles cause cancer, lead poisoning, and a variety of bronchial and respiratory illness, as well as acid air pollution (Greenpeace 1995; Spowers 2001). Many urban residents perceive noise as one of the most significant problems associated with road traffic; elevated noise levels contribute to stress, cardiovascular disease, and hearing loss (O'Meara Shee-han 2001).

Auto manufacturers are among the largest multinational corporations in the world, and the automotive industry is one of the largest manufacturing industries in the world. Working together with their allies in the petroleum, cement, rubber, and steel industries, the automobile industry has successfully lobbied in favor of more and larger roads and against increased fuel efficiency and stronger, more effective hazardous waste laws.

Socioeconomic inequalities in urban areas are exacerbated by inequitable transit options and the disproportionate burden of negative impacts experienced by lower-income residents. A study conducted by Northwest Environmental Watch in Seattle, Washington, showed that the average American spends twenty-seven hours a month paying for the thirty-two hours a month spent driving their car (Durning 1996). Two of the many social injustices related to transit are (a) lack of access to work and education opportunities for those who do not have access to automobiles and (b) the amount of money used to support a car. Additional social costs include waste generation, land values lost to roads and parking facilities, traffic policing, traffic jams, road rage, and emergency services related to auto accidents (Center for Sustainable Transportation 1998).

Sustainable Urban Transportation Planning

In recent decades, every major city in the world has had to confront the problem of what to do about increasing air pollution, congestion, and demand for travel. As these problems increase, planners are gradually beginning to understand that the pervasiveness of automobile transportation to move people and their goods is one of the major contributors to decreased quality of urban life (Blowers 1995, Evans et al. 2001). The environmental and social costs of unrestrained growth in car ownership and use are causing planners to become concerned about the impact of the automobile on air and water quality, disturbance of the natural or built environment, loss of wildlife habitat and open space, increased traffic congestion, accidents, noise, and carbon emissions effecting climatic change. As importantly, a small, but growing, number of planners are slowly recognizing that developing policies that reduce automobile dependence can be popular with the public (Evans et al. 2001).

The European Union's 1992 report entitled *Transport Europe* concluded that a city without cars would be up to five times cheaper to run than a city with cars and would actually be a viable proposition (Smith et al. 1988). A recent U.S. study found that the cost of driving-related air and water pollution, climate change, noise, and accidents (at $125 billion) was nearly three times greater than the $42 billion paid by car drivers in highway users fees (O'Meara Sheehan 2001). A study by Taylor et al. confirmed that increases in public transport ridership are linked to heavy public spending on transit, innovation among transit systems and projects, and growing congestion on roads and highways (2002).

Increasingly, studies are showing that nonmotorized transport, such as bicycles and bicycle-pedaled carts and wagons, offer significant benefits to an urban area because they are less expensive to build, purchase, and maintain, are more flexible forms of transit, are nonpolluting (zero emission vehicles), and are popular with the public. As problems stemming from automobile use increase, discussions about transportation planning have expanded from a narrow focus on the extraordinary benefits of road and highway infrastructures and their associated economic development and growth benefits to include an understanding that motorized traffic growth has significant negative effects on the economy through congestion and defensive expenditures related to health care, road traffic accidents, and other diseconomies of urban life in crowded cities (O'Meara Sheehan 2001). In terms of quality of life, there is increasing realization that transport has significant societal, environmental, and social justice implications and that crowded, polluted, and noisy cities are both unacceptable and avoidable (Whitelegg and Williams 2001).

In *Reinventing Transportation: Exploring the Paradigm Shift Needed to Reconcile Transportation and Sustainability Objectives*, Todd Litman discusses how moving toward urban sustainability will require rethinking how we understand and measure transportation options and how we identify and evaluate solutions to existing and future transport problems (1999). Sustainable transportation planning challenges the notion that increased vehicle travel reflects legitimate consumer demand. It recognizes that attraction to the car or scooter is strongly influenced by spatial arrangements that separate land uses, the lack of viable public transit alternatives, and market distortions that underprice the cost of driving.

Conventional transportation planning typically treats vehicle movement as an end in and of itself, obsessively focusing on vehicle movements, congestion delay, average speed of travel, and traffic efficiency. In sharp contrast, sustainable transportation planning focuses on access, not vehicle travel. *Access* reflects the purpose of travel, the need to reach goods, activities, and services. Access can be improved in many ways, including such strategies as land use management, eliminating market distortions that encourage automobile use and inefficient travel, reducing urban sprawl, improving electronic communications, and utilizing strategies that reduce the need to travel altogether by designing local environments that increase the proximity between people, goods, and services (Litman 1999).

As Litman points out, although achieving a sustainable transportation system will require significant changes in transportation planning and policy in most cities, the path toward cleaner and more equitable transportation systems is clear. Transportation planners must shift from being traffic engineers concerned only with vehicle flow to public space architects concerned with balancing diverse and often conflicting uses of road environments. Streets are more than just conduits for vehicle traffic; they are part of the public realm where people meet and interact. Roadway design must not focus on traffic movement objectives at the expense of slow-moving uses (i.e., walking, biking, and wheelchairs) of streetscapes. Transportation planners must recognize that their decisions determine transit patterns. Increasing highway and road capacity will stimulate car-dependent transport and land-use patterns; investments in public transit, pedestrian, and bicycle infrastructures and facilities will create multimodal transit behaviors and uses (Litman 1999).

As Hank Dittmar points out in "A Broader Context for Transportation Planning," professionals and the public must profoundly shift their perceptions about transit (1995). Rather than prioritizing individual transport decisions, individual decisions and benefits must become subordinate to larger social and environmental needs. There must be an integrated approach to decisions about transportation policy and land use. Individual transport decisions must become subordinate to a community or city's long-term strategic objectives to improve quality of life for the area's residents. The underlying presumptions should be that (1) capacity expansion is not the preferred option; (2) the expansion of existing transportation systems should not destroy houses or land or disrupt community activities unless absolutely necessary; and (3) the priority should be to conserve natural and built environments (Dittmar 1995).

Sustainable transportation planning will require a comprehensive analysis of impacts and consideration of a broader range of solutions than has typically occurred. It will require public participation to determine alternatives, reflect community values, and support changes in community design and individual behavior. The paradigm shift will even involve changes in language. Litman shows, for example, how many transportation planning terms are biased in favor of automobile travel. Projects that increase road or parking capacity are often called "improvements" even though they may be harmful to many activities and people, degrade the local environment, reduce adjacent residential property values, and/or reduce the safety and mobility of pedestrians and cyclists (Litman 1999). The term *efficient* is frequently used to imply increased vehicle traffic speeds based on the (false) assumption that speed increases overall efficiency. In fact, high vehicle speeds can reduce total traffic capacity, increase resource consumption, increase costs, increase automobile dependency, and reduce overall economic efficiency. Increased speeds also result in more fatal road accidents (Litman 1999).

The Role of Language in Transportation Policy and Planning

Todd Litman illustrates how "biased" versus "objective" language in transportation planning can bias planners and policymakers in favor of policies which support increased automobile use. Biased language implies automobile accommodation exclusively and reveals nothing about the weaknesses of the proposed policy initiative. Objective language reveals the options for both motorists and pedestrians and reveals the problems proposed initiatives would generate for pedestrians. Examples are provided below:

Bias language: Level of service at this intersection is rated "D." The proposed improvement will cost $100,000. This upgrade will make our transportation system more efficient by enhancing capacity and preventing deterioration of traffic conditions.

Objective language: Level of service at this intersection is rated "D" for motorists and "E" for pedestrians. A right-turn channel would cost $100,000. This road widening project will increase motor vehicle traffic speeds and capacity but may reduce safety and convenience for pedestrian travel.

Source: Litman 1999

Urban planners and policymakers have considerable powers to influence transportation decisions and developments. They must begin to use their influence on decisionmaking related to land use, infrastructure, transit, parking, transportation demand management, and investments to encourage mass transit and bicycle use in cities. Increasing highway capacity will stimulate automobile-dependent transport and land use patterns, whereas investments in transit, pedestrian, and bicycle facilities will stimulate multimodal transportation systems and reduced reliance on the car (Moore and Thorsnes 1994). The major shifts involved in solving contemporary urban transportation problems will be to (1) focus on accessibility and affordability, (2) give urban residents more travel choices, and (3) ensure that transportation decisions are informed by a sense of good design, context, and community needs (Dittmar 1995). A sustainable transportation planning approach is designed to support a transport system that has the following essential characteristics and meets the following essential criteria:

- It allows the basic access needs for individuals and societies to be met safely and in a manner consistent with human and ecosystem health.

- It is affordable, operates efficiently, offers choice of transport mode, and supports a vibrant economy.

- It is capable of delivering required capacity and performance and is compatible with the desired lifestyle of the population it serves.

- It limits emissions and waste within the planet's ability to absorb them, uses inexhaustible energy (renewable energy) sources, minimizes consumption of non-renewable resources, reuses and recycles its components, and minimizes the use of land and the production of noise.

- It is clean and affordable for the vast majority of users; it does not pollute air, land, or water beyond the planet's ability to absorb and cleanse; this is especially the case with regard to CO_2 emissions.

- It makes use of land in a way that has little or no impact on the integrity of ecosystems.

- It uses energy sources that are essentially renewable or inexhaustible.

- It uses other resources that are renewable or inexhaustible and achieved in part through the reuse of items and the recycling of materials used in vehicles and infrastructure.

- It produces no more emissions and waste than can be accommodated by the planet's restorative ability.

- It meets basic human needs for health, comfort, and convenience.

- It allows for and supports development at a human scale and provides for a reasonable choice of transport modes, housing, community, and living styles.

- It produces no more noise than is acceptable by communities, is safe for people and their property, and provides cost-effective service and capacity.

- It is financially affordable in each generation and supports economic activities (Center for Sustainable Transportation 1997; Wadhwa 2000).

Sustainable transportation planning will require urban authorities to support planning and policy initiatives that reduce the transit infrastructures' reliance on nonrenewable energy resources. This will require changes in the design and production of light vehicles and their energy sources as well as ecological improvements in roadways and parking areas so that the materials utilized reduce the use of other resources, do not leach, and allow percolation of groundwater rather than runoff (Dittmar 1995). The use and reliance on the private automobile can and must be reduced, and the use of other more efficient travel modalities can and must be encouraged by localities charging the full costs of road travel to road users; though it is controversial and has problems, this may well be the most effective strategy for moving toward more sustainable urban transportation systems.

The fact that users do not pay the full cost of road travel (infrastructure, environmental damage, public health impacts, accidents, fuel, and so on) has resulted in an overuse of the automobile and a subsidized road transportation system. If road users were required to pay for the full cost of travel, they would be motivated to reduce their use and reliance on the private automobile and use more efficient travel modalities (Litman 1999; Wadhwa 2000; Argalis et al. 2000).

As discussed earlier, the wealth of a city is not sufficient in and of itself to explain the degree of automobile dependence in different cities. Some wealthy cities in Asia and western Europe have reduced reliance on the private automobiles and are making great strides in mass transit. Some less prosperous cities are promoting policies that strongly encourage automobile ownership and use. Thus, it is clear that it is public policy that shapes the urban system into a much less (or more) auto-dependent and higher (or lesser) mass transit-use form (Wadhwa 2000). It is urban form, and in particular higher urban density, that is highly correlated with lower levels of car ownership and car use, higher levels of mass transit use, and lower total costs of operating urban passenger transportation systems. The cost of cars is an important policy factor to consider in any efforts to reduce automobile dependence and increase transit use, but policies to increase the cost of car ownership and car use must be combined with physical planning strategies that emphasize development patterns oriented to transit, as well as walking and cycling (Litman 1999; Wadhwa 2000; O'Meara Sheehan 2001). Public transit use in industrialized nations is most strongly correlated with land use patterns and government support for transit-oriented modalities. Kenworthy and Laube's research on urban automobile and transit use in the United States, western Europe, Canada, Australia, and Asia reveals that public policy, urban density, and the cost of cars are the determining factors in reducing automobile use and increasing reliance on public transportation (1999).

Planners and other urban authorities must begin to accept the fact that solid investment in public transportation is the best strategy for addressing the social and environmental problems that stem from overreliance on private automobiles and for reducing a city's and urban resident's psychological and physical dependence on the automobile. Sustainable transportation planning goes way beyond minimizing petroleum use; it includes using nontoxic materials in roadway construction that have been recycled or that can be recycled and are more long-lasting as well as applying life-cycle costing methodologies and utilizing different materials. Mass transit options must be abundant, affordable, and accessible, and the routes covered by mass transit must get people to and from all the places where they need to go. In industrialized countries, planning and policy must be directed toward revitalizing existing bus and rail systems and steering new developments to locations easily reached by a variety of transportation, including walking, bus, rail, bicycles, park-n-rides, and car- and van-pools, not only by one-passenger cars, and providing residents with affordable, high-quality mass transit options (O'Meara Sheehan 2001).

Although technological developments designed to improve the automobile and road congestion are important, reducing the negative environmental impacts of urban transportation will require significant improvements in public transportation and a larger role for cycling and walking. All new developments should be required to encourage and accommodate alternative transportation modalities like the bicycle. Parking spaces should be limited whenever feasible in favor of mass transit, cycling, and walking transport modalities. In order to encourage walking and cycling, roads must be reconfigured to provide safe, convenient, attractive access opportunities for pedestrians and cyclists, even if this means slowing down automobile traffic or sacrificing some performance.

The next section of this chapter describes planning and policy approaches and technological changes that can be used to promote a more sustainable urban transportation system; the focus is on (1) increasing mass transit options and mass transit ridership, (2) increasing the role of bicycles, (3) increasing the role of work bikes and cycle rickshaws, (4) creating a pedestrian friendly infrastructure, and (5) alternative automotive systems, fuels, and design.

Increasing Mass Transit Options and Mass Transit Ridership

Increasing mass transit options and mass transit ridership are the most important components of sustainable urban transportation planning and management. To promote sustainable urban development, mass transit modalities must be increasingly designed to limit emissions and waste, use renewable energy sources, minimize consumption of nonrenewable resources, reuse and recycle components, minimize the use of land and production of noise, be accessible to and affordable for the vast majority of users, and get people where they need to go. Though the obstacles and opportunities to support mass transit in prosperous, industrialized nations with extensive road and rail networks are different from those in developing nations with fewer financial and material resources and weaker transportation infrastructures, the challenge is the same—to provide people with accessible, reliable, affordable, high-quality mass transit options.

Mass Transit in Industrialized Nations

Prosperous, industrialized nations would benefit enormously from increasing mass transit options and extending mass transit routes. Reducing car use has multiple social, economic, public health, and environmental benefits. Transit services increase urban development, job growth, and tax revenues. Rents are higher, and office vacancy rates are lower, near transit stations (Weyrich and Lind 1996). Extending mass transit to areas experiencing economic decline can revitalize an area.

A study by the European Commission describes how urban authorities in the city of Zurich, Switzerland, were motivated to implement changes in transportation planning and policy as a result of the dramatic increase (75 percent) in automobile use and in commuter workday car trips from the outlying areas of the city into the city center; in 1970 there had been one car park per fifteen employees; by 1990 there was one car park per five employees (European Commission 2002). A 1987 public opinion poll in Zurich showed a 61 percent approval rate for drastic measures to reduce private motorized traffic. Over the course of a few years, city officials introduced a series of public policies that functioned to constrain car traffic, integrate all modes of transport, upgrade and prioritize segregated tram and trolley routes and complimentary bus and tram systems, restrict parking, establish bus lanes and bus-only access to pedestrian areas, and introduce a computerized operational control system and selective vehicle detection system at 80 percent of traffic signals on bus and tram routes. The policies were particularly designed to reduce air pollution and noise levels.

The city of Zurich's transit policy is currently based on four measures and themes that define the development and management of the system

(European Commission 2002). First, all inhabitants of the city must be within reach of a metro line. This required the city to improve the network of routes to the stations as well as to create new and extended bus routes. Second, the system must meet basic standards of accessibility and comfort. A transport access point must be within 300 meters (328 yards) of living and working places. Tram and buses must run minimally between 6 a.m. and midnight; waits can be no longer than thirty minutes on all routes. Maximum traveling time shall not exceed one hour between any two stations in the city area. Passengers will be guaranteed a seat on public transit at off-peak time. Ideally, the goal is to improve the system further by providing passengers with more space between seats, interval times waiting for trams or buses of only six to eight minutes, extended routes to avoid passengers having to change modes of travel, and coordinated services so that door-to-door journeys are possible on a single ticket. Third, the system should support the provision of parking facilities for vehicles and bicycles. Fourth, car use should be discouraged to improve air quality and noise levels. Measures in this category include reducing the number of parking spaces, providing preferential car parks for small cars, channeling traffic through the main roads, limiting new road construction projects, redistributing road space in favor of public transit and pedestrians, banning car traffic in certain residential areas, and calming traffic to a speed no more than thirty km per hour (nineteen miles an hour) in residential areas.

In 2002 Zurich's transportation system was serving over 300 million passengers a year, and public transport had become the predominant feature of the city's transportation system (European Commission 2002). From 1985 to 1990, when the metro was opened, use of public transport services increased by over 30 percent. Public transport is used for 80 percent of journeys in the central city areas and for 50 percent of journeys from the suburbs and hinterlands areas into the city. Zurich's transport policy is an excellent illustration of a sustainable approach because this combination of planning and policy initiatives (1) consistently promotes public transport, (2) reduces motor vehicle transport, (3) shifts motor vehicle transport to main roads, (4) supports traffic calming measures in residential areas, (5) reduces public car parking spaces, and (6) promotes policies for environmentally friendly transportation modalities, particularly walking and cycling (European Commission 2002).

The city of Houston, Texas, was able to reduce traffic congestion by developing and implementing a transportation system strategy that relies on public transportation services, specifically buses and ride share programs, with a renewed emphasis on using transit centers and park and ride connections (Mass Transit 1999). As population and employment opportunities increase, the city plans to more than double its fleet of buses, increase the number and quality of transit facilities located near high-occupancy lands to better serve bus patrons, car-pool and van-pool passengers waiting in windy or rainy weather, and design waiting stations in ways that deter crime and increase personal safety.

A unique feature of the Houston design plan was its reliance on what is called a "crime prevention through environmental design approach," which posits that crime can be prevented by designing a physical environment that positively influences human behavior. The approach is based on four core strategies: (a) territoriality, (b) natural surveillance, (c) activity support, and (d) access control. The idea is to create an environment that people who use the area perceive as being safe and people who might commit crimes perceive as a highly risky place to commit crimes (Mass Transit 1999). The design approach uses building structures, landscaping, lighting, public art and signing, and ongoing public activities located in close proximity to the transit facilities, combined with regular maintenance. In this case, the city created a facility made of translucent windscreens that are durable, attractive, and that people can see through from clear solid glass blocks that are three inches thick. In addition, the facility includes low landscaping, high-powered halogen lights and other lights with high levels of illumination, and a closed-circuit television surveillance system and automatic electronic gates. According to city officials, the initial capital expenditures will lead to long-term savings related to less money spent on repeated maintenance and repair work as a consequence of vandalism (Mass Transit 1999).

Mass Transit in Developing Countries

In almost every major city in Asia, Latin America, and Africa, non-motorized urban transport is being threatened by urban planners and other officials who are justifying the expansion of the automobile infrastructure by arguing that motorized vehicles are more attractive and efficient and that slow-moving nonmotorized vehicles like bicycles and cycle rickshaws are a problem because they obstruct faster cars and buses, cause congestion, and project the wrong image for cities wishing to attract foreign investment (Whitelegg and Williams 2001). In these cities the emerging pattern of automobile, motorcycle, and truck transit replacing bus, rail, bicycle, and foot traffic must be slowed down considerably (and ideally, reversed) before it transforms transportation systems in developing countries completely (Whitelegg and Williams 2001).

Rather than encouraging increased automobile dependency, planners in developing countries should support policies that improve the quality of the diverse range of affordable, accessible, non- and less polluting transit options that are currently in place and popular with users. Planning and policy measures to discourage private automobile and motorcycle use and encourage use of public transit are essential to reducing traffic congestion, its associated public health impacts, and controlling urban sprawl (Rebelo 2002). Land use planning should pursue two complimentary paths: (1) to encourage urban forms which minimize transport needs, and (2) to improve existing public

Using Bus Systems to Promote Traffic Management

Planners in Abidjan, Cote d'Ivoire's capital city, developed a comprehensive traffic management plan in order to improve the quality, speed, and efficiency of bus transportation. The city created special bus lanes and new road links for a high-speed express bus network, new facilities for buses consisting of depots, terminals, and bus stops, footbridges to facilitate the movement and safety of pedestrians, and new traffic signals to improve traffic management.

Planners in Singapore's main city used an area licensing scheme, combined with an efficient shuttle bus system, to deal with central area traffic problems. The licensing scheme utilizes private car restraints and efficient shuttle buses. The program includes high annual license fees for private cars; fees for low-occupancy vehicles; limits on low-occupancy vehicles entering the central city zone; significant parking charges within the restricted areas; strict enforcement against illegal parking in the central area; and shuttle buses which carry passengers from residential areas to the city center. This combination of policies has substantially reduced congestion during the morning and evening rush hour periods and increased use of public transportation.

Source: Armstrong-Wright 1997

transit services to make them faster, safer, more comfortable, convenient, and affordable for low-income riders (Rebelo 2002).

In developing countries, the emphasis on mass transit should be on buses, not on rail. Buses are vastly less expensive to implement and maintain than rail; they can cover a much wider geographic area (including going into small localities off the beaten track); they are more affordable for passengers; and they create more employment opportunities. since there are typically more buses than trains utilized in a transportation system (Rabinovitch and Leitman 1996).

Curitiba, Brazil provides one of the most important examples of how municipalities in developing nations can provide residents with affordable, high quality, attractive, modern bus-based public transit options that meet the needs of a growing urban population. Since the 1960s, urban planners in Curitiba, Brazil, have used land-use policies and the transit system to promote high levels of public transit, guide urban growth, and improve quality of life for urban residents. Curitiba's road network and bus-based public transportation system are probably the most important elements accounting for the city's shape and development over time.

In an article entitled "Urban Planning in Curitiba," urban planners Jonas Rabinovitch and Josef Leitman describe how Curitiba's road network is organized around three parallel roads and five main axes along which the city has grown (1996). The central road contains two express bus lanes flanked by local roads; one block away on each side, there are high-capacity one-way streets that go in to and out of the central city. This land-use transportation pattern ensures that buses are able to move quickly and efficiently. Interdistrict and feeder bus routes complement the express bus lands along the structural axes. Large- and medium-sized bus terminals allow passengers to transfer easily from one line to another; a single fare allows passengers to transfer from the express routes to the local routes. At some stops, passengers pay their fare in advance in order to increase the speed and efficiency of boarding; quick boarding is facilitated further by two extra-wide doors on each bus. Double- and triple-articulated buses allow drivers to carry many more passengers (Rabinovitch and Leitman 1996).

The rationale behind a bus-based transportation system is based on economics and efficiency. Building a subway system would have cost the government roughly $60 million to $70 million per kilometer; the express bus highways that Curitiba's planners designed cost $200,000 per kilometer (Rabinovitch and Leitman 1996). Bus operation and bus maintenance were familiar tasks that the urban authorities knew the private sector could handle. Several different private companies received contracts to operate buses on particular routes. Bus companies are paid by the number of kilometers they travel rather than by the number of passengers they transport; this eliminates competition for passengers (Rabinovitch and Leitman 1996).

Curitiba's high-quality, efficient, affordable bus system covers an extensive land network that riders can use to quickly get almost anywhere in the city. As a result, although Curitiba has more cars per capita than any other city in Brazil besides the capital city of Brasilia, three quarters of all commuters (more than 1.3 million passengers a day) take the bus. Though

Ecological Urban Transportation Planning: Curitiba, Brazil

The city of Curitiba has seventeen new parks, ninety miles of bike paths, trees everywhere, and garbage and traffic systems that officials from other cities come to study. One of the city's most well-known and successful urban planning and infrastructure developments is its highly integrated, affordable, attractive, and efficient bus system. The system is based on the concentric circles of local bus lines that connect to five lines that radiate from the center of the city in a spider web pattern. On the radial lines, triple-compartment buses in their own traffic lanes carry up to three hundred passengers each. The buses, which are clean and attractive, go as fast as subway cars, but at 1/80th the construction cost. The buses stop at Plexiglas tube street stations; this system eliminates paying on board, which results in faster loading and unloading, less idling, and air pollution, and has a sheltered place for waiting. Passengers pay their fares, enter through one end of the tube, and exit from the other end. Bus fares are low, and passengers get unlimited transfers. Despite high quality and affordability, the system still pays for itself. Private companies own and operate the buses and keep part of each fare. The city gets the rest to pay for roads and terminals; they use some of the funds to purchase old buses, which are then refurbished and used as traveling classrooms, job training centers, libraries, daycare centers, and clinics.

Source: Meadows 1995

the buses run on diesel fuel, the number of car trips eliminated by the bus system has lowered overall emissions. Ideally, buses would be powered by alternative fuel sources like biodiesel. In order to ensure maximum efficiency, municipal authorities retire most buses after several years, recycling them for use as mobile vocational schools or using them to take small numbers of people to city parks and tourist sites. A very important additional benefit is that the city can self-finance its transit system instead of going further into debt to pay for the construction and operating subsidies that a rail system would have required (Rabinovitch and Leitman 1996).

Increasing the Role of Bicycles

In stark contrast to motorized vehicles, which are decreasing air quality in almost every city in the world, bicycles are nonpolluting (zero emission) vehicles that actually improve environmental quality by reducing air contamination, noise, and congestion resulting from so many motorized vehicles on the road. In many urban areas, bicycles are more convenient than public transportation (such as buses) because passengers don't have to wait hours for them to arrive, can ride around traffic jams, and save money. Even the most expensive bicycles are much less expensive than cars. On average, a new car costs about sixty times as much as a new bicycle; long-term cost savings are even greater when one factors in savings related to the ongoing cost of gas, repairs, auto registration, and insurance (Winner 1995).

Bicycles are an efficient transit option for people traveling and carrying lightweight goods short distances. Assuming reasonable terrains and travel distances, bicycle use can lead to improvements in public health because drivers get an aerobic workout while they travel. While there are obvious limitations for some drivers, bicycles can be adapted to accommodate many body types, and unless the terrain is difficult, most people will quickly accommodate to riding a bike short distances. Adaptations include three-wheel bikes, which are great for those who need more balance support, and bicycles that allow a driver to push a person sitting in a wheelchair attached to the front of their bike. In terms of weather constraints, one study showed that a committed cyclist biking in England, where it rains frequently, will only get really soaked through by bad weather twelve days out of every year (McClintock 1992).

Nevertheless, although bicycles are a popular form of recreation and transportation, several factors prevent most people who own bicycles from riding their bikes on a regular basis. In contrast to motorized vehicles, (a) bicycles are less appealing to most people because they take more work to drive and are slower, (b) they may not function well on certain terrains, (c) they expose the driver to natural elements like cold and rain, (d) they do not easily accommodate more than two passengers, and (e) heavy weights are difficult to carry without an attached cargo carrying system, which many people find difficult or awkward to drive and which are unaffordable for some riders (Winner 1995). Arriving at work or school hot and sweaty can also be a deterrent for some people.

Safety is the major factor that discourages people from using their bicycles on a regular basis (Pucher and Dijkstra 2000). Most city streets are designed only with cars in mind, and biking along them can be very dangerous. Finding a place to park a bicycle safely can be very difficult. Very few cities have safe bike riding lanes, and in most cities, conditions along the route discourage people from cycling. Additionally, motorized vehicles convey a much higher social status than the bicycle; as soon as most people have enough money to finance a car, motorbike, or scooter they do so.

But despite personal preferences for cars, bicycles are not only a viable alternative to motorized vehicles, they are an essential component of the transportation system in most developing nations, are slowly gaining popularity in industrialized countries, and are an integral part of a sustainable urban transportation system. The benefits of cycling include zero-pollution emissions, essentially nonhazardous to other riders, low-cost purchase and maintenance, easy access to urban grid, exercise and stress reduction, and the ability to carry passengers and cargo.

Increasing bicycle use will require transportation and land-use planners to reevaluate how they want to use the street grids in their cities. To increase walking and cycling, planners will need to immediately begin to promote traffic-free cycle routes, traffic-calmed roads and minor roads, urban cycling routes that connect important road networks throughout the city, safe parking facilities, and enforcement of existing and new regulations that require cars to share the road with bicycles.

Asia continues to be the dominant bicycle market. Between 1997 and 2002, bicycles topped all other means of transport, including cars and public transport in Beijing, China; in 2001 the city had ten million bikes and 1.2 million cars (Anonymous 2002). In 1999 China, Taiwan, and India produced 62 million bicycles and claimed 86 percent of the global bicycle export market (Vital Signs 2001). The amount of people and cargo moved by bicycle in Asia alone outweighs that moved by motor vehicles in all of Europe combined (Workbike Research 2001). Examples of planning and policy approaches and strategies to promote urban cycling in Japan, the Netherlands, England, and Peru are discussed below.

Planning to Increase Bicycle Use in Japanese Cities

More than 15 percent of commuters in Japan ride bicycles to work or to rapid transit stations where they safely park their bikes in guarded parking areas and then board trains that will take them to work each day (Winner 1995). In an article entitled "Bicycles as Transportation Policy," Michael Replogie describes how land-use planning, transport systems, and economic policies in Japan encourage bicycle ridership and are leading to bicycles becoming a major part of Japan's urban transportation system (2002). The cost of owning a car in Japan is high: fuel taxes double those of the United States account for almost half of the price of gas and automobile tax levies and vehicle inspection fees amount to an average of almost $2,000 annually. Employers provide incentives for biking. One company doubled its contributions for commuting by bicycle in the year 2000, while allowances for automobile commuters were halved. The use of bicycles as feeders into the main transit lines is popular in Japan; convenient bicycle access to transit stops helps railways compete with automobiles. An estimated three million bicycles are parked daily at rail stations throughout the country (Replogie 2002).

City officials in Japan advocate for land use and transportation planning that encourages bicycle use and supports bicycle-friendly programs. From 1997 to 1998, the Japanese Central Planning Agency conducted a study on the possibility of shared bicycle usage. Eighty bicycles were distributed to eighteen different government organizations. During this period, over 5,800 people made journeys totaling approximately 15,000 kilometers. In 1998 the city of Fukuoka experimented by allowing bicycles on one of the six train cars in the city's rail system. In 1999 government employees working in central Tokyo began using bicycles for short trips within the Kasumigaseki district, which is home to many government offices. A public appeal was made to employees to switch from automobiles and other forms of transportation to bicycles for short trips within the area. In 1999 a group of elected representatives in the Japanese Diet (Parliament) demonstrated their support for cycling by joining in a mass morning ride sponsored by the Federation of Representatives Promoting Bicycle Use (Replogie 2002).

After thirty years of transportation planning based on an ordinance for road structure that viewed pedestrians and cyclists as nuisances who obstructed the traffic of automobiles, constructed sidewalks based on car traffic volume, and gave no consideration to pedestrians and cyclists, the Japanese Construction Ministry substantially revised the Government Ordinance for Road Structure. The new revised Road Structure Ordinance stipulates that new roads constructed in urban areas should provide bicycle-only roads and wider sidewalks. The width of sidewalks will be determined by the amount of pedestrian traffic. The emphasis is on the safety of pedestrians and bicycle users, in the ever-growing advanced-age society. In August 2000, the Construction Ministry announced that newly constructed roads in urban areas shall be obligated to provide sidewalks and bicycle-only roadways (Replogie 2002). The Road Council, an advisory organization for the Minister of Construction, submitted a report in November 2001 entitled *Future Road Policy for Reducing Global Warming.* In the report, the council encourages bicycle usage for short distances (less than five kilometers) and promotes bicycle-friendly environments, such as lanes and parking. The report encouraged the development of interconnected bicycle roadways throughout the city. To support the construction of a nationwide bicycle road network, the ministry requested cities to submit their proposals for the creation of bicycle-friendly environments. Of thirty-three cities, fourteen were selected and are scheduled to take part in the program, with a major part of the construction work to be completed by the fiscal year 2003. The city of Akita Prefecture proposed recycling one thousand abandoned bicycles for public use. The Niigata Prefecture area of Japan, characterized by large amounts of rain and snow that fall in the area, proposed a system which would provide rental rainwear and drying facilities for wet clothes (Replogie 2002).

Over a dozen Japanese companies have emerged that specialize in manufacturing and installing bicycle storage facilities, ranging from simple rack sets to high-rise and underground automated garages. The average bicycle parking facility at Japanese rail stations holds more than 275 bicycles, and there are fifty-five bicycle parking garages holding over two thousand bicycles each and accounting for six percent of nationwide total parking. One city issued special cards to participants in a bicycle parking program, which are used to get in and out of automated gates equipped with sensors that read the cards. A host computer at the municipal office and personal computer terminals at each parking lot keeps track of the users payment, and records are verified as the gate opens or closes automatically by remote control. Parking charges are automatically settled through the user's bank accounts. Several rental bicycle agencies located near train stations called "Rent-a-Cycle Ports" have emerged. These companies employ fleets of identical minicycles, which are bicycles with twenty-inch wheels, adjustable seats, a front basket for parcels, a light, a bell, and a built-in locking device. The bicycle is normally painted a bright color so as to avoid theft. Most people rent bicycles on a monthly basis (Replogie 2002).

Planning to Increase Bicycle Use in Western European Cities

Many western European cities have created bike infrastructures that include bike-only lanes and roads, bike routes over and under dangerous intersections, secure bike parking, and workplace shower facilities for riders. For example, the Dutch government has prioritized pedestrian and bicyclist safety and has implemented a wide range of planning and policy measures to improve safety. Measures include better facilities for walking and bicycling, urban design sensitive to the needs of nonmotorists, traffic calming of residential neighborhoods, restrictions on motor vehicle use in cities, rigorous traffic education of both motorists and nonmotorists, and strict enforcement of traffic regulations to protect pedestrians and cyclists (Pucher and Dijkstra 2000).

Up to 50 percent of all trips in cities in the Netherlands are made on bicycles (Winner 1995). In some western European countries, the elderly make half their trips by either walking or biking (48 percent in the Netherlands, 55 percent in Germany) (Pucher and Dijkstra 2000). This high rate of bike use clearly indicates that people are using their bikes on a daily basis to support a wide range of transit needs related to work and non-work activities. In a review of policies designed to make walking and cycling safer, Pucher and Dijkstra describe how widespread bicycle use in the Netherlands is linked to two essential components of the Dutch transportation system. First, over the past twenty-five years, the Dutch government has consistently implemented policies that make bicycling (and walking) safer. Second, transportation planners in the Netherlands have focused on how increasing cycling use could facilitate increased rail use (Rietveld 2000). All of the policies proposed by Dutch planners required physical changes to the existing transportation environment. They include:

- Auto-free pedestrian zones.

- Clearly marked crosswalks; sidewalks on both sides of all streets.

- Pedestrian and bicycle traffic lights (including traffic lights that have priority signaling for bikes).

- Intersection modifications (including special bicyclist-activated traffic signals at key intersections).

- Streets that are designed one-way for cars but two-way for bikes.

- Reserved bus lanes that can be used by cyclists but not by cars.

- Street networks with deliberate dead ends and circuitous routing for cars but direct, fast routing for bikes (including special cut-through shortcuts off the road network altogether).

- Permission for cyclists to make left and right turns where prohibited for motor vehicles; special bike lanes leading to intersections that allow cyclists to pass waiting cars and proceed directly to the front, while the cars must wait at a considerable distance from the intersection; bicycle streets, bike lanes, and bike paths.

Dutch transportation planners focus heavily on how increasing cycling use can facilitate increased rail use (Rietveld 2000). Their thinking is based on the rationale that the train is often not chosen as a travel alternative to the car due to a lack of accessibility to the railway stations both at the home end and at the activity end of trips. For travelers considering the choice between a car trip and a train trip, the problems of low speeds of entry modes, bad connections, uncomfortable waiting, probability of missing a connection, uncomfortable departure times, and so on most often lead them to choose the car. But when walking and biking are feasible alternatives due to the origin and destination of the trip being relatively close to the railway station and/or when the trip is long distance, motivation to use the rail will increase. To get riders to act on this motivation, planners in the Netherlands made the cycling infrastructure and conditions more attractive. The strategies they use include creating safe and efficient bicycle parking facilities at railway stations, access to a supply of services such as rental centers for use of bicycles at the activity end, and facilities to take bicycles on the train. Planners also give priority to nonresidential land-use types near railway stations; these include office, education, shopping, and cultural facilities (International Bicycle Fund 2001a).

In an article entitled "The Nottingham Cycle-Friendly Employers Project: Lessons for Encouraging Cycle Commuting," Cleary and McClintock describe how transportation planners promoted cycling in Nottingham, England (2000). The Nottingham Cycle-Friendly Employers Project in England was designed to promote cycling to work for workers employed by eight large city employers in order to reduce automobile use and its associated congestion and pollution. The program developed when the Department of Transport invited groups throughout England to submit proposals to promote and facilitate bicycling for local journeys. After receiving 230 proposals, the department funded sixty-two projects, one of which was the Nottingham Cycle-Friendly Employers Project. At the time the program was implemented, over 32,000 employees were affected by the program.

The incentives introduced include workplace showering and changing facilities for both men and women, secure cycle parking at the workplace including cycle lockers, cycle stands, and shelters offering weather protection. The program also provides employees with interest-free loans, repayable over two years, for the purchase of bikes and equipment and/or the option to use company "pool" bikes for short official business trips and site visits.

Publicity materials were produced describing the personal health and environmental benefits of cycling. Promotional events were sponsored including bikers' breakfasts, barbecues, bike-to-work days, and the establishment of bicycle-user groups. Seven firms were motivated to become involved for four principal reasons: the program helped to reduce the increasing employee demand for workplace parking spaces, provided firms with a "greener" image for their organization, led to a more fit and healthier workforce resulting in less absenteeism through illness, and responded to existing demands from workers already interested in cycling to work. The Nottingham Cycle Program has proved highly successful, as measured by 42 percent of employers increasing their cycle commute to and from work. The program's success is based on the following conditions:

- An enthusiastic facilitator willing to champion the project and steer it through difficult challenges.

- A forum for discussion and exchange of ideas within the organization between those implementing the program and those affected by it.

- Encouraging the bicycle-user groups from different organizations to network and share important information, ideas, and experiences.

- Supporting, but not pressuring, potential cyclists to become involved in the program.

- A demonstrated commitment to the program's goals and objectives on the part of senior management.

- Careful identification of disincentives and strategies to overcome these problems.

- Promoting the accessibility, flexibility, and benefits of cycling.

- The most important external condition was a more cycle-friendly road environment. This was accomplished through measures to reduce the speed and volume of motorized traffic.

Planning to Increase Bicycle Use in Lima, Peru

The municipal government in Lima, Peru, has embarked on a twenty-year program to encourage bicycle transport. *Programa de*

Transporte Popular de Vehiculos No Motorizados (*Popular Transport Program of Nonmotorized Vehicles*) contains three core components: (a) infrastructure, (b) development of standards, and (c) education (International Bicycle Fund 2001a). The initial phase of infrastructure development included constructing seven priority bike routes covering a total distance of seventy kms (forty-three miles) and construction of 500,000 bicycle parking spaces. The medium-term goal includes extending the bike routes over 140 kms. The long-term goal calls for extension to 210 kms of bike routes. Technical standards are being developed to inform the planning and design of bike routes. Public education programs use pamphlets and radio spots to promote cycling and safety. A related program provides low-cost, affordable bicycles to low-income people living in the densely populated Cono Norte area of Lima and working in the Lima-Callao industrial area. This program involves credit facilities that enable the purchase of bicycles for low-income workers and a public information campaign to promote cycling and educate motorists about how to share the road with cyclists (International Bicycle Fund 2001a).

Cars and Bicycles in the United States

- After purchasing the vehicle, the typical cost for a typical commuter to own and operate a bicycle in the United States is from $20–$300 a year. The typical cost to own and operate a car is from $3,303 to $6,523 a year.

- Every bike rider not only removes a car from the road, it also frees a park-and-ride space. In the United States, a bike rack costs $250 per bike (the rack can hold two bikes if need be in a pinch) compared to a parking lot space which costs $20,000 per car to build.

- Fourteen bikes can fit in one car parking lot space.

- The bicycle as an urban vehicle offers no pollution, less congestion, quieter streets, and a healthier populace.

- People with autos make about one thousand round trips in the car that are less than five miles in distance each year. In other words, the majority of car trips are short distances.

- Average velocity for short trip urban driving is less than twenty miles per hour.

- Although cars are sold as vehicles that can easily accommodate many riders, drivers average 1.3 passengers per automobile; individual car use is increasing throughout the world.

- Using parking lanes as an obvious choice for bike lanes in cities is always voted down because urban authorities do not want to lose parking meter money.

Source: International Bicycle Fund 2001a

Increasing the Role of Workbikes and Cycle Rickshaws

Workbikes

Workbikes (alternatively known as *cargo-carrying bikes, commercial or utility vehicles,* and/or *human-powered delivery vehicles [HPUVs]*) are defined as "a human powered vehicle with two to four wheels, a steering mechanism, a saddle seat, pedals by which it is propelled and a load carrying area" (Workbike Research 2001). Utilized throughout the mid-1800s to deliver newspapers, baked goods, milk, and groceries in both Europe and the United States, workbike use dropped dramatically with the advent of the automobile but is now making a comeback. Workbikes are used throughout India, China, and southeast Asia, and in many parts of Africa. There are now more than ten million workbikes in use throughout the world, and both use and production are increasing (Workbike Research 2001).

Workbikes have the potential to be widely used in urban areas because they have the capacity to traverse crowded, local urban road networks where congestion is more likely to be encountered. Although vans and trucks may be economical and efficient over long distances, the local road network part of the journey is both costly and cumbersome for delivery trucks because of time delays and extra fuel consumption related to traffic congestion and street parking problems. It also contributes to higher air and noise pollution levels in local areas. "The use of workbikes for urban delivery and distribution services offers a new angle from which to view the issues of sustainable transportation. Current government policy views sustainable distribution as focusing solely on using the existing distribution network more efficiently . . . this is a step in the right direction but it does not deal with the fact that the existing resources that are being used are part of the pollution problem. What is needed is a switch to a newer, greener, transportation resource that makes better use of the delivery networks. . . . City center distribution is a massive hurdle for all efficient transport networks to overcome. . . . Utilizing workbikes would allow existing networks to be streamlined and operate in a more rational and sustainable manner" (Anonymous 2002, 2).

Workbikes are currently being used by small businesses, large industries, and local and federal governments. Commercial cargo cycling and cycle courier companies are increasingly using trailers and cargo cycles to deliver goods within cities. Their services are used by government agencies, private companies, and even individuals to pick up and deliver packages, food, and other goods. Many human-powered delivery vehicles throughout the world are now being used to deliver car parts, newspapers, groceries, prescriptions, office supplies, household goods and furniture, print shop products, produce, videos and video equipment, flowers, books, recycling goods, computers, bread, fresh vegetables, and even a stray bride and groom to destinations throughout urban areas (Workbike Research 2001).

A bakery in Columbia, South America, replaced its entire fleet of two hundred motorized delivery vans with eight hundred workbikes, resulting in huge savings in transportation costs for the company and increased quality of life in the city. The Swiss postal service uses more than 3,700 delivery bikes. The Danish postal service uses forty *Christiania Trike* bikes in its daily service delivery. A post office truck distributes additional loads to workbikes once drivers have exhausted the bags they are carrying; the truck essentially operates as a depot away from the main post office of the area being served. A program in the Netherlands gives tax breaks to employers who buy company bicycles instead of company cars for their employees (Workbike Research 2001). The postal service in England operates a fleet of roughly 35,000 bicycles, all of which are built to carry twenty-five kilograms of letters over the front wheel. The city of Eugene, Oregon, tried out a tricycle recumbent bike to use as a parking patrol vehicle because it allowed them to carry the equipment they needed to "block" the wheels of certain vehicles as well as easily maneu-

URBAN TRANSPORTATION PLANNING AND MANAGEMENT

ver and park to fine parking violators (Workbike Research 2001). The city of Vancouver has a police department bicycle squad that acts as the first line of defense to protect visiting dignitaries and others requiring high security protection (Gardner 1998).

Most workbikes operate in bike-friendly cities and towns where the transportation infrastructure allows bikes carrying trailer systems to move easily throughout an urban area. If human-powered delivery vehicles are to be used more widely, land use and transportation planning focused on facilitating bicycle and cargo-bicycle transport is essential. Cities need to encourage infrastructure developments that provide safe bike ways and parking, high-density and mixed-use development and road-sharing strategies, government support for utilizing cargo bikes, and economic incentives for cargo bike transport systems.

One important planning initiative is to move toward integrating transport so that workbikes can work in tandem with other transit systems. A combination of a cargo bike picking up packages in one town and delivering them to a train station and another cargo bike at the other end picking them up and delivering them to their destination is being used in England (Workbike Research 2001).

To encourage the use of workbikes as part of an integrated transport system, cities will need to create depots where goods can be picked up and unloaded; for example, creating depots which function as the drop-off and pick-up points for the van to workbike interface. Creating this kind of interface has numerous advantages including reduced polluting emissions, decreased traffic congestion, decreased noise and vibration disturbance, increased efficiency on crowded, urban road networks, and reduced energy use (Anonymous 2002).

The social, environmental, and economic benefits are obvious. Workbikes cost considerably less to purchase, operate, and maintain than trucks or vans. They reduce harmful emissions and accidents. According to information provided by two courier services in England, in their first year of operation, their workbikes were able to substitute for 13,500 motorized van deliveries and carry a total weight of 220,000 kilograms of consignments in one city annually. With average journeys roughly three miles in length, these figures show these couriers are responsible for 40,500 zero emission delivery miles, with hopes of raising their capacity to 90,000 miles (Anonymous 2002). If workbikes are to going to be integrated into the urban transit mix,

165

planners must recognize that infrastructure capacity is critical to workbike business. Ideally, planners would create an urban infrastructure that incorporates the following components:

- Separated bike paths, especially between cities—transcity bike routes that accommodate cycling from one city into another and help people get there on the fastest possible routes.

- Raised level cycling areas.

- Wide bike paths that allow the passage of both standard bikes and workbikes and of more than one workbike at a time.

- Dedicated "Class 1" lanes (separated bike lanes) for cyclists.

- Lighting and synchronization of traffic lights that, if possible, include loop detectors that are located under the pavement that will detect cyclists coming along on a lane and switch the traffic light to green so the cyclists can keep cycling.

- Signage that alerts motorists to cyclists, tells riders the mileage from one place to another, and so on.

- Bike parking supports including plentiful bike racks (including bike racks outside businesses to accommodate cargo bike deliveries) and supervised bike parking facilities to avoid theft of bikes or cargo.

The public and city planners need to be educated to think of bicycles (1) not simply as one person on a machine, (2) to understand that bike lanes need to be more than "car door" lanes, and (3) to recognize the need to accommodate real substantial lanes that can accommodate wider vehicles. Truly integrating workbikes into the transit mix would result in the creation of multimodal transportation mixes that would allow workbike riders and other riders to pick up and drop off cargo at rail, bus, and boat stations and take it where it needs to go. These benefits would increase the quality of cycling for all, in particular those most vulnerable to traffic (i.e., children, people in wheelchairs, and the elderly) and would also encourage walking.

Pedal Express Bicycle Delivery Service

Pedal Express Bicycle Delivery Service was formed in 1994 by the members of an organization called the Auto Free Bay Area Coalition. After meeting with members of a cargo bike company based in Eugene, Oregon, called Pedalers Express, members of the coalition were convinced that workbikes could be used to deliver goods and services in the Bay Area. Three members of the coalition started the company in 1994 with relatively little capital. They purchased two long-haul cargo bikes (at the price of $1,200 each), chose the name Pedal Express and had it printed up and glued on to the side of the cargo bikes, made a brochure describing their services, designed a t-shirt that became the company's first uniform, found clients, and started pedaling.

A long-haul cargo bike is ideally designed for fast-paced urban environments. From the back wheel to the handlebars, the bike looks like a mountain bike, but the other half looks like a converted tandem. It has a beautiful frame that allows for the attachment of a cargo fiberglass container that is aerodynamically designed with a very low center of gravity which promotes stability. The long-haul uses a twenty-one-gear system and linkage steering (a low tube comes out of the bottom with a front wheel attached to a rod that goes underneath the container and attaches to the steering column to control the front wheel). The back wheel is twenty-six inches, the front wheel is twenty inches; this allows the container to be low to the ground, which keeps the bike more stable.

Pedal Express's first client was a baker who wanted bread delivered to food markets in the city of Berkeley. He loved bikes, had seen them used to deliver goods in other countries, and had tried to deliver his bread by bike himself but had run into trouble with the city's health department for not having a closed, lockable container. So he was thrilled when Pedal Express assured him that they could reliably deliver hundreds of breads of different kinds and sizes every day at an affordable price. Their second client was a free local newspaper that needed to have mail delivered daily from their post office box to their office several miles away. Their third client was the city of Berkeley, which needed to have information packets sent to members of various committees and commissions in preparation for upcoming meetings.

Benefits to the clients include competitive prices, which are often lower than truck-based delivery services; working with an innovative, reliable, accountable local business; and supporting an environmentally and socially responsible business that employs local residents. Eight years later, Pedal Express operates a fleet of more than ten utility vehicles and has seven employees; the company brought in more than $100,000 worth of business in 2002. There are now more than six Pedal Express companies in the United States, as well as many other people using workbikes, including: policemen, city groundskeepers, industry employees, curbside recycling pickup workers, and mobile bike repair service people.

Source: Pedal Express 2003

Cycle Rickshaws

Cycle rickshaws are nonpolluting bicycle-pulled vehicles used to carry passengers and goods. Cycle rickshaws are used in many parts of India, throughout southeast Asia, and in many other developing countries, where they play an important role in the transit system through income maintenance for the poor, transportation for vulnerable groups, and pollution reduction.

There are three main problems with cycle rickshaws. First, the heavy weight of the cycle rickshaw, coupled with the lack of a multispeed gear system, makes the driver act like a gearbox, producing differing amounts of torque in relation to the loading and road conditions which are often extremely difficult and taxing for the driver. Second, the lack of suspension on most cycle rickshaws makes for a bumpy and unsafe ride for the driver and other riders. Third, the street grids in most cities are inadequate for cycling and do not protect cycle rickshaw drivers and passengers from motorized vehicles (Pope 2001). Yet despite these problems, cycle rickshaws are used widely in many parts of the world and are both functional and highly popular with riders. With the improvements suggested, cycle rickshaws could become an efficient, affordable part of the mass transit mix in some cities.

Based on their study of nonmotorized transport in Calcutta, India, Whitelegg and Williams describe why cycle rickshaws are a critical part of the transportation mix in developing countries (2001). First, cycle rickshaws provide greatly needed employment for very low-income residents in many cities in developing countries. The income rickshaw drivers earn supports hundreds of thousands of their dependents in cities around the world (i.e., Calcutta, Delhi, Bangkok, Jakarta), in the home areas of workers who migrate to the big city to fill the jobs of rickshaw pullers and, to a lesser extent, the rickshaw peddlers. Second, cycle rickshaws provide inexpensive, reliable, and consumer-friendly transport options in an urban context where buses are dirty, crowded, and often dangerous and arrive irregularly and the car and taxi are unaffordable forms of transport for the majority of urban and periurban residents. Cycle rickshaws are particularly useful for women, children, the elderly, and the disabled who may not be able to access buses easily or comfortably. Cycle rickshaw drivers will pick up and take customers where they need to go any time of the day or night, will work during the worst of the monsoons, and will travel through the most water-logged and muddied streets. In some cities, local rickshaw drivers take children to and from school on a daily basis in communities and situations where personal care and reliability are highly valued. Third, cycle rickshaws are zero-emission vehicles that do not contribute to air and noise pollution in local areas (Whitelegg and Williams 2001).

Despite these three critical benefits, urban authorities in many developing countries are beginning to ban cycle rickshaws and encourage motorized vehicle use. Rickshaw bans are typically justified on the ground that the slow-moving vehicles cause traffic jams. Calcutta's mayor-in-council (roads) Anup Chatterjee stated, "We must be fair to the one million cars and buses which crawl on the choked roads causing traffic jams everywhere every day" (Abdi 2002, 11). But the main problem for cycle rickshaws is that they are being judged by public authorities in non-Western countries who have internalized Western stereotypes about hand-pulled vehicles symbolizing a nation's "backwardness" and lack of development (Whitelegg and Williams 2001). From a Western perspective, cycle rickshaws are simply not in tune with a vision of a city that is modernizing, prospering, and progressing (Sen 1998).

Whitelegg and Williams describe the economic and environmental consequences of banning cycle rickshaws in Calcutta (2001). They discuss how the characteristics of the cycle rickshaw facilitate optimum use of most vehicles. Because cycle rickshaws are heavy and physically demanding to drive, they are made to carry only two adults, and the majority of trips are for one person only or an adult with small children. Because the work is hard, many cycle rickshaws are shared by two drivers who work on a shift basis, increasing the number of vehicle trips per day. Because they are heavy to pull, the distances traveled are short, averaging one kilometer for hand-pulled cycle rickshaws and 1.5 kilometers for cycle-pulled cycle rickshaws. Because of these characteristics, the total number of passenger kilometers traveled per day in greater Calcutta is a minimum of 1.847 million trips at ten trips per day and a maximum of 3,695 million at twenty trips per day; this is an average value of 2,771 million trips a day in Calcutta alone (Whitelegg and Williams 2001).

From an environmental perspective, every cycle rickshaw journey is a journey that is not made by another form of more polluting motorized transport. This is particularly true for the cycle riskshaw's most common replacement—the three-wheeled auto-rickshaw, which is powered by fossil fuels. Whitelegg and Williams's research reveals that as motorized cycle rickshaws, motorcycles, and cars have increased in use and importance in the city of Calcutta, the city's air quality and associated public health problems have worsened significantly (2001). A study that analyzed the impact of replacing bicycle-driven cycle rickshaws with auto-cycle rickshaws in Agra, India, concluded that if all cycle rickshaw trips in Agra were reallocated to highly polluting two-stroke IC engines like the auto-cycle rickshaw, the annual totals of pollutants in Agra would increase by eleven tons of lead, four thousand tons of particulates, 20,000 tons of carbon monoxide, and 150 tons of nitrogen oxide (Hook 1996).

Cycle rickshaws play an important role in reducing pollution emissions that are harmful not just to the environment and humans, but to built structures like the Taj Mahal that are being structurally degraded by polluting emissions from motorized vehicles (Hook 1999). M. K. Mehta and his colleagues at the Asian Institute of Transport Development (AITD) and the Institute for Transportation and Development Policy led a project designed to promote the use of cycle rickshaws around the Taj Mahal in Agra, India. The project was developed in response to the haze of dust and smog caused by belching smokestacks and the exhaust fumes from cars, trucks, and auto-cycle rickshaws. The Taj Mahal and other world-famous monuments in India are being discolored with orange, black, and brown staining from suspended particulate matter and hydrocarbon emissions, which come mainly from motor vehicles and internal combustion power generators. The negative effects of these pollutants are quite localized, which means that the immediate threats to the monuments can be reduced by controlling access to the Taj Mahal area by motorized vehicles (Hook 1999). According to Mehta, "The rickshaw is a cheap, non-polluting vehicle and a viable mode of transport for narrow lanes and places around the Taj Mahal where the use of motor vehicles is now banned; by making cycle rickshaws more comfortable for the passenger and the rickshaw puller we think that more people will use them to get around" (Iijima 2000, 57).

With funding from the U.S. Agency for International Development, AITD staff worked with the New York-based Institute for Transportation and Development Policy to design a more comfortable, lighter, and safer rickshaw. The new cycle rickshaw weighs on average 30 percent less than traditional cycle rickshaws due to an integral tubular frame; this makes it easier for the driver to pull. The center of gravity has been lowered by about a third, improving stability, and a multigear system specially designed for cycle rickshaws was added (Pope 2001). An added benefit of the project has been the creation of a new industry and employment sector for skilled local workers; production is now entirely in the hands of local entrepreneurs. The cycle rickshaws have been so popular and successful with passengers and drivers that they are now being integrated into other cities in India, including Delhi, Lucknow, and Chandigarh, with plans to introduce the new cycle rickshaws into other countries such as Indonesia. Interest in using the new cycle rickshaws has spread as far as Europe and the United States. The reduced weight and stability has improved speed, safety, and comfort as well as improved the image of the rickshaw. "The vehicle is no longer seen as a rickety, unsafe, and degrading machine but as an environmentally-friendly and comfortable means of transport. The passenger has a better ride and the driver has a status previously unheard of" (Pope 2001, 47). Future plans include wider seats and local subsidies so that more cycle rickshaw pullers can afford to buy the newly designed cycle rickshaws.

Creating Pedestrian-Friendly Infrastructures

In an article entitled "The Built Environment and Human Activity Patterns," planners Lawrence Frank and Peter Engelke describe how three essential components of the built environment—transportation systems, land development patterns, and microscale urban design—increase or decrease walking and biking behavior (2001). Fundamentally, transportation systems provide connections between human and economic activities. Within urban centers and communities, the layout of the street network and distribution of space for different modes of travel within a given right of way impact the directness and quality of travel. It is at this scale that the ability to walk or bike between places of residence, commerce, employment, and recreation is determined.

Land development patterns define the arrangement of activities and impact the proximity between travel origins and destinations. Increased compactness and concentration of uses (density) reduce trip lengths and reduce vehicle ownership. Increased mode choice options are a fundamental component for shortening the distances between activities and increasing the ability of people to walk for utilitarian, social, and recreational purposes. Microscale urban design features are more noticeable to pedestrians and cyclists than motorists. "Motorists have a limited ability to process detail in the environment because speed demands concentration; therefore, the ideal environment for a motorist is low in complexity. Conversely, pedestrian and bicycle travel, being much slower, afford the ability to notice differences in the streetscape. A rich pedestrian environment . . . is one that maintains the pedestrian's visual and sensory attention" (Frank and Engelke 2001, 210).

The perception of safety is critical; streets with sidewalks, bike lanes, crosswalks, open spaces, low landscaping, and social and commercial activities will provide pedestrians with a higher sense of personal security and greater incentive to walk (Litman 1999). The state of Maryland's Department of Transportation *Bicycle and Pedestrian Master Plan* focused on a wide range of complementary planning and policy measures to encourage walking in their cities:

- Require traffic calming measures in residential areas.

- Create pedestrian-only streets in commercial areas.

- Promote neighborhood-scale small business development in residential areas.

- Promote higher density residential development.

- Keep auto-oriented development in specific zones along major arterial roadways.

- Encourage affordable housing and senior housing within five hundred feet of transit facilities and bus stops.

- Require existing site plans to propose how pedestrian (and bicycle) facilities and amenities could be integrated into existing development.

- Include pedestrian (and bicycle) access in all development proposals related to substantial changes to an existing land use.

- Require that pedestrian (and bicycle) access be considered in all new development proposals.

- Develop specific design standards for pedestrian (and bicycle) development. These standards can be included for bicycle lane width and composition; sidewalk width and composition; bicycle land, sidewalk, and multi-use paths locations in relation to buildings, parking lots, transit facilities, signs and streets; setback and natural buffer requirements for multi-use paths; landscaping requirements; lighting; benches, rest-rooms, and bike racks, parking, and storage requirements.

- Offer incentives for land uses and developments that incorporate high-quality pedestrian (and bicycle) facilities and amenities.

- Carefully consider how improvements can be made in existing traffic circulation, roadways, intersections, traffic conditions, traffic control, and so on that will encourage walking.

Alternative Automotive Systems, Fuels, and Designs

Auto exhaust contributes significantly to air contamination and to global greenhouse gas production. Reducing automobile emissions is essential to promoting sustainable energy use in cities. Alternative automobile designs are critical because they can reduce emissions that are harmful to human and environmental health. At the same time, it is important to point out that the only *sustainable* solution to automobile transportation is to reduce dependence on private cars. Having said this, strategies to reduce environmental and public health damage from cars, while still driving cars, can be divided into three categories: (a) alternative ownership, (b) alternative energy sources, and (c) alternative auto designs.

CHAPTER FOUR

Alternative Ownership

Alternative automobile ownership, particularly urban car sharing, is an intriguing option. Programs like the Yokohama Project in Japan, City Car Share in the San Francisco Bay Aarea, and Zip Car in the Washington, D.C., area allow registered users to rent cars owned by a car-share company. Members receive computerized keys and reserve vehicles by phone or electronically for anywhere between a few minutes to several days. Groups of cars are spaced throughout the area, often close to mass transportation hubs; users may use cars in any existing location, choosing whichever is most convenient. Very low monthly fees secure membership, and use fees are based on time and mileage. Programs like these create more transportation options for individuals and households who may use car-sharing instead of owning private cars or who may use car-sharing instead of buying a second (or third!) car. Businesses may also subscribe to car-sharing services, eliminating or reducing the need for a corporate auto fleet. Many car-sharing organizations are investing in the alternative fuel vehicles that will be discussed next, further reducing members' transportation-related environmental damage.

Alternative Fuel Vehicles and Energy Sources

Electric: Electric cars use electricity stored in large battery banks to power vehicles. Although their main advantage is that they produce little or no emissions, they still have significant disadvantages. Emissions savings from the auto are somewhat offset by the continuous requirement for electricity to charge the batteries, because the world's electricity is still derived largely from fossil-fuel-powered generation plants, and the emissions savings at the vehicle level are to a certain extent simply transferred to emissions from the plant that generates the electricity to charge the batteries. Electric cars also suffer from limitations in range between charges and lack of infrastructure (charging stations) to recharge batteries.

Hybrid: Hybrid cars rely on a combination of traditional combustion engines and electric power. Combustion engines rely on batteries to start the engine, but as soon as the car is started, the combustion process takes over. The car's alternator then recharges the battery for the next start. Traditional combustion engines produce an excess of electricity through the alternator, which is usually wasted. Hybrid cars take advantage of this energy to recharge larger battery banks, and they have an alternate engine system that allows the cars to be powered by the electricity. These cars are not zero emissions vehicles but, because they run on electricity at least part of the time, they have significantly higher fuel efficiency and correspondingly lower emissions than non-hybrid cars. The combination of fuel and electric engines eliminate the limitations in range of the pure electric cars, and the batteries do not require plugging in to recharge because they are charged by the alternator from the fuel engine.

Hydrogen Fuel Cell Technology: While hybrid cars lower emissions by raising fuel efficiency, newer technology, particularly the fuel cell, have the potential to reduce emissions even more. The fuel cell works by combining hydrogen and oxygen to produce electricity and water. Theoretically, clean water could be the only emission from fuel cell vehicles. In practice, the generation of the hydrogen can either come from a wind-powered process (for the lowest environmental impact), from methanol, or from petroleum-based electricity or fuels, which have some emissions impact. In the Proton Exchange Membrane Fuel Cell, hydrogen and oxygen are fed into opposite sides of the cell. The hydrogen reacts with a catalyst that removes the atom's electron, leaving a positively charged hydrogen ion. This ion travels on toward the oxygen and eventually the two combine to form water. Meanwhile, the electron from the hydrogen atom travels through an electrical circuit that powers the vehicle's motor (Renzi and Crawford 2000). Hydrogen fuel cells have been described as "solid state nonmoving parts, no-combustion devices that silently, efficiently, and reliably turn hydrogen and air into electricity, water, and nothing else" (Spowers 2001, 56). Ten thousand fuel cell vehicles running on hydrogen not generated from fossil fuels would reduce oil consumption by 31.41 million liters per year. In an article entitled "Dream Machines," author Roy Spowers reports that if a mere ten percent of cars in the United States were powered by fuel cells, sixty million tons of carbon dioxide and one million tons of air pollutants would be eliminated; if ten thousand fuel cell vehicles were fueled by non-petroleum fuel oil, consumption would be reduced by 8.29 million gallons (31.41 million liters) annually. An added benefit would be that, as the price of fuel cell technology went down, these vehicles could be used to generate electricity when they were parked, feeding it back to the national grid, ushering in the era of clean, sustainable energy systems (Spowers 2001).

Electric, hybrid, and fuel cell systems lower emissions by moving away from the internal combustion engine; but there are also strategies to lower automobile emissions by using different fuel in traditional combustion engines. The idea is to reduce or eliminate the need for diesel or gasoline; they include, among others, biodiesel, methanol and ethanol.[3]

Biodiesel: Biodiesel is a cleaner burning alternative fuel produced from vegetable oil. It can be blended with petroleum diesel or used by itself with little or no modifications to diesel engines. Biodiesel blends are labeled *BXX* (*XX* represents that percentage of biodiesel in the blend). *B20* is 20 percent biodiesel and 80 percent petroleum diesel. It can be made from any fat or oils, such as soybean, canola, linseed, rapeseed, sunflower, even hempseed oil. In the United States, fuel grade biodiesel must meet strict industry specifications; fuels must be tested by the Environmental Protection Agency and registered as a legal motor fuel for sale and distribution. The B20 blend of biodiesel has been demonstrated to have significant environmental benefits while requiring a minimal increase in cost to consumers. While any blend of biodiesel meets the clean diesel standards of the U.S. California Air Resources Board, only 100 percent biodiesel is designated as an alternative fuel. *B100 biodiesel* used in a conventional diesel engine reduces emissions of unburned hydrocarbons (67 percent), carbon monoxide (48 percent), and particulate matter (47 percent) compared with petroleum diesel (National Biodiesel Board 2002). Biodiesel also reduces cancer risks compared with regular diesel. Pure biodiesel reduces polycyclic aromatic hydrocarbons (PAH) by 80 percent and nitrated polycyclic aromatic hydrocarbons (nPAH) by 90 percent; PAH and nPAH compounds are the compounds in diesel exhaust thought to cause cancer (National Biodiesel Board 2002).

Biodiesel: Questions and Answers

What are the benefits of biodiesel?

Biodeisel produces 93 percent fewer hydrocarbons (a major precursor to ground-level ozone, the main component of smog).

Biodeisel produces between 30 percent to 85 percent less particulate matter.

Biodeisel produces 50 percent less carbon monoxide.

Biodeisel produces 50 percent to 85 percent less carcinogenic aromatics, like benzene and toluene.

Biodeisel has zero sulfur oxides and sulfates (contributing factors to acid rain).

Can biodiesel be used in any regular diesel vehicle, or must a vehicle be modified first?
Biodiesel can be used in any regular unmodified diesel engine. The engine must be diesel; if it is, you can pour your biodiesel directly into the fuel tank. It mixes with diesel fuel at any ration so you don't need to drain your fuel system at any point.

Why can't biodiesel be put into a car that runs on unleaded or leaded fuel?
Vehicles that run on gasoline have spark-ignition engines. These engines use spark plugs to ignite the fuel. They are designed to use very thin, explosive fuel. Diesel engines are compression-ignition engines, instead of spark plugs; they use super-compressed air to ignite the fuel. The engine is generally heavier and sturdier and designed to run on thick, viscous fuels like vegetable oil-derived biofuels.

Why not just use grease in the diesel engine instead of processing it into biofuel?
You can do this in a pinch. However, most diesel engines are not designed to run on straight vegetable oil; they can "choke up" the engine and simply stop working because the oil is thicker and less combustible.

What kind of emissions does biodiesel give off?
There are no sulphur dioxide emissions from biodiesel since biodiesel does not contain sulphur. Soot emissions are 40 percent less, while carbon monoxide and hydrocarbon emissions are cut by between 20 percent and 60 percent. Vehicles running on biodiesel still emit the same amount of carbon dioxide (CO_2) but there are no new carbon dioxide emissions added to the Earth's atmosphere since the next batch of crops grown to make biodiesel will absorb the CO_2. In other words, unlike fossil fuels, in which you dig up fossilized carbon and dump it into the sky, biodiesel recycles carbon and oxygen through the ecosystem. This is why it is called a renewable fuel.

Can any kind of vegetable oil be used to make biodiesel?
Any type of vegetable oil or animal fat can be used to make biodiesel.

If the demand were there, could enough vegetable oil be produced to make biodiesel a significantly viable option for the mass of autos?
Yes. In Germany there is enough biodiesel to offer the fuel at five hundred service stations across the country. Biodiesel can be made from several sources, including vegetable oil, animal fat, and a fast-growing, naturally occurring strain of algae.

What are the byproducts of making biodiesel; are there any issues related to its disposal?
The byproduct of the biodiesel process is glycerin soap. You can use it to clean your biodiesel processor or give it in jars as a gift.

Sources: Tickell and Tickell 1999

Biodiesel Fuels:
Berkeley's Ecology Center's Recycling Truck Fleet

In 2001 a community-based nonprofit environmental organization responsible for collecting an average of eight thousand tons of curbside recycling every year in the city of Berkeley, California, switched the fuel it uses to run its fleet of recycling trucks from diesel to biodiesel. The transition was easy. It required inspecting the fuel tanks in each tank for cleanliness, ensuring that no natural rubber was used as a component in the fuel system, and changing the truck's fuel filters three to five days after making the transition. The organization now works with a supplier that brings a single tanker truck of biodiesel fuel to Berkeley every three months, which the Ecology Center uses to fill its above ground storage tanks. Ideally, the Ecology Center uses biodiesel made from spent used "yellow grease" (vegetable oil) collected from the nation's food industry companies, an example of materials reprocessing at its best!

Switching from diesel to biodiesel reduced the fleet's soot emissions by 80 percent; reduced its fine particulate emissions by 50 percent, and completely eliminated aeromatic hydrocarbons like benzene and toluene. The Ecology Center is particularly enthusiastic about the reductions in fine particulates since they directly contribute to asthma and other respiratory illnesses in the local community.

The cost of switching to diesel is becoming more affordable every day as more manufacturers identify biodiesel as a niche market. The Ecology Center was paying $1.87 per gallon in 2003, but staff members expected to pay much less within a very short time. In the two years since they began their program, the city of Berkeley switched its entire fleet to biodiesel and was able to purchase biodiesel for seventy cents per gallon less by working with a different supplier. The long-range plan is to work with other big municipal fleets to purchase biodiesel in a consortium; this would bring the price down and, more importantly, would dramatically reduce harmful emissions in the region. It would also provide an infrastructure that would make it easy for other small and large fleets to switch to biodiesel and would facilitate the eventual sale of biodiesel in local gas stations.

Having an infrastructure and large demand for biodiesel would make it economically viable for a company with the resources to open a biodiesel manufacturing plant in the area. This would allow yellow grease produced in the area to be sent to a regional manufacturing plant to be processed into biodiesel, creating a closed-loop regional system that reprocessed food and organic waste to create an alternative energy source to fuel the Bay Area region's heavy and light vehicles.

Source: Ecology Center 2003

Methanol: Methanol is cleaner burning and more energy-efficient than gasoline. Methanol is a simple alcohol that can be combined with gas (*M85*) for use in most methanol-powered vehicles, or used pure (*M100*), usually as a diesel substitute. Most M85 methanol vehicles can also be powered by pure gasoline, making it possible to use the vehicles in which methanol infrastructure does not exist. M85 fuel reduces hydrocarbon emissions by 30 to 40 percent, and M100 fuel by up to 80 percent; particulate matter is eliminated in M100 fuel, while M85 has some particulate matter emissions because of its gasoline content. Methanol is usually produced from natural gas, but it can be produced from renewable sources such as wood and waste paper (USEPA 2002).

Ethanol: The Model-T Ford operated on either ethanol or gasoline. Ethanol is still a common gasoline additive used to reduce gasoline carbon monoxide emissions. Pure grain alcohol, ethanol is produced from plant sugars and can be made from waste paper, brewery waste, and other food waste products in addition to corn, potatoes, wood, and wheat. Ethanol is usually mixed with gasoline to form E85 (85 percent ethanol, 15 percent gasoline). Heavy duty trucks can use E95 or E93. E85 produces fewer total toxics, reduces volatile organic compounds (*VOCs*) 15 percent, carbon monoxide 40 percent, particulate emissions 20 percent, nitrogen oxide 10 percent, and sulfate 80 percent.

Several modern biogas systems have been designed to produce ethanol from sugary and starchy plants. Both Brazil and Zimbabwe use commercial ethanol from sugar cane for transportation fuels (Petesch 1992). The process involves fermentation and distillation, both of which require considerable energy inputs that typically come from conventional sources. However, if sugar cane is unavailable, the waste products of the sugar industry known as *bagasse* can be used instead. The alcohol that is produced can be used as fuel either by itself or mixed with gasoline (Pasztor and Kristoferson 1992).[4]

Alternative Vehicle Designs

Alternative automobile designs concentrate as much, if not more, on changing the structure of the car as they do on using alternative energy sources and fuels related to the changing structure of the engine.

Hypercar: The Hypercar was designed by a team of scientists at Rocky Mountain Institute in the United States. The goal of the Hypercar is to reduce the number of natural resources used in the production and use of an automobile. The Hypercar concept advocates a car using ultralight materials, aerodynamic design, a hybrid engine (or fuel cell when the technology is practical), and efficient accessories to improve automotive design. Traditional vehicles built with steel are twenty times heavier than the driver. In order to move the heavy vehicle, engines are larger than they would be in a lighter vehicle. In contrast, the Hypercar uses ultrastrong carbon, Kevlar, and glass fibers that are embedded in specially molded plastics; this reduces the weight of the car without reducing safety, because these particular materials absorb five times more energy per pound than steel. When weight is reduced, other features, such as power steering, are not required. In addition, all parts of the Hypercar are recyclable. These Hypercars are still in the concept phase and not yet produced for the market.

Smart Car: DaimlerCrysler's Smart Car brand produces small light cars marketed for urban driving. The tiny cars use recyclable plastic body panels, which are significantly lighter than steel. They run on gas engines, but their size and weight contribute to fuel efficiency: they get about fifty miles to the gallon. In order to travel at freeway speeds and maintain maximum safety given their tiny size, the cars rely on twin air bags and a protective steel cage around the driver (Everett 2000).

Summary

This chapter outlines the problems stemming from dependency on the automobile. Problems include green houses emissions and associated climate change problems, injuries and death from accidents, delays and stress for travelers, negative public health impacts, political conflicts, and environmental degradation. The chapter discusses how transportation plays a critical role in urban design and form. Transportation infrastructures and the characteristics of transportation supply and performance impact the physical structure and spatial arrangements of a city and its surrounding area, influence personal and employment related travel patterns, generate economic opportunities, increase or decrease people's sense of community, and have the potential to improve the quality of living and efficiency in an urban area. The chapter also discusses how land-use development and transit planning exert a very strong influence on individual transportation choices.

The chapter emphasizes that people living in cities around the world travel through urban areas for many different reasons and use different transportation modalities to do so. Today's global transportation mix includes walking, animal- and hand–pulled vehicles, boats, ships, rail, buses, minivans, trolleys, trucks, automobiles, motorcycles, helicopters, airplanes, and paratransit vehicles. Paratransit vehicles include shared taxis, converted pick-ups, cars and vans used as shared transport, scooters used as motorized cycle rickshaws, and bicycle-pedaled vehicles such as pedal-cycle rickshaws

The chapter describes how a sustainable transportation planning approach is designed to support a transport system with five essential characteristics. It allows the basic access needs for individuals and societies to be met safely and in a manner consistent with human and ecosystem health. It is affordable, operates efficiently, offers choice of transport mode, and supports a vibrant economy. It is capable of delivering required capacity and performance and is compatible with the desired lifestyle of the population it serves. It limits emissions and waste within the planet's ability to absorb them, uses inexhaustible energy sources (meaning it is powered by renewable energy resources), minimizes consumption of non-renewable resources, reuses and recycles its components, and minimizes the use of land and the production of noise. It is clean and affordable for the vast majority of users and does not pollute air, land, or water beyond the planet's ability to absorb and cleanse; this is especially the case with regard to CO_2 emissions.

Clearly, the characteristics of the spatial environment are related to mobility and choice of mode of transport. "The rise in demand for car travel is fueled more by the increased spatial separation of homes and workplaces, shops and schools than by any rise in trip making" (Cooper et al. 2001, 103). Studies of transport patterns in industrialized countries, where car use is highest, confirm that the number of car trips is very largely correlated to personal travel related to shopping, taking children to and from school, and social activities (Meurs and Haaijer 2001). Reliance on car trips will only be reduced when shopping, jobs, and housing are located closer together. "Reducing car mobility will be achieved when facilities for daily and other shopping and schools are located close to the home, the road network in the neighborhood is laid out for slow traffic (by bike and on foot) that is unsuitable for the car, and the accessibility of locations outside the neighborhood (including the main road and places for shopping) discourage car use. The reduction in car use is greatest when this occurs in a densely built up area" (Meurs and Haaijer 2001, 445).

Transportation policy needs to be oriented toward helping to revitalize communities by incorporating mixed transit uses and providing pedestrian-friendly environments. It is critical to ensure that the location and price of transportation modalities and facilities do not negatively impact low-income neighborhoods and the people who live there. Transportation systems must be integrative, using a synergistic mix of incentives and restrictions as necessary. Incentives should be used to promote higher-density mixed-use development, environmentally friendly transit modes, and reduced car use. Planning and policy should be used to constrain urban sprawl through stricter land-use policies, limits on car driving, speed limits, parking, and higher fuel taxes (Wegener 1995).

Public transport must be encouraged in cities throughout the world. Planning and policy should focus on improving the network and quality of services supplied by providing an efficient route network, high punctuality and regularity, sufficient speed, short intervals, security and safety of passengers, and a wide range of transit services offered. Automobile and motorcycle traffic must be controlled by regulating parking options using economic methods such as determination of limited parking zones, comparatively high fees, and limited time for parking. Car pool incentives, traffic management, and parking strategies should be used to discourage solo driving and encourage car pools. Providing employees with a "cashing out" policy that gives those who don't drive the equivalent of their parking subsidy can also substantially reduce private automobile commutes.

Operationally, a sustainable transportation system must meet eight criteria. It makes use of land in a way that has little or no impact on the integrity of ecosystems. It uses energy sources that are essentially renewable or inexhaustible. It uses other resources that are renewable or inexhaustible and achieved in part through the reuse of items and the recycling of materials used in vehicles and infrastructure. It produces no more emissions and waste than can be accommodated by the planet's restorative ability. It meets basic human needs for health, comfort, and convenience. It allows and supports development at a human scale and provides a reasonable choice of transport modes, housing, community, and living styles. It produces no more noise than is acceptable by communities. It is financially affordable in each generation and supports economic activity.

Chapter Questions

The chapter provides readers with information to address six essential questions related to planning for sustainable urban transportation planning and management:

1. What problems have resulted from automobile dependency?

2. What can be done to reduce reliance on the one passenger car and other light vehicles?

3. What policies and measures need to be introduced to support cycling, cargobike delivery services, and walking in cities?

4. What are the advantages of human-powered vehicles?

5. What alternative automotive systems, fuels, and designs are proposed to reduce the harmful environmental and human health effects of automobiles?

6. What are the essential components of a sustainable urban transportation system?

Notes

1. In some industrialized countries, *paratransit* refers to vehicles retrofitted for special needs like wheelchairs, but in this book the term is used it to refer to vehicles traditionally used in the public transit mix of developing countries. Paratransit

includes shared taxis, converted pick-ups, cars, and vans used as shared public transport, and both motorized and bicycle-pedaled cycle rickshaws.

2. It is important to note that while the trend in Polish cities is definitely toward increased motor vehicle ownership and use, there is also a growing movement to encourage bicycle use throughout Poland, and cycling has increased in many parts of the country (International Bicycle Fund 2001b).

3. Other fuels characterized as "alternative fuel sources" include Fisher-Tropsch, an alternative to diesel which like biodiesel is interchangeable with petroleum diesel, requiring little or no vehicle modifications, and may be blended with petroleum diesel in any ratio. But, unlike biodiesel, Fischer-Tropsch fuels are petroleum-based. "Fischer-Tropsch technology converts coal, natural gas and low-value refinery products into high-value, clean-burning fuel" (EPA, Clean Alternative Fuels). Natural gas and propane are also considered alternative fuel sources.

4. Like other petroleum fuel sources, *bagasse* can be used to power many different kinds of processes and technologies in the transportation and manufacturing sectors. Cuba is currently using *biogasse* produced from sugar cane waste to provide power in sugar-producing facilities.

CHAPTER FIVE
URBAN FOOD PRODUCTION

To move towards sustainability and integrated natural resource management, planners and other urban authorities must begin to put social and
economic processes into place that function to close the open loop system
where consumables are imported into an urban area and their remainders
and packaging are then dumped as waste into the bioregion and bios-
phere. Urban agriculture is one of these social and economic processes because it has the capacity to contribute to the food needs of urban
populations, provide individuals and families with alternative sources of
income and job training opportunities through local food production,
stimulate community participation, and contribute to more sustainable
waste management and water use.

—Jac Smit and Joe Nasr, "Urban Agriculture for Sustainable Cities:
Using Wastes and Idle Land and Water Bodies as Resources," 1992

Food

In the foreword to the book *Rain Forest in Your Kitchen,* Jeremy Rifken
notes that "eating, more than any other human activity, binds us to the
world of nature; the vital bridge that connects human culture with the
larger environment" (in Teitel 1992, ix). Eating, he notes, has motivated
some of the most important human innovations: "The earliest uses of
physics-based power were centered around food, water wheels to grind
grain, for example, or sailboats to trade food and spices . . . [and today] so
much of our interaction with the natural world has to do with getting
food, as we clear grasslands and forests for crops and animals, dam and divert river and lake waters for irrigation and terrace mountains into crop-
land. Every person needs to eat in order to live. The fortunate among us
eat every day. No matter how urbanized we may be, we maintain immediate and direct contact with the natural, biological processes of the world
through our daily meals" (Teitel 1992, x).

For centuries men and women throughout the world have cared for a
diversity of crops that provide nutrition and medicine for people all over the
world (Shiva 2000). For the first eight thousand years of settled agriculture,
farmers used ecologically sound agricultural practices to domesticate several
hundred different crops and develop thousands of crop varieties (Anonymous 2001). These practices include diverse crop production, crop rotation,
letting land lie fallow, nutrient recycling, soil regeneration, and conservation

of biological diversity. But over the course of the last century, farming and food production have changed profoundly.

Environmental and Social Impacts of Industrial Agriculture and Corporate Food Systems

In a report entitled "Roots of Change," the Funders Agriculture Working Group describes how in an attempt to control the forces of nature and increase yields, the general trend in agriculture has been to industrialize farming and increase the formulaic control of cultivation (Anonymous, "Roots of Change" 2001). Traditional food production systems have been utterly transformed as basic ecological principles have been abandoned and replaced by new processes and technologies that degrade the natural resources and ecosystems upon which farming depends, rapidly exhausting natural resources that have been replenished for thousands of years. "Today's conventional—or industrial farming—relies on synthetic fertilizers, chemical weed controls, monocropping, mechanical tillage and harvesting, and a complex worldwide web of distribution channels. Everything from fertility amendments to pest controls and water systems depend on prescribed quantities of synthetic additives. . . . The dependence on high inputs of synthetic chemical fertilizers and pesticides, energy, and water causes extensive environmental damage including soil contamination and degradation, water waste and degradation, and air pollution" (Anonymous, "Roots of Change" 2001, 1–2).

Conventional agriculture (alternately referred to as *industrial agriculture*) is among the single greatest contributors to water pollution, aquifer depletion, and air contamination and is a significant source of toxic exposures to humans (especially those who work and live closest to fields using chemical inputs). Despite increased yields, millions of people throughout the world, in both developing and industrialized nations, are hungry and/or malnourished.

Chemical fertilizers and pesticides used on farms in urban regions worsen urban water problems. Excessive fertilizer use has led to nutrient runoff into rivers and oceans, causing algae blooms that can use up all the available oxygen in the water as the algae decomposes, and to dead zones with no sea life in some areas. Although irrigation dates back six thousand years and has always been associated with increased yields, farmers are now pumping groundwater faster than nature is replenishing it. Aquifer depletion is now widespread in much of the western United States (where the majority of the nation's and about a quarter of the world's food is produced), central and northern China, northwest and southern India (particularly serious in India's principal food-producing states of Punjab and Haryana), parts of Pakistan, North Africa, the Middle East, and the Arabian Penisula; worldwide, one out of every five hectares (12.36 acres) of irrigated land is damaged by salt (Postel 2000).

A growing number of scientific studies link exposures to agricultural pesticides to cancer, birth defects, reproductive damage, and neurological diseases, as well as other chronic and acute illnesses, yet despite this documentation, pesticide use increased 50 percent in the last thirty years, with the use of pesticides that cause cancer increasing 129 percent in recent decades (Anonymous, Pesticide Watch 2001). In addition to environmental and public health impacts, industrial agriculture has also resulted in the loss of family farms and farm livelihood.

World food supply has increased significantly as a result of industrial inputs such as water and fertilizers; yet half of the world's people are hungry and/or malnourished. As we entered the twenty-first century, about 800 million people (approximately 15 percent of the world's population) and one third of all children under five years of age in developing countries were living a life of permanent or intermittent hunger, chronically undernourished and hungry (Conway 2000). More than 38 percent of all children in Pakistan, 53 percent of all children in India, and 56 percent of all children in Bangladesh are undernourished; 48 percent of children in Ethiopia and 39 percent of children in Nigeria are underweight (Brown 2001). Hunger and malnutrition are not limited to developing countries. Ten percent of households in the United States, home to nearly one in five American children, experience hunger on a regular basis; more than 40 percent of low-income, pregnant African-American women in the United States have chronic iron deficiencies (Gardner and Halweil 2000).

As the corporate-controlled food system gains a foothold in almost every city in the world, increasing numbers of urban residents are replacing diets associated with good health and lengthy adult life expectancies (diets rich in whole grains, vegetables, fruits, and nuts, supplemented by small amounts of animal products) with diets that are linked to health problems. People who overconsume fat, animal-based protein, and calories and eat nutrition-poor foods are at much greater risk of heart disease, stroke, diabetes, and various cancers—the four sets of diseases responsible for more than half the deaths in the industrialized world (Gardner and Halweil 2000). Roughly half of the world's diseases are linked to poor diet, and some of these diseases, like diabetes and obesity, are spreading rapidly in both developing and industrialized nations. Fast food items, high in fats, sugar, cholesterol, and salt, are rapidly replacing nutritious fresh foods.

In cities throughout the world, people are eating fewer varieties and breeds of food, and greater amounts of processed food, dairy, meat, and seafood as their food choices are increasingly connected to the requirements of industrial agriculture, mass production, economies of scale, marketing prerequisites, and market performance (Gardner and Halweil 2000; Teitel 1992). French fries and potato chips now make up one fifth of the "vegetables" eaten by people in the United States; urbanites throughout the developing world are being tempted by the same foods that are jeopardizing health in the industrial world; four out of the five restaurants that McDonald's opens every day are located outside the United States (Gardner and Halweil 2000).

The Connection between Food and Other Urban Planning Concerns

Hunger and malnutrition are not limited to rural populations; an astonishingly high and increasing number of the world's hungry and malnourished people live in cities (Brown 2001). Farming (which includes crop and fruit production, as well as raising livestock, poultry, and aquaculture) is not an activity that occurs exclusively on rural land. Globally, about 200 million urban dwellers are urban farmers, providing food and income to about 700 million people (Cook and Rodgers 1996). In wealthy, industrialized countries, there is an abundant amount of food, yet many low-income urban residents in the United States have difficulty accessing a supermarket as a result of food industry consolidation and supermarket redlining of low-income areas, which results in significant barriers to their families obtaining healthy food (Cook and Rodgers 1996). Food sector establishments and food wholesalers are an important contributor to local economies and employ a great number of city residents (many of whom are part of lower-income households). Almost all urban households spend a significant portion of their income on food purchase. Food waste is a significant portion of the household, commercial, and institutional waste streams. If food packaging is included, food wastes make up close to a third of the total waste that ends up in many city landfills in developed countries. A significant number of energy resources are dedicated to transporting food from farms and to and from processing and packaging centers, food outlets and markets, and households. Clearly, food and food-related issues are urban concerns (Pothukuchi and Kaufman 2000).

As urban planners Kameshwari Pothukuchi and Jerry Kaufman point out in an article entitled "The Food System: A Stranger to the Planning Field," food system issues (understood as the chain of activities connecting food production, processing, distribution, consumption and waste management, as well as all the associated regularly institutions and activities) are central to urban development in a myriad of ways (2000). Pothukuchi and Kaufman remind us that the discipline and field of urban planning is identified with a concern for improvement of human settlements (focused on making places better serve the needs of people) and with the interconnections among distinct community facets, incorporating linkages among physical, economic, natural, and social dimensions, as well as linkages among sectors (i.e., transportation and land use, housing and economic development) and with public and private enterprises (2000). Further, the urban planning field claims to be comprehensive in scope, future-oriented, public-interest driven, and dedicated to enhancing the livability of human settlements and quality of life in cities. Thus attention to the complex, integrated range of food system issues should be high on the list of urban planning concerns (Pothukuchi and Kaufman 2000).

Pothukuchi and Kaufman suggest that urban planning's focus on interconnections among distinct community facets should lead planners directly to a concern about food systems, as the food system is so intricately connected to land and land use and so central to health and to the goal of improving human settlements (Pothukuchi and Kaufman 2000). Unfortunately, as their survey of the urban planning literature reveals, the discipline of urban planning has paid almost no attention to the food system or to planning for community food needs. Pothukuchi and Kaufman discuss how this lack of food system analysis has led planners to neglect the critical role that food plays in urban households and that agriculture plays in regional systems. They describe four of the most problematic consequences of this lack of attention to urban food systems.

First, it leads urban planners to fold grocery store and market development and location into the broader category of commercial-retail development without considering the higher priority that food merits among household needs. Second, it leads to a failure to systemically devise community-wide plans for composting food wastes, resulting in food waste being dumped into landfills, thereby making landfills 12 percent to 15 percent larger than they otherwise would be and depriving households and farmers of a valuable organic fertilizer. Third, although urban planning is attentive to issues related to the loss of agricultural land surrounding cities and to the accompanying loss of both urban coherence and regional self-reliance, this orientation to food issues conveys neither the significance of food as a community issue nor the importance of its links to other activities and systems, such as wholesale trade, transportation, energy use, and waste management. Fourth, although urban planning as a discipline claims to focus on the improvement of human settlements, with an emphasis on making cities better serve the needs of the people, concern about food has rarely been expressed (Pothukuchi and Kaufman 2000).

Increasingly, people living in cities throughout the world are eating more food grown far outside their region. Food is being transported by air and shipped from countries on the other side of the world while local crop varieties are being replaced by a few commercial types popular with food corporations and supermarkets (Howe and Wheeler 1999). Agribusiness food products typically travel over one thousand miles before they even reach the consumer (Cook and Rodgers 1996).

Transporting food over long distances has many ecological and social consequences: air pollution from trucks and planes contributes to climate change and ill health; food has to be preserved for the long distance travel and is often overprocessed, overpackaged, and sprayed with pesticides; small farms and rural jobs are threatened by cheaper food imports and squeezed out by corporate buying policies that favor large farms and bulk supplies from large producers; and limited land and resources in developing countries are used to produce cash crops for export instead of food for local people (Foodmiles 1994). It is in this context that urban agriculture represents a unique urban land use and opportunity for urban planners to put social and economic processes into place that will move cities toward sustainable development in an integrated, holistic manner (Smit and Nasr 1995; Pothukuchi and Kaufman 2000; Pinderhughes 2003).

Urban Agriculture

"Urban food growing provides a powerful vehicle for helping to move towards sustainable patterns of urban living. Its outstanding quality is its ability to simultaneously tackle a range of linked issues—environmental, social and economic issues" (Howe and Wheeler 1999, 15). The environmental benefits of urban food production include ecological restoration, preserving biodiversity, turning organic waste into a resource, and reducing transport (Pinderhughes 2003). Social benefits include preventing hunger, providing food and income for low-income households, improving nutrition, reducing poverty, reversing urban blight, creating jobs, developing the local economy, and supporting local food economies (Cook and Rodgers 1996; Howe and Wheeler 1999; Pinderhughes 2003).

Gradually, professionals working in the fields of urban planning and development are recognizing that urban agriculture can contribute to the food needs of people living in cities. According to a United Nations Development Program official, "Urban agriculture has been underrated in all but a handful of countries—and mostly overlooked by the international development community . . . by putting simple laws into effect, urban agriculture can become a formidable economic force of the 21st century" (Cook and Rodgers 1996, 31).

The term *agriculture* includes horticulture, aquaculture, arboriculture, poultry, and animal husbandry; it can also include the production of a number of products that are not edible, for example, medicinal plants, fuel material, wood for other uses, and animal feed. *Urban agriculture* involves the production of crops and/or livestock on land that is administratively and legally zoned for urban uses or at the periphery of urban areas, including on land that is being rezoned from rural agriculture to urban land (Mbiba 1995). The *urban agricultural sector* is a production sphere that includes preproduction and postproduction processes, as well as water and waste recycling processes (United Nations 1996). The sector produces, processes, distributes, and markets food, fuel, and raw materials in response to the daily needs and demands of consumers. These activities occur on land (agriculture) and in water (hydroponics and aquaculture) dispersed throughout urban and periurban areas by applying intensive production methods through the use and reuse of natural resources and urban wastes and with the goal of yielding a diversity of crops and livestock (United Nations 1996).

The term *urban* encompasses the entire area in which a city's sphere of influence (social, ecological, and economic) comes to bear daily and directly on its population. Members of the United Nations Development Programme and the Urban Agricultural Network (TUAN) suggest that an approximate definition of the city's *zone of metropolitan intensive agriculture* be understood as the agricultural product that gets to city markets or to consumers the same day it is harvested. The *urban agriculture zone* can also be construed more narrowly, as food and livestock production that takes place within city or municipal limits.

Urban agriculture takes place in vacant lots; in back, front, and side yards, balconies, and rooftops; in tanks, ponds, and containers; on roadsides and right of ways; on private, public, and quasipublic lands; in open spaces that are vacant, idle, or unsuited for urban development; in community gardens; and on land specifically allocated for urban agricultural uses (Smit 1996; Pinderhughes 2003). These areas are used for crop cultivation and/or raising small livestock for family consumption and for sale directly to consumers and in local markets (United Nations 1996).

Urban agriculture typically includes small-scale intensive production of crops and/or the raising of small livestock or milk animals within or at the edges of urban areas, as well as the postproduction and waste recycling processes, barter in an informal economy, and/or sales in neighborhood and local urban markets. The food cultivated and/or the livestock raised are used for family consumption and/or for sale directly to consumers and in local markets. Typically, urban agriculture products get to city markets and/or urban consumers the same day they are harvested (United Nations 1996).

Ancient Traditions and Current Practices

Farming intensively within and at the edges of cities is both an ancient tradition and a current practice (Smit et al. 1996; Mougeot 1994). Throughout the world, civilizations have developed systems of agriculture within or on the edge of urban areas. Agriculture was a vital, well-supported element of urban life in ancient cities. In many early cities, intensive production of fruits and vegetables, small livestock, fish, and poultry were essential to the development and stability of urban life. Archaeological evidence has revealed cultivation of fruits, vegetables, grains, and livestock in ancient Aztec, Mayan, and Inca cities, as well as in early civilizations in Java and the Indus Valley (Mougeot 1994). Many precolonial cities in Africa produced much of their local population's food. Several West African cities were surrounded by concentric zones of agriculture in which a large part of the urban population worked each day. In Eastern and Central Africa, large portions of urban space were devoted to farming, frequently separating city quarters so that immense gardens were located in between other urban land uses (Rokadi 1988).

In many ancient systems, climatic variations were addressed through techniques that included irrigating the soil to regularize the supply of water and warming the soil and air to stretch the growing season. In desert climates, such as those found in the Tigris and Euphrates delta, sun reflectors were used to heat the soil. In Peru standing water in aquaterra systems held off the mountain frost in Machu Picchu. In Bolivia the ancient tradition of storing the sun's heat in the adobe walls of greenhouses was utilized extensively (Mougeot 1994).

The separation of agriculture from cities is very recent in urban history and occurred most rapidly over the past century as increasing emphasis was placed on separating farming from urban settlements and cleaning cities by removing waste via sanitary sewers rather than by incorporating wastes into existing urban agricultural systems. Before the development of modern sanitation systems, urban agriculture was the principal method of treatment and disposal for urban organic (biodegradable) wastes. Colonial cities used urban waste for enriching soils in both urban and rural areas. Many colonial cities were planned and managed to have food production at the edge of cities, and urban areas incorporated the principle of using urban waste for enriching soils in urban and rural areas. Since the twentieth century, the trend has been to sanitize cities around the world through the introduction of modern sanitation systems. These efforts resulted in the shift of increasing volumes of waste from one location to another within the urban ecosystem, putting immense pressure on the sanitation infrastructure (United Nations 1996). Most cities gradually began to import their food and export their biological waste rather than continue to grow their food locally and utilize urban wastes as valuable farming inputs.

Incorporating Urban Agriculture and Food-Related Issues into Urban Planning Concerns

Supporting urban agriculture will require urban planners to analyze the connections between food and other planning concerns, access the impact of current planning on the local food system, integrate community food security into urban planning and policy goals, greatly expand their ideas about what constitutes good land use, integrate waste management concerns into their thinking about the food system, provide support to the various components of the urban infrastructure that sustain urban agriculture in cities, and educate future planners about food system issues[1] (Pothukuchi and Kaufman 2000; Pinderhughes 2003).

One problem planners and policymakers will have to overcome quickly is the almost total lack of association most urban officials have between cities and food production. The term *urban agriculture* does not resonate with most planners because in the fields of urban studies, professionals in urban planning, management, and policy have consistently associated food and livestock production with rural areas and activities and defined urban areas as locations explicitly associated with the nonexistence of agriculture. As a consequence, the status and potential of urban agriculture has been trivialized. Urban agriculture is seen as making a minute contribution to national food stocks when compared with agricultural production in rural areas; this is especially the case when urban agricultural efforts are compared to modern commercial farms and industrial agriculture. When compared with high value urban land uses, such as industry, commerce, transportation, and housing, urban agriculture is seen as a land use of considerably lesser value (Mbiba 1995). Very little emphasis has been placed on the role that a well-planned, well-supported urban agricultural sector can play in reducing poverty, food insecurity, and waste in cities (Pinderhughes et al. 2001).

Multiple Benefits of Urban Agriculture: Waste Reduction, Soil Health, Public Health

Urban agriculture has multiple benefits for cities and urban residents (Pinderhughes 2003). It can alleviate hunger and malnutrition and improve public health by augmenting the limited food budgets and incomes of low-income individuals and households. It can contribute to sustainable waste management by recycling wastes that would otherwise be discharged in to the environment in landfills or surface water. It can provide individuals and families with alternative sources of income and job training opportunities through local food production and the eventual sale of food to urban consumers in their locality. It can stimulate and support new

195

patterns of community participation by involving people in community gardening and urban farmers markets.

By utilizing intercropping and integrated farming techniques that make efficient use of both horizontal and vertical space, intensive urban farming has the potential to yield several times as much produce per area as conventional rural agriculture. As a result, urban agriculture can provide those with very limited access to land with significant benefits. Depending upon the technology applied, urban agriculture can provide as much as fifty kilograms of fresh produce per square meter annually. Although yields vary widely based on inputs, resources, and farming knowledge, productivity in urban agriculture can be as much as fifteen times the output per hectare of conventional rural agriculture (FAO 2003).

The *French-intensive* method of gardening, characterized by double-dug raised beds with large applications of manure and compost, can produce huge amounts of produce from a small space year-round in soil that is heated with the aid of heavy manure applications (United Nations 1996). In Chile urban farmers produce vegetables, fruits, herbs, and flowers by planting crops in containers that they stack up in pyramids. Plants also grow on the walls, their vines providing a ceiling of shade as well as crops. By using containers, walls, and air space, twenty square meters can provide three times as much productive farm space. In Hong Kong vegetables are grown in containers that sit on top of floating cages used for raising fish. In Poland the garden structure is often a three-layer system with fruit trees at the top, berries below, and vegetables on the lowest layer (Smit et al. 1996). Greenhouses can be structured to produce fifteen to twenty times as much per acre as crops grown under normal field conditions, although greenhouses and other facilities require more labor and capital (Kneen 1995).

These and other small-scale urban agricultural techniques reduce strain on land and water resources. Limited availability and the cost of resources like land, water, and inputs in urban areas have led to the development of farming techniques that require less water and fertilizer than that needed for tractor-cultivated rural farms per unit of production. Because urban agricultural products are sold close to the fields in which they are grown, the produce is fresher and the transportation and storage needs lower, reducing overall consumption of fossil fuels and associated CO_2 emissions (Rodrigues and Lopez-Real 1999). The United Nations Food and Agriculture Organization estimates that producing the food needs for a nutritious, low-meat diet requires about 1,600 cubic meters of water per person per year (United Nations 1996). In humid climates this can be provided by rainfall, but in drier climates and those with wet and dry seasons, a portion of water used for crop production needs to come from irrigation water drawn from rivers, lakes, or aquifers.[2]

Urban agriculture has the potential to incorporate vast amounts of solid and liquid waste, reducing both waste management problems and costs in urban areas. Before modern urban sanitation systems were developed in the latter part of the nineteenth century, urban agriculture was the principal method for the treatment and disposal of urban wastes. In many places, human- and animal-powered carts delivered food to urban markets and returned the city's wastes to the fields (United Nations 1996). Producing food in or at the edge of urban areas allows for the utilization of wastes as inputs to the process, recycling nutrients that would otherwise be discharged to the environment in landfills or surface water (Rodrigues and Lopez-Real 1999).

Composting, a process wherein microorganisms break down organic materials, has multiple benefits in urban agriculture.[3] Composting diverts organic waste from dumping sites and landfills, enriches soil, and increases its ability to hold and retain moisture (Rodrigues and Lopez-Real 1999). In urban areas, nontoxic household organic waste can be diverted, processed into organic fertilizer, and returned to urban garden plots and farmlands. Using appropriate techniques, composting can generate heat with pile temperatures reaching 70 degrees Celsius; at temperatures this high, waste can be sanitized as pathogens are killed off by the heat (Rodrigues and Lopez-Real 1999).

As discussed in the chapter on urban waste management, one essential principle of sustainable waste management is that wastes generated as outputs by one producer should be used as inputs by other producers. Urban agriculture has immense potential to fulfill this principle and there are numerous examples of how it is functioning. In Metro Manila the Philippine Business for the Environment administers a program wherein shrimp heads generated as wastes by shrimp exporters are being used as inputs by animal feed milling companies. Staff match sellers and buyers with one another. The program has minimized wastes and pollution of rivers and landfills and increased environmental awareness in the industrial sector.

A program in Italy utilizes urban agricultural food industry wastes, in this case the leftovers from citrus fruits and the residuals of sugar-beet processing and abundant seaweed, to make ecological, recyclable, and biodegradable paper. When compared to the traditional well-established paper-making technology, the use of seaweed and agricultural food leftovers to make paper saves trees, mineral fillers coming from quarries, water, and energy.

In order to reduce pathogen, nutrient, sediment, and pesticide runoff into the city's water supply system, the New York City Department of Environmental Protection worked with farmers to devise a plan to put the best management practices into place to reduce agricultural pollution. The plan is designed to remove the necessity of installing a costly filtration system for New York City's water supply. The program reduces pollution at the source rather than treating the resulting impacts. Each of these examples illustrate how urban agricultural wastes can be used as inputs for other production processes, how wastes from nonagricultural sources can be used as inputs in agriculture, and how best management practices in agriculture can reduce waste streams into urban areas.

Edible Buildings

Approximately 800 million people are currently engaged in urban agriculture worldwide, and about 200 million of these farmers are growing food for commercial reasons. Much of this food growing takes place on, in, and around buildings. Throughout history, people have used their dwellings, workplaces, and communal spaces to produce food. In Yemen, some towns and cites have integrated high-rise architecture with organic urban gardens over many centuries. These gardens use traditional techniques of stacking layers of shrubs, vegetables, herbs, and root crops under a canopy of date palms—mimicking the ecological structure of natural forests. Residents in Mexico City cultivate cactus on rooftops for home consumption and income generation.

Source: Petts 2002

Food Production in Cities

In recent decades, farming within and at the periphery of cities has been increasing throughout the world at a rapid rate in both poor and wealthy nations. Millions of residents in Africa, Asia, Latin America, and increasingly in North America are growing crops and tending livestock in urban areas. In developing countries, urban agriculture has been shaped by several factors, including rapid urbanization, the migration of large numbers of low-income people to cities, the continuity of historical agricultural and cultural practices, export-oriented agricultural policies, and the inability of rural food production and distribution systems to adequately meet the food needs of low-income urban populations (Smit 1996).

Worldwide, about one quarter to two thirds of urban and periurban households are involved in agriculture (FAO 2002). According to a report produced by the Food and Agriculture Organization of the United Nations, the demographic characteristics of urbanites that produce food include just about everyone. The report confirms that people engage in urban agriculture for different reasons and in varied socioeconomic and political contexts but suggests that urban farmers can fit into six categories: (1) *Household self-sufficiency*, in which a household provides staple foods for its members throughout the year and is less dependent on the market to provide food, is among the most important. (2) *Augmentation of household budget*, in which the household buys much of its food in the market but regularly consumes food cultivated and/or raised, is very common. (3) *Absolute necessity*, in which the food households grow and raise is their principal source of food, is among the most important of factors motivating urban agriculture in many parts of Africa, Asia, and Latin America. (4) *Commercial production*, in which food grown and raised in urban areas is principally for sale, is increasing. (5) *Occupational and job training opportunities*, in which people are paid to work in urban agriculture, are increasing in popularity throughout the United States. (6) *Recreation*, in which the principal reason for gardening and/or raising livestock is for pleasure, is popular throughout the world.

Though many people associate urban agriculture with new immigrants to cities, a review of the literature shows that urban agriculture is practiced by both new immigrants to cities and by long-time urban residents, and of the two, more likely to be practiced by longer-term residents (United Nations 1996). Women tend to engage in urban agriculture more often than men. Using a combination of national census data, household surveys, and individual research projects, the authors of the Food and Agriculture Organization report concluded that urban agriculture is most often carried out by women on a part-time basis as they combine food production activities with child care and other household responsibilities (FAO 2002). In many parts of the world, both women and men work in cultivation; some studies indicate that women tend to be associated with raising livestock, medicinal plants, and aromatic plants while men are more associated with cultivation, although this is clearly not the general pattern throughout the world.

Urban agriculture is practiced across class lines and income groups, and people of all classes and incomes are engaged in food production in cities. However, as would be expected, differences in access to capital and land affect the types of agriculture being practiced, types of food produced, amounts of food produced, and the degree to which food is produced for household consumption versus sales to urban consumers.

Many wealthy people own land in cities that they may use for personal or commercial agriculture within the boundaries of metropolitan areas. Mougeot discusses a number of surveys that show that wealthy households are extensively involved in urban agriculture in parts of Africa; one survey of 1,800 farmers in six Tanzanian cities showed that top executives are making money from animal breeding in the capital city of Dar es Salaam (1994). According to the Food and Agriculture report, urban gardeners are typically not the poorest urban residents but rather those with families that have lived long enough in a city to secure land and water and become familiar with the market channels for selling surpluses (FAO 2002). According to researchers at the Minzingira Institute in Kenya, food in African cities is produced in the backyards of middle-income and high-income people, but the poorest urbanites cannot produce food easily since they are crowded in high-density areas or squatter settlements. It is certain that a large proportion of urban residents involved in urban agriculture are of low income, though how low remains a question. No matter how difficult, research on urban agriculture in cities around the world confirms that in the last half of the twentieth century, throughout Africa and Asia, and in many parts of Latin America, millions of low-income urban dwellers have turned to urban agriculture as a result of the need to augment their household diet and earnings.

Urban Agriculture in Africa

Urban agriculture occurs in cities throughout Africa. Research among people living in squatter communities in Lusaka, Zambia, reveals that throughout the 1970s and 1980s, urban gardening was widespread among the very poor. In households surveyed, more than 50 percent cultivated home and distant gardens (Rokadi 1988). Sanyal's research in Zambia confirmed that urban agriculture was an important part of food security for low-income urban Zambians. Forty-five percent of 250 low-income households surveyed cultivated food in their back and front yards or in the urban periphery, and an additional 15 percent cultivated both (Sanyal 1984). Tripp's research in the Buguruni and Manzese Ward areas in Tanzania showed that about 40 percent of those who went into urban farming had no other employment (Tripp 1990). A 1991 study in Kenya showed that 29 percent of urban households grow crops in town and 17 percent keep livestock (Mbiba 1995). A second study of 1,576 families in six urban areas revealed high levels of urban agriculture, including crop cultivation, livestock, and fuel wood production. Sixty-two percent of households surveyed grew a portion of their household diet, 29 percent cultivated in the urban area where they lived, 17 percent kept livestock, and 63 percent of households cultivated food outside of the city (Stren and White 1992). Of those urban families who have access to land, nine out of ten families engage in food production. Seventy-seven percent of all urban farmers grow food for their own use. In smaller towns, 100 percent of families supplement their diets by gathering indigenous vegetables that grow wild (Eberlee 1993). A survey of 330 households consisting of 2,675 respondents in periurban Maputo, Mozambique, revealed that 37 percent of households engage in urban food production, growing multiple crops including beans, vegetables, and yellow corn. Twenty-nine percent of households sampled raised livestock, mainly ducks and chickens (Graham 1999). A study in Kampala, Uganda, found that about 30 percent of all residents engage in urban agriculture, growing staple foods such as cassava, coco-yams, plantains, maize, and beans. The most popular livestock are chickens. Households involved in urban food production showed a significantly improved level of health among women and children (Memon and Lee-Smith 1993). Foeken and Mwange describe farming in contemporary Nairobi as "an activity of people of all socioeconomic classes growing food whenever and wherever possible—along roadsides, in the middle of roundabouts, along railway lines, in parks, along rivers, under power lines, in short in all kinds of open spaces crops are cultivated and animals like cattle, goats and sheep are roaming around" (1998, 3). In Malawi, goats are now a regular feature of urban life, and the government has encouraged people to plant trees to be used for fuel. In Lesotho, urban agriculture includes dairy, livestock, maize, vegetable, and fruit production (Mbiba 1995). Residents in Lome, the capital city of Togo, produce enough vegetables to meet the local population's needs and supply produce to neighboring countries (Lachance 1993).

Growing Food in Cities: Africa

Poverty in Accra, Ghana, is widespread, and food costs are a considerable portion of household budgets for most families. Families engage in urban agriculture to support household needs, augment family income, and to have an asset (livestock) to sell in case of an emergency. Farmers are mostly men, and farming is not an activity limited to the poor. Staple crops include maize, cassava, peppers, okra, and tomatoes. Greens and sweet potatoes are also grown, but in smaller quantities. Families keep livestock, primarily chickens or ducks, with goats and sheep raised to a much lesser degree. Most farming takes place on household property, but informal access to land is also important. Families practice intensive crop rotation to maximize use of small household plots, maintain soil fertility, and manage pests and disease. Vegetable farmers use cow dung and chicken droppings to augment the soil; mulching is practiced; some farmers use agrochemicals to treat crops for pests. Unfortunately, some urban farmers are using water contaminated by human, animal, and industrial waste, which could lead to serious health problems.

Source: Armar-Klemesu and Maxwell 2000

Urban agriculture in Dar Es Salaam, Tanzania, provides an indispensable part of the diet. About 70 percent of the city's population live in unplanned settlements with marginal access to tap water, sewage systems, and infrastructure or basic social services. In 1970 the government gave people plots and encouraged cultivation in every available piece of land. Private and public land, residential plots, and industrial and institutional areas are under cultivation. When there is no pumped water, farmers rely on rainfall. Vegetable production, including leafy vegetables, eggplant, sweet and hot peppers, okra, tomatoes, and fruits like oranges, mangoes, bananas, papaya, and pineapple are most common, followed by livestock for dairy and poultry. Some people in the inner city cultivate green maize and rice in the long, rainy season. Farmers use hoes, bush knives, and watering cans for subsistence production.

Source: Jacobi et al. 2000

Urban Agriculture in Asia and Southeast Asia

Throughout Asia, urban residents have small lots where plants, livestock, and sometimes fishponds are cultivated together. The Chinese are famous for their highly intensive urban cropping systems, and to this day many of their large cities are largely supplied by food produced in periurban areas administered by the city (Yi-Zhoang and Zhangen 2000). The Chinese government has encouraged urban authorities to produce a significant percentage of their local population's vegetable consumption. In Shanghai, a city populated by 13 million people, the government is pursuing capital-intensive urban agricultural development with a high degree of mechanization and intensive use of land, labor, and inputs. The emphasis is on cereals, grains (wheat and rice), and vegetables. In addition to food production, urban agriculture is seen as a way to reduce air pollution by maintaining green open spaces (Yi-Zhoang and Zhangen 2000). In Singapore and Hong Kong approximately 30–50 percent of families grow food in small gardens (Sommers and Smith 1994). Urban Singapore produces almost all of its own meat, consuming about 140 pounds per person per year (Schurmann 1996). In Ho Chi Minh City, Vietnam, money spent on food is as high as 80 percent; many people grow food near their homes to augment limited incomes (Cook and Rodgers 1997). In Bangladesh livestock and fish food are being grown in urban sewage-fed ponds; as much as 10 percent of total family income is derived from small urban gardens (Sommers and Smith 1994; Smit et al. 1996).

Growing Food in Cities: Asia

Cagayan de Oro, Philippines, is a rapidly growing city in the southern Philippines. Population density is high, and 82 percent of the population lives in urban areas. Farmers produce rice, maize, bananas, coffee, root crops, fruit, and vegetables for both home consumption and market. Production is characterized by monocropping on small acreage. Most of the land is owned by private individuals who hire tenant farmers to farm their urban and periurban fields. Farmers are limited by what they can produce due to the heat, pests, limited knowledge of appropriate inputs, poor infrastructure, limited access to land, and limited resources. Nevertheless, farmers grow vegetables, particularly eggplant, squash, string beans, tomatoes, peppers, and bitter gourd. Surveys reveal that about 46 percent of farmers extract water from nearby streams and rivers,

20 percent from deep wells, 11 percent from irrigation canals, and 12 percent depend entirely on rainfall. Eighty-six percent reported they use chemical fertilizers to control pests, diseases, and weeds. Ninety-six percent of schools in Cagayan de Oro maintain a school garden which is cultivated by students as part of their curriculum and supervised by teachers and principals. School administrators have adopted biointensive farming methods specifically designed to teach students about urban agriculture.

Source: Potutan et al. 2000

Jakarta, Indonesia, is home to almost ten million people during the day and 8.5 million people at night. The climate is humid and warm, with good rainfall. Soils are fertile, the land is relatively low and flat. The vast majority of people are poor; most rely on a diet of vegetables since meat, fish, and eggs are too expensive for most families to purchase on a regular basis. Urban farming is spreading in response to a severe economic crisis. Many urban farmers own their land, but many do not. In 1998 hundreds of people took over land on a horse-racing track and a cattle ranch owned by ex-president Suharto to grow vegetables. The police came and struggled with them, but in the end the governor of Jakarta gave the city's poor the permission to use the idle land to grow food, urging them to obtain permission rather than grabbing the land next time. Most farmers are men; they grow rice, vegetables, and fruit.

Source: Purnomohadi 2000

Urban Agriculture in Latin America and the Caribbean

Throughout Latin America and in many parts of the Caribbean, urban households spend a large portion of their household income on food. Households in Lima, Peru, spend 70 percent of household income on food. In Sao Paulo, Brazil, urban households devote about 50 percent of their income to food. In this context, growing food augments household budgets significantly. To promote urban food production in Latin America, the Latin American Urban Agriculture Research Network (AGUILA) was established in 1997. The organization promotes policies, technologies, and methods to improve the productivity, accessibility, and sustainability of urban production systems. Located in the Andes (Colombia, Peru, Bolivia, and Ecuador), the Southern Cone (Argentina, Chile, Brazil, Paraguay, and Uruguay), Central America, and the Caribbean, AGUILA helps low-income urban residents set up small gardens and greenhouses in which to grow food to supplement household diet and sell extra produce. A study of urban agriculture in Santiago, Dominican Republic, estimated the number of urban gardens at three thousand, the majority of cultivators being members of very low-income households. Fifty-two percent of urban gardeners had monthly incomes below the poverty level; 33 percent had incomes in the low- to mid-income group. Only one out of seven gardeners produced food to sell, and when they did so, food was sold within the neighborhood itself. One out of every five gardeners said they had only gardened in the city. Fifty percent reported that their main reason for growing food was to feed the family; 16 percent reported that food produced and sold added to family income which would then be used for purchasing additional food (Graham 1999).

Growing Food in Cities: Latin America

Lima, Peru, is home to seven million people, the majority of whom are poor. Home gardens make a major contribution to the food security, nutrition, and socioeconomic well-being for the city's low-income households. The system of "easy hydroponics" has been introduced by FAO-Chile. It tries to make use of the slope of a plot in order to water the vegetables without using electric pumps. Discarded wood can be used to make the table; different types of plastic containers can be used to hold plants. A standard formula mix of macro- and micronutrients is applied. Families are also breeding guinea pigs in cages made of locally available bamboo. Urban agriculture is especially popular in the fast-growing periurban areas of the city.

La Paz, Bolivia, has a population of 1.5 million. It is one of the cities with the most extreme climatic differences in the world. Many people have migrated to the city from rural areas, and many live in informal settlements; 79 percent of households live below the poverty line. Urban agriculture exists in every corner of the city, near the center as well as on the outskirts. Hens cackle, pigs grunt, and sheep graze on the size of the road. Yet when asked about urban agriculture, public officials say that it does not exist in the city. One church official who insisted that agriculture did not exist in the city had a productive greenhouse in the courtyard opposite his office. People primarily grow vegetables and raise livestock in their backyards and in open fields. Irrigation is essential due to the climate, and water supply is one of the biggest challenges for farmers. The soil is heavy clay and different practices to preserve soil health are essential; they include animal manure, kitchen waste, ashes, sand, and lime inputs. Since the climate is cold, composting is a difficult and lengthy process; some people compost in holes to quicken the process. Farmers grow potatoes, beans, and maize, as well as vegetables. Covered nursery beds and wooden fences are often used to shield plants from the wind.

Source: Kreinecker 2000

Urban Agriculture in Europe, Canada, and the United States

Many Eastern Europeans raise food and small livestock in urban and periurban areas. In 1997, Poland commemorated one hundred years of its urban allotment food production. Urban agriculture in Poland originated in the era of industrialization and the relocation of peasants from countryside to city; the now landless workforce grew food to supplement their meager incomes, especially during times of high unemployment (Bello 1998). Currently, 28 percent of urban families in Poland engage in urban agriculture growing food in over 900,000 plots on 42,000 hectares of land, with an estimated 700,000 additional families waiting to obtain a garden plot; urban agriculture in Poland provides one out of every fifteen kilograms consumed; for retired persons, it provides one out of every seven kilograms (Smit and Nasr 1995).

In Yerevan, Armenia, small food gardens are a major part of a family's food source. Seedlings are raised in homes during the long, cold winter. As soon as it becomes slightly warmer, people plant the small starts. A typical garden contains a multilayer mixture of Mediterranean type vegetables, spices, herbs, fruit trees, and grapevines. Once harvested, many of the crops are processed and stored for eating over the long winter (Sommers and Smith 1994). In Moscow, the number of urban resident families engaged in food production increased from 20 percent in 1970 to 65 percent in 1990. Approximately 30 percent of food in Russia is being produced on only three percent of the land in periurban and suburban dachas (Schurmann 1996).

Urban agricultural activities are increasing throughout western Europe. In the Netherlands it is estimated that urban agriculture is 33 percent of total agricultural production. The Dutch government is planning a "rim city," with Rotterdam to Amsterdam as the "tire" and urban agriculture as the "hub" (Sommers and Smith 1994). In Berlin, UNDP estimates that there are 80,000 community gardens with 16,000 people on the waiting list for a garden plot (Schurmann 1996). In Canada and the United States, urban agriculture has been promoted through the community gardening movement. *Community gardening,* in which plots of land are allotted to members of a local community and basic agricultural resources are shared, is increasing in popularity in both countries.

Growing Food in Cities: Europe

Sofia, Bulgaria, is the largest city in the nation and home to about 15 percent of Bulgaria's population. Urban agriculture has been an essential part of life in Bulgaria for centuries and is typical for all cities, including the capital. People produce food in privatively owned gardens and backyards. About 50 percent of all households in the city cultivate fruit, vegetables, and spices, and more than 90 percent make preserves and pickles out of homegrown and purchased agricultural produce. People grow cabbage, potatoes, onions, and beetroot among other vegetables and some livestock. Most households process food (canning, pickling, and stewing are the most common) to keep for the winter.

Source: Yoveva et al. 2000

London, England, has had a long history of gardening and there about 30,000 households in London who are active allotment holders growing food in the city. There are also eight productive farms in London. The farms serve a largely educational role, receiving visits from schoolchildren and families. In addition, there are seventy-seven community gardens located throughout the city. Almost all of the food grown by home gardeners is grown using sustainable agriculture methods and practices. The government is increasingly supportive of urban gardening, promoting farmers markets and organic urban agriculture. Farmers and gardeners grow vegetables, raise bees for honey, and also keep chickens for eggs.

Source: Garnett 2000

The Role of Urban Authorities

Urban authorities vary considerably in their approach to urban agriculture. In most developing countries, urban agriculture has proceeded for decades without the formal support or approval of officials; lack of government support stems largely from the fact that many public officials perceive agriculture as unsuitable in urban areas (FAO 2002). Concern about competition for land and water and incompatible land uses has resulted in government officials discouraging urban food production in the belief that, in addition to competing with other land uses, urban agriculture contributes to public health and traffic problems (Eberlee 1993). Many public authorities perceive agriculture as a traditional and backward activity (as opposed to modern and progress-oriented activity) that is antithetical to their notion of a modern city.[4]

In a few countries, aggressive government tactics have been used to curb urban agricultural activities. In Kenya the Local Government Act gives every town the authority to restrict or permit urban agriculture. Cultivation is prohibited on many streets in Nairobi, but authorities have allowed nongovernmental organizations to support urban agriculture projects. However, because the government has not provided support for urban food production, it remains uncoordinated and unplanned. In Uganda municipal laws dating from the colonial period ban cultivation in the city with the exception of small vegetable and flowers gardens; authorities tolerate food cultivation but use restrictive legislation to ensure that residents do not keep livestock without permission from the city council because they are fearful that unconfined livestock could spread diseases such as salmonella and brucellosis, and, by damaging drainage projects, potentially malaria as well (Memon and Lee-Smith 1993). Until very recently, federal and municipal governments in Harare, Zimbabwe, actively discouraged urban agricultural activities. The situation was eased somewhat when there was a public outcry when maize planted on public land in response to drought was routinely being destroyed by police working for the Harare City Council (Mbiba 1995).

Yet despite negative perceptions about urban agricultural land uses, planners and government officials usually tolerate food production because it is integral to the economic survival of the urban poor in their localities. Although the general tendency has been for urban authorities to reject urban agriculture as an urban land use, some national governments are encouraging urban agriculture. A few national and local governments have explicitly supported urban agriculture by creating incentives to attract people to grow food in cities.

In the early 1960s, officials in the Chinese government instituted a series of policies designed to encourage and support urban agriculture in order to ensure that China's cities could produce a significant proportion of their local populations' food needs. In the 1970s, government officials in Ghana sponsored Operation Feed Yourselves, designed to assist urban dwellers to grow food in cities and near factories based on the premise that much of the country's food imports could be grown within the country (Armar-Klemesu and Maxwell 2001). In the 1980s, governments in Papua New Guinea and the Philippines provided land for allotment gardens, forcing landowners to cultivate unused lands or allow others to cultivate it in the owner's absence. Public lands adjacent to highways were also designated for cultivation (Rokadi 1988). In South Africa, the National Department of Agriculture, the Department of Water Affairs and Forestry, and the Department of Land Affairs consider the use of open space by low-income families to produce food a policy priority. The South African Department of Land Affairs, responsible for land reform and land redistribution programs, has a land grant program through which new urban agriculturists can get access to municipal common land and a grant for training and support. Governments in Zaire and Nigeria support urban farming through Zaire's subsidizing access to water and drainage and Nigeria's making basic agricultural inputs tax free (Lachance 1993). In Sao Paulo, Brazil, the metropolitan master plan formally includes agriculture as a planned land use.

Urban agriculture is increasingly being recognized in Europe as a realistic and desirable land-use option in urban areas and an integral part of the urban productive system. The recently established European Support Group on Urban Agriculture is working with the European Coordination of Gardeners Associations, International Coalition for Local Environmental Action, European League of Local Authorities, and other organizations to promote urban agriculture throughout cities in Europe. The goals are to (1) stimulate dialogue on urban agriculture between city councils, citizens, farmers, and other stakeholders at the local, regional, and European level; (2) discuss policy developments pertaining to sustainable urban agriculture and development; and (3) facilitate regional and European networking among stakeholders in urban agriculture and in the development of urban farming systems and integration of urban policies and planning related to urban agriculture (de Zeeuw and Dubbeling 1997).

Planning and Development to
Support Sustainable Urban Food Production

The best example of urban infrastructure planning and development to support sustainable urban food production is found in Havana, Cuba. Urban agriculture in Cuba emerged as the government systematically responded to severe food shortages that came about as a result of the fall of the Soviet Bloc in 1989 (Murphy 1999). For almost three decades, Cuba had relied on the Soviet Bloc countries for food, medicines, and farm inputs ranging from petroleum to pesticides. Following the Cuban Revolution in 1959, the new Cuban government viewed access to nutritious food as a basic human right and prioritized eliminating hunger and poverty through an elaborate national food distribution system (Murphy 1999; Pinderhughes et al. 2001). This system functioned well to distribute needed food goods to the Cuban population, but it was highly dependent upon food imports; 57 percent of total foods consumed in Cuba were imported from the Soviet Bloc.

With the demise of the Soviet Bloc in 1989, all food imports were lost, resulting in the Cuban population experiencing immediate food shortages. Cuba also lost critical agricultural imports upon which its national food production system had become dependent—fertilizers, pesticides, tractors, spare parts, and petroleum to provide fuel energy. Reductions in access to petroleum brought the food distribution system to a halt; severe fuel shortages meant that food could not be refrigerated or transported by trucks from the periurban and rural areas where food was produced to the urban areas where the majority of the population resided. The U.S. Congress made the situation more difficult with the passage of the Torricelli Bill in 1992. The bill banned trade between Cuba and foreign subsidiaries of U.S. companies threatening to confiscate ships that touched port in both Cuba and the United States within six months. Since most of this trade had been in food stuff, after the Toricelli bill was passed, food shortages worsened considerably.

By the end of 1992, food shortages had reached crisis proportions throughout Cuba, including in the capital city of Havana, home to 2.2 million Cubans and the largest city in the Caribbean. Like many large cities, Havana was a food-consumer city, completely dependent upon food imports brought in from the Cuban countryside and abroad. Havana had no food production sector or infrastructure and almost no land dedicated to the production of food. Worsening food shortages motivated urban residents in Havana to plant food crops in their yards, patios, balconies, rooftops, and vacant land sites near their homes. In some cases, neighbors got together to plants crops—beans, tomatoes, bananas, lettuce, okra, eggplant, and taro. If they had the space and the resources, some households began to raise small animals—chickens, rabbits, even pigs. Within two years there were gardens and farms in many Havana neighborhoods. By 1994 hundreds of Havana residents were involved in food production. The majority of these urban growers had little or no access to much needed agricultural inputs—seeds, tools, pest controls, and soil amendments, nor did they have knowledge about the small-scale, agro-ecological techniques that urban gardening requires (Murphy 1999). In a report published by the Institute for Food and Development Policy entitled *Cultivating Havana: Urban Agriculture and Food Security in the Years of Crisis*, Catherine Murphy describes how the Cuban government responded to the food crisis by systematically creating an infrastructure to support urban food production (1999).

The government responded to people's need for agricultural information and agricultural inputs by working with the Cuban Ministry of Agriculture to create a new institution—the Department of Urban Agriculture, headquartered in Havana. The department's goal was to put all of the city's open land into cultivation and provide a wide range of extension services and resources such as agricultural specialists, short courses, seed banks, biological controls, compost, and tools. The department secured land-use rights for all urban growers by adapting city laws to gain legal rights for food production on unused land. Hundreds of vacant lots, public and private, were officially sanctioned as gardens and farms. In some cases land ownership titles have been accorded, but in most instances land has been, and continues to be, handed over in *usufruct*, a planning concept that grants free and indefinite right to use public land for gardening. The issuing of land grants of unused vacant space in the city resulted in the conversion of hundreds of vacant lots into food producing plots (Pinderhughes et al. 2001).

In addition to land grants, the Cuban government created an economic infrastructure for farmers and incentives for urbanites to grow/raise food that was based on the creation of farmers' markets and direct farmstand sales from farmers to consumers (Murphy 1999). The department also set up a network of extension agents organized to respond to the varied needs of urban growers and assist them in all aspects of farming. The majority of extension workers are women who live in the neighborhoods in which they work; they know the residents of the neighborhoods, keep track of ongoing needs and concerns, and continually encourage people to consider using available land for food production. Extension agents teach urban growers about small-scale agriculture techniques suited to urban food production and promote sustainable methods and practices—biofertilizers, composting, and green manure for increasing organic matter in soil, companion planting, biological controls, and permaculture methods. Currently, there are sixty-eight extension agents working in small teams of two to seven people in thirteen of Havana's fifteen urban districts. The emphasis is on sustainable agriculture methods and processes.

The Department of Urban Agriculture also set up seed houses (*tiendas del agricultor*). In 2003, there were twelve seed houses in Havana that sold garden inputs, seeds, ornamental and medicinal plants, tree samplings (mostly fruit-bearing), tools, books, biological control products, biofertilizers, biological pest and disease controls, packaged compost, worm humus, and other needed agricultural inputs. The department also worked with Cuba's agricultural research sector to develop a new emphasis on providing information and resources for small-scale, sustainable urban agriculture. Two hundred and twenty-two small-scale centers now produce biological control products to support sustainable organic agriculture throughout the nation. These centers harness microorganisms that perform useful functions in natural ecosystems and reproduce them in forms that can be used as biopesticides; other laboratories produce a variety of organic biofertilizers and pheromones.

This planned government strategy gave rise to the only nationwide infrastructure for urban agriculture in the world and resulted in over eight thousand farms and food gardens in the city of Havana alone. State-supported infrastructure for urban agriculture allowed thousands of Cubans to become involved in food production in the nation's capital. The goal of the Cuban government for the urban vegetables and herbs program was to produce three hundred grams of fresh vegetables daily per capita by the end of 2000. In 1997 urban farms and gardens in Havana provided 30,000 tons of vegetables, tubers, and fruit, 3,650 tons of meat, 7.5 million eggs, and 3.6 tons of medicinal plant materials. Farmers in Havana also began to grow rice. This small-scale rice production was completely unprecedented and unexpected because historically rice production in Cuba had been conducted on large farms using industrial methods. Nationwide, small-scale urban rice production is now producing as much rice as large-scale state-owned farms in rural and periurban areas. In 1999 vegetable production in *organoponicos* and intensive gardens alone provided Cubans with 215 grams per day per person of fresh horticultural crops. By 2003 about 30 percent of Havana's available land was under cultivation and there were more than 30,000 people growing food in the city of Havana.

The size and structure of these urban farms and gardens varies considerably. There are small backyard and individual plot gardens cultivated privately by urban residents (*huertos populares*). There are larger gardens based in raised container beds by individuals and state institutions (*organoponicos*). There are workplace gardens that supply the cafeterias of their own workplace or institution (*autoconsumos*). There are small family-run farms (*campesinos*), and there are farms owned and operated by the state with varying degrees of profit-sharing with workers (*empresas estatales*) (Murphy 1999).

The growth and success of urban agriculture is due to the Cuban government's decision to make use of unused urban and periurban land available to Cubans interested in farming. The issuing of land grants of vacant space in the city resulted in the conversion of hundreds of vacant lots into food-producing plots. Although there is now competition for land uses in Havana, new planning laws place the highest land-use priority on food production. In addition to land grants, the Cuban government created an infrastructure for farmers' markets and direct sales from farmers to consumers and a series of incentives for urbanites to grow/raise food. Unlike anywhere else in the world, in Cuba deregulation of prices, combined with high demand for fresh produce, has allowed urban farmers to earn more than many of Havana's professionals (Pinderhughes et al. 2001).

Outside of Cuba, people are concerned about the degree to which Cuba will be able to maintain its commitment to urban agriculture and sustainable methods as the country increasingly enters the global economy and faces pressures to restructure its economic and political system. Certainly there are signs of competing urban land uses, such as residential housing and the tourist industry. As the economy opens, multinational food corporations will try to flood the Cuban market with cheap imported food products that could undermine local food production. Understanding these pressures, the Cuban government has developed land-use policies that are designed to ensure that urban food production will continue. For example, any new constructions that would displace an existing garden must finance the relocation of that garden. This includes not only finding a new location but also constructing new garden beds, fences, bringing in compost and tree samplings, and so on. To encourage people to become involved in urban food production, the Cuban government has developed strategies that allow urban growers to earn a very good income based on direct consumer sales. The Urban Agriculture Department is developing policies and strategies to ensure sufficient access to water for irrigation. There is ongoing public education about urban food production using television, radio, and print media.

Although urban agriculture in Cuba came about as a response to an acute food shortage, the benefits have been far reaching. These advances are directly due to the Cuban government's commitment to food security, which in Cuba has come to mean not only providing people with access to food, but providing them with healthy food produced without chemical inputs harmful to human and environmental health. The Cuban government's systematic development of an infrastructure for urban agriculture illustrates the role that urban planners and other urban authorities can play in developing strategies and policies that support small-scale sustainable farming methods and inputs, allow urban farmers to thrive, increase local food security, and promote ecological sustainability.

Summary

This chapter focuses on the role that food production in cities can play in moving forward the goal of sustainable urban development in cities around the world. Urban agriculture has critical socioeconomic and environmental functions. By providing nonmarket access to food for low-income consumers, urban agriculture can augment household budgets, increase household and community food security, and improve health through increased access to fresh food. Urban agriculture can also function to create income, employment, and job training opportunities for low-income urban residents. In terms of environmental protection, urban agriculture has obvious environmental benefits ranging from recycling wastes to reducing inputs related to transportation, storage, and packaging. Urban agriculture also contributes to public health by increasing intake of fresh fruits and vegetables (Pinderhughes 2003).

The chapter discusses the work of urban planners Pothukuchi and Kaufman, whose work reveals that the discipline of urban planning has paid almost no attention to the food system or to planning for community food needs and that this lack of food system analysis has several very problematic consequences. It has led urban planners to fold grocery store market development and location into the broader category of commercial retail development without considering the higher priority that food merits among household needs. It has resulted in missed opportunities to develop community-wide plans for composting food wastes, contributing to a solid waste crisis that has already reached crisis proportions and missing a vital opportunity to contribute to soil health. It has led planners and other urban authorities to misunderstand the significance of food as a community issue as well as its links to other activities and systems, such as wholesale trade, transportation, energy use, and waste management.

The chapter emphasizes the multiple benefits of urban agriculture and describes how it represents a unique land use and opportunity for urban planners to integrate food concerns into their focus on enhancing the livability of human settlements. Doing so will require urban planners to analyze the connections between food and other planning concerns, access the impact of current planning on the local food system, integrate food security into urban planning and policy goals, educate future planners about food system issues, and provide support to the various components of the urban infrastructure that sustain urban agriculture in cities.

Chapter Questions

The chapter provides readers with information to address eight essential questions related to urban food production:

1. Why should the food system be an important focus for urban planners?

2. What problems are associated with industrial agriculture processes and inputs?

3. How does urban agriculture contribute to an urban areas waste management capacity?

4. Does urban agriculture have the potential to contribute to poverty reduction?

5. How can existing models help planners to develop an urban agricultural sector that increases food security and environmental protection?

6. What would an infrastructure to support sustainable urban agriculture look like?

7. What are the most important characteristics of the infrastructure that supports urban agriculture in Havana, Cuba?

8. What are the consequences of proposing food production as a major urban land use?

Notes

1. Community food security refers to all people having access to culturally acceptable, nutritionally adequate food through local non-emergency sources at all times.

2. If approximately one third of the 1,600 cubic meters per person is needed to be supplied by irrigation, annual water demand to support food needs would average about 530 cubic meters per person (Postel 1997). This is estimated to be about 240 cubic meters per capita per year needed to support worldwide household, municipal, and industrial water uses. Assuming an average of two hundred cubic meters per capita per year for household, municipal, and industrial uses, and adding this to the fresh water required for food production, Postel assumes a requirement of about 730 cubic meters per capita per year (1997). In order to meet instream needs, the total amount of runoff must be two to three times higher than the amount required to meet irrigation, industrial, and household water demands; the amount of total annual runoff per capita works out to about 1,700 cubic meters per year, making it clear that many countries will not be able to meet their population's water needs (Postel 1997).

3. *Composting* is the controlled biological decomposition of organic material in the presence of air to form a humus-like material. Controlled methods of composting include mechanical mixing and aerating; ventilating the material by dropping it through a vertical series of aerated chambers, or placing the compost in piles out in the open air and mixing it or turning it periodically (USEPA 2002).

4. This is similar to the perceptions that urban authorities have about cycle-rickshaws that were discussed in chapter 4 on urban transportation planning and management.

Photograph by Raquel Pinderhughes

CHAPTER SIX
TOWARD SUSTAINABLE
DEVELOPMENT PLANNING IN CITIES

The emergence of the concept of sustainable development marks the end of the industrial civilization of fordist production, of the logics of economies of scale. But it also signals that societies based on a vulgar Darwinistic principle of survival of the fittest, of ruthless egoism of the few who mercilessly and thoughtlessly exploit their fellow human beings as they exploit nature, will not survive. Either humanity will eventually succeed in establishing the truly humane principles or it will vanish from Planet Earth. . . . Sustainability indicates the end of the affluent industrial society and points, at the same time, to a future which is not yet clear. It is, however, clear that the basic problem lies in social organizations, in social institutions, in the way and how decisions are made, to whose profit and at whose cost. . . . The bottom-line is that humanity can not and will not survive beyond the limits set by the reproductive abilities of nature; above all, humanity will have to reduce its total consumption of natural resources.

—Bernd Hamm and Pandurang Muttagi,
Understanding Sustainable Development, 1998

Alternative Urban Futures

Sustainable development requires a commitment to provide goods and services that are essential to people's ability to live healthy, productive lives using processes and technologies that minimize the use of natural resources and limit the harmful environmental and social impacts of human activities. Whereas the development paradigm is based on degrading the world's natural resources, exploiting human labor, and compromising the carrying capacity of the globe and the health of humans and other species, the sustainable development paradigm rejects policies and practices that support current living standards by promoting social inequality and depleting the natural resource base, leaving future generations with poorer prospects and greater risks (Repetto 1986).

Pragmatically, moving toward sustainable development will require planning and policy initiatives designed to eliminate profound disparities between and within nations and deal with rapid degradation of the natural resource base and ecosystems upon which humans and other species depend (Mbeki 2002). Prosperous nations will need to reduce inefficient and wasteful use of natural resources, change unsustainable patterns of production and consumption, and assist nations that need additional resources to fight poverty and strengthen their capacity to deliver essential infrastructure services related to water, waste, energy, transportation, food, adequate housing, health care, and education, so that the basic needs of billions of people around the world can be met. Assistance will have to include support to transfer appropriate technologies to developing countries.

Ultimately, achieving sustainable development will require radical changes in the way we think about economic activity and its associated production and consumption processes. Sustainable development "can only take place when predatory development, which destroys nature and threatens the survival of the human race, is replaced by progressive governance which emphasizes democratic processes and the participation of the population in decision-making processes" (Henrique Cardoso 2002, 6). We will need to move away from what the Balaton Group calls the *hypermarket*, which emphasizes competition, globalization, individualism, and technological progress as a solution to scarcity, high inputs, and information as both property and power, and toward *regional stewardship*, which emphasizes holism, partnerships, democratic governance, decentralization, ecological carrying capacity, transparency of information, and cooperation (Hollantai 1999).[1]

As a global community, we will need to consume fewer resources, reduce dependency on fossil fuels, increase reliance on renewable energy sources, and produce less waste. Economic activity will need to be measured differently and government subsidies and tax systems will need to be reorganized so that they reward sustainable development activities and create disincentives for unsustainable economic activities. Investing in properly designed and well-managed sustainable urban infrastructure development will contribute to economic development, reduce adverse local, regional, and global environmental impacts, lead to improvements in public health and the natural resource base, and increase quality of life for urban residents (Choguill 1996).

In the area of urban water management, inefficiency and overuse of water in wealthy, industrialized countries must be addressed immediately. Industrialized countries must decrease their drawdown of water supply by reducing water consumption for agriculture and landscaping, using gray water systems that capture and reuse water, treating wastewater for reuse, using constructed wetlands and living machines, and integrating appropriate technologies such as non-leaking low-flush toilets, aerated shower heads, and top-loading washing machines into all households. Globally, more than one billion people lack access to safe drinking water and more than three million people die every year from diseases caused by unsafe water (Moosa Valli 2002). Developing countries must be assisted to develop an infrastructure that provides clean water for all urban residents and to do so utilizing sustainable water management strategies to deliver adequate and safe water supply.

In the area of urban waste management, excessive consumption and waste in prosperous nations must be reduced significantly. Economic activities must be reorganized around a "resource recognition" approach, which promotes the reduction of waste in production and distribution processes and the enhancement of waste through reuse and recycling processes. Incentives to move toward resource recognition include financial savings from byproduct opportunities, more land becoming available for other uses, reduction of greenhouse gases, increase of efficiency and reduction of costs related to the disposal of toxic and hazardous waste, and improved public health and environmental quality. Policies that encourage materials exchange/reprocessing and pollution prevention strategies must be promoted in order to facilitate large and small institutions and businesses to trade, sell, and/or give away unwanted materials to one another in order to use them as raw materials in manufacturing or reuse them in their existing form. Reusing metals, paper, glass, plastic, textiles, organic waste, and water will result in reductions in the demand for energy, raw materials, fertilizers, foreign exchange, and freshwater sources. At the same time, it is critical to prevent wealthy nations from sending their hazardous waste to poorer nations under the guise of recycling.

In the area of urban energy management, we must move toward an energy system that is flexible and adaptable to different regions and needs, increasingly relies on renewable energy sources, emphasizes energy efficiency, and ensures affordable, consistent access to modern energy sources for all households. The emphasis must be on efficient use of both renewable and conventional energy supplies in all sectors.

Cities must begin to use a diversity of energy sources provided by various combinations of hydroelectric power, intermittent renewable power sources (wind, solar-thermal electric, and photovoltaic power), biomass power, and geothermal power. We have the capacity to produce massive quantities of energy with wind and solar technologies. Intermittent renewable energy sources can provide as much as one third of total electricity requirements cost-effectively in most regions without the need for new electrical storage technologies. If we invest in research and development, we will soon be able to affordably harness energy from biomass sources grown using sustainable farming methods and processes and converted efficiently to electricity and liquid and gaseous fuels using appropriate technologies. Electricity produced from renewable sources could easily be fed into large electrical grids and marketed by electric utilities. Achieving the complementary goals of energy efficiency and expanding markets for renewable energy technologies will require the passage of new policy initiatives that would be specifically developed to encourage innovation and investment in renewable energy technologies. It is especially important to remove subsidies that artificially reduce the price of fuels (fossil, nuclear, and hydro). It is particularly important to tax fossil fuels and to introduce taxes, regulations, and other policy instruments that ensure that consumer decisions are based on the full cost of energy, including environmental and other external costs not reflected in market prices. Within developing countries, a third of the world's total population (two billion people) have no access to modern energy sources. According to the G8 Renewable Energy Task Force, bringing renewable energy to households in the developing world could be a major source of employment and business creation on the local and national levels (Moody-Stuart 2002). Support for renewable energy will have to come from many sectors— government, the private sector, research institutions, and international finance institutions. All conventional energy sources have benefited from enormous subsidies for research, development, and infrastructure capacity, and they continue to be heavily subsidized today. Encouraging a flexible energy mix will require reducing subsidies for fossil fuels and increasing subsidies to promote research, development, capacity building, and affordability of renewable energy sources.

In the areas of urban transportation and land use, it is essential to develop land-use planning policies that explicitly shape the urban environment in socially and ecologically responsible ways. Planners and policymakers must begin to support land uses that have lower impacts on the integrity of ecosystems. They must promote transportation modalities that use energy sources that are renewable or inexhaustible and produce no more emissions and waste than can be accommodated by the planet's restorative ability. Increasing amounts of renewable energy sources and recycled materials should be used to support the existing and necessary infrastructure for motorized vehicles. Land-use planning should focus on supporting urban development at a human scale and providing urban residents with affordable, high-quality transportation choices that are viable alternatives to the one-passenger automobile. Automobile use must be reduced considerably, using public policies and planning initiatives that support the use of mass transit and bicycling and discourage use of the private automobile. It is particularly important to create an infrastructure that encourages bicycling and walking, which are highly beneficial to human and environmental health. With regard to the popularity of automobiles, it is important to develop infrastructures that support alternative fuel sources for light motorized vehicles (i.e., biodiesel, methanol, ethanol, hydrogen, and methane [biogas] derived from biomass) as well as changes to the structure of the vehicle itself.

In the area of urban food systems, urban planners have paid almost no attention to urban food systems, planning for community food needs, or to the role that urban agriculture can play in reducing socioeconomic and environmental problems in cities. This lack of food system analysis has meant that planners and policymakers have missed opportunities to develop community-wide plans for composting food wastes, contribute to soil health, increase food security, and improve urban food systems (Pothukuchi and Kaufman 2000). This has led planners to misunderstand the significance of food as a community issue as well as the linkages between food production and energy and water use, transportation, and waste management. Urban agriculture represents a unique land use and provides planners with an opportunity to integrate food concerns into their focus on enhancing the livability of human settlements. Urban agriculture can augment household budgets, increase household and community food security, improve health through increased access to fresh food, create income, employment, and job training opportunities for urban residents. In terms of environmental protection, urban agriculture has obvious environmental benefits stemming from recycling wastes and reducing inputs related to food production, transportation, storage, and packaging. Planning and policy measures designed to create an infrastructure that supports urban food production must be put into place whenever feasible.

Much of the information that planners need to understand how to deliver essential urban services (safe water supply, sanitation services, energy, housing, transportation, food supply, and so on) in ways that reduce (rather than create) environmental degradation and adverse social impacts is provided in this book. But adopting the sustainable alternatives described in the chapters will require planners to go way beyond simply implementing alternative technological processes. William Rees says that "to pursue sustainable development planners must reject the false assumptions of modern neoclassical economic theory, a theoretical framework uninformed by ecological principles, wherein the economy is understood as mechanical rather than biological or ecological based. Neoclassical economic theory advances the ideology that economic growth is the principal vehicle for development and that, somehow, increases in economic growth measures will benefit the poor and generate surpluses for ecosystem protection. By accepting this false ideology, planners end up promoting and supporting policies that are based on the continued exploitation of human and natural resources, rather than developing and implementing policies that (1) fight poverty through redistribution and sharing resources and (2) fight environmental degradation through natural resource reductions in prosperous countries. Planners will not be able to achieve sustainable development without identifying and analyzing the root causes of poverty, social inequality, and ecological decline. Fundamentally, planners must recognize that the solution to the global ecological crisis resides within the same social and economic structures that created the problems in the first place" (Rees 1998). Planners must acknowledge that human activities do not occur independently of nature and that the environment is not a static backdrop to economic and social activities (Herfindahl and Kneese 1965). Urban planning must focus on adopting new approaches and appropriate technologies designed to deliver and manage urban infrastructure services in ways that minimize a city's impact on the environment. Fortunately, as the chapters in this book have shown, the paradigms, processes, and technologies that we need to proceed have all been developed. Now it is a matter of commitment to change, cooperation between nations, and planning for sustainable development in cities throughout the world.

Note

1. The Balaton Group is an informal association of people working in their home countries around the world toward a sustainable society. Their name comes from the fact that they meet yearly for five days on the shore of Lake Balaton in Csopak, Hungary (Hollantai 1999).

BIBLIOGRAPHY

Acknowledgments

Drakakis-Smith, David
"Third World Cities: Sustainable Urban Development." *Urban Studies* 32, nos. 4 and 5 (1995): 657–77.

Drakakis-Smith, David
"Third World Cities: Sustainable Urban Development III. Basic Needs and Human Rights." *Urban Studies* 34, nos. 5 and 6 (1997): 797–823.

Preface

Annan, Kofi
Public remarks leading up to the 2002 World Summit on Sustainable Development (WSSD), Johannesburg, South Africa, August, 2002.

Anonymous
Introduction in "Sustainable Cities: Meeting Needs, Reducing Resource Use and Recycling, Re-use and Reclamation." *Environment and Urbanization* 4, no. 2 (1992).

Couch, C.
Urban Renewal: Theory and Practice. London: Macmillan Education, 1990.

Fox Quesada, Vincente
"Development with a Human Face." *Our Planet* (United Nations Environment Programme magazine) 13, no. 4 (2003): 6–7.

Goodland, Daly, and El Serafy, eds.
Environmentally Sustainable Economic Development Building on Brundtland. Environmental Working Paper No. 46. Washington, D.C.: World Bank Environment Department, 1991.

Gossaye, A.
"Inner-city Renewal and Locational Stability of the Poor: A Study of Inner-city Renewal Program in Addis Ababa, Ethopia" In *The Sustainable City: Urban Regeneration and Sustainability*. Southampton, U.K.: WIT Press, 2000.

Hamm, Bernd, and Pandurang Muttagi
Introduction. In *Understanding Sustainable Development* in *Sustainable Development and the Future of Cities*. London: Intermediate Technology Publications, 1998.

Jensen, M. B., B. Persson, S. Goldager, O. Reah, and K. Nilsson
"Green Structure and Sustainability: Developing a Tool for Local Planning." *Landscape and Urban Planning* 52 (2000): 17–33.

Moosa Valli, Mohammed
"African Renaissance." *Our Planet* 13, no. 2 (2002): 13–14.

Priemus, Hugo
"The Dutch Experience." *International Planning Studies* (June 1999).

Rees, William
"Understanding Sustainable Development." In *Sustainable Development and the Future of Cities*, edited by B. Hamm and P. Muttagi. London: Intermediate Technology Publications, 1998.

United Nations
Sustainable Human Settlements Development: Implementing Agenda 21. United Nations Centre for Human Settlements, 1994.

United Nations
United Nations Environment Programme Magazine 13, no. 2 (2002): 10.

White, Rodney, and Joseph Whitney
"Cities and the Environment: An Overview." In *Sustainable Cities*. San Francisco: Westview, 1992.

Introduction: Planning for Sustainable Urban Development

Adams, W.
Green Development: Environment and Sustainability in the Third World. London: Routledge, 1990.

Adriaanse, A., S. Bringezu, A. Hammond, Y. Moriguchi, E. Rodenburg, D. Rogich, and H. Schutz
Resource Flows: The Material Basis of Industrial Economies. Washington, D.C.: World Resources Institute, 1997.

Anonymous
Introduction in "Sustainable Cities: Meeting Needs, Reducing Resource Use and Recycling, Re-use and Reclamation." *Environment and Urbanization* 4, no. 2 (1992).

Bartone, C., J. Bernstein, J. Leitmann, and J. Eigen
"Toward Environmental Strategies for Cities: Policy Considerations from Urban Environmental Management in Developing Countries." UNDP/UNCHS (Habitat) World Bank Urban Management Program (UMP). Washington, D.C.: World Bank, 1994.

Basiago, Andrew
"Economic, Social and Environmental Sustainability in Development Theory and Urban Planning Practice." *The Environmentalist* 19 (1999): 145–61.

Briassoulis, Helen
"Who Plans Whose Sustainability? Alternative Roles for Planners." *Journal of Environmental Planning and Management* 42, no. 6 (1999): 889–902.

Choguill, Charles
"Ten Steps to Sustainable Infrastructure." *Habitat International* 20, no. 3 (1996): 389–404.

Commission on Sustained Development
Overall Progress Achieved since the United Nations Conference on Environment and Development. New York: Economic and Social Council, 1997.

Couch, C.
Urban Renewal: Theory and Practice. London: Macmillan Education, 1990.

Daly, Herman, and Cobb, J.
For the Common Good: Redirecting the Economy toward Community, the Environment, and a Sustainable Future. Boston: Beacon Press, 1989.

Diamantini, Corrado, and Bruno Zanon
"Planning the Urban Sustainable Development: The Case of the Plan for the Province of Trento, Italy." *Environmental Impact Assessment Review* 20 (2000): 299–310.

BIBLIOGRAPHY

de Roo, G., and D. Miller
Compact Cities and Sustainable Urban Development. Newport NSW, Australia: Ashgate, 2000.

Douglass, Mike
"The Political Economy of Urban Poverty and Environmental Management in Asia: Access, Empowerment and Community Based Alternatives." *Environment and Urbanization* 4, no. 2 (October 1992): 9–32.

Drakakis-Smith, David
"Third World Cities: Sustainable Urban Development II. Population, Labour and Poverty." *Urban Studies* 33, nos. 4 and 5 (1996): 673–701.

Durning, Alan
How Much Is Enough: The Consumer Society and the Future of the Earth. New York: W. W. Norton, 1992.

Gibbs, David
"Integrating Sustainable Development and Economic Restructuring: A Role for Regulation Theory?" *Geoforum* 27, no. 1 (1996): 1–10.

Glasby, G. P.
"Concept of Sustainable Development: A Meaningful Goal?" *The Science of the Total Environment* 159 (1995): 67–80.

Goddard, Haynes
"Promoting Urban Sustainability: The Case for a Tradable Supplementary License System for Vehicle Use." *Urban Studies* 36, no. 13 (1999): 2317–31.

Goodland, Robert
"The Case That the World Has Reached Limits." In *Environmentally Sustainable Economic Development Building on Brundtland*, edited by Daly Goodland and El Serafy. Environmental Working Paper No. 46. Washington, D.C.: World Bank Environment Department, 1991.

Gossaye, A.
"Inner-city Renewal and Locational Stability of the Poor: A Study of Inner-city Renewal Program in Addis Ababa, Ethopia" In *The Sustainable City: Urban Regeneration and Sustainability*. Southampton, U.K.: WIT Press, 2000.

Hamm, Bernd, and Pandurang Muttagi
Introduction. In *Understanding Sustainable Development* in *Sustainable Development and the Future of Cities*. London: Intermediate Technology Publications, 1998.

Human Settlements Program
Identifying the Groups Most Vulnerable to Urban Environmental Hazards.
Briefing Paper No. 2. London: International Institute for the Environment
and Development, 2001.

Ingram, Gregory, and Christine Kessides
"Infrastructure for Development." *Finance and Development* 31, no. 3 (1994).

Krizek, K., and J. Power
"A Planning Guide to Sustainable Development." *American Planning Association.* Planning Advisory Service Report Number 467.

Leitmann, Josef
"Browning the Bank: The World Bank's Growing Investment in Urban Environmental Management." *Environmental Impact Assessment Review* 16 (1996): 351–61.

Miller, D., and G. de Roo
Integrating City Planning and Environmental Improvement: Practical Strategies for Sustainable Urban Development. Aldershot, U.K.: Ashgate, 1999.

Newman, Peter
"Sustainability and Cities: Extending the Metabolism Model." *Landscape and Urban Planning* 44 (1999): 219–26.

Pereira, A., L. Oliveira, and M. Reis
"Waste Recycling and the Sustainable City." In *The Sustainable City: Urban Regeneration and Sustainability.* Southampton, U.K.: WIT Press, 2000.

Petesch, Patti
North-South Environmental Strategies, Costs and Bargains. Washington, D.C.: Overseas Development Council, 1992.

Priemus, Hugo
"The Dutch Experience." *International Planning Studies* (June 1999).

Rees, William
"Revisiting Carrying Capacity: Area-based Indicators of Sustainability." *Population and Environment* 17, no. 3 (1996): 195–215.

Rees, William
"Understanding Sustainable Development." In *Sustainable Development and the Future of Cities,* edited by B. Hamm and P. Muttagi. London: Intermediate Technology Publications, 1998.

BIBLIOGRAPHY

Reid, W., J. Barnes, and B. Blackwelder
Bankrolling Successes: A Portfolio of Sustainable Development Projects. Environmental Policy Institute and National Wildlife Federation, 1988.

Repetto, R.
World Enough and Time. New Haven, Conn.: Yale University Press, 1986.

Rotmans, J., M. van Asselt, and P. Vellinga
"An Integrated Planning Tool for Sustainable Cities." *Environmental Impact Assessment Review* 20 (2000): 265–76.

Ryan, John, and Alan Durning
Stuff: The Secret Lives of Everyday Things. Seattle, Wa.: Northwest Environmental Watch, 1997.

Smith, M., J. Whitelegg, and N. Williams
Greening the Built Environment. Washington, D.C.: Earthscan, 1988.

Tinbergen, J., and R. Hueting
"GNP and Market Prices: Wrong Signals for Sustainable Economic Success That Mask Environmental Destruction." In *Environmentally Sustainable Economic Development Building on Brundtland,* edited by Daly Goodland and El Serafy. Environmental Working Paper No. 46. Washington, D.C.: World Bank Environment Department, 1991.

Tjallingii, Sybrand
ECOPOLIS: Strategies for Ecologically Sound Urban Development. Leiden: Backhuys, 1995.

Turner, B. L.
"The Sustainability Principle in Global Agendas: Implications for Understanding Land-use/Cover Change." *The Geographic Journal* 163, no. 2 (July 1997): 133–40.

United Nations
Sustainable Human Settlements Development: Implementing Agenda 21. United Nations Centre for Human Settlements, 1994.

United Nations
Global Environmental Outlook 3. United Nations Environment Programme (UNEP) 2001. Available at www.unep.org (accessed September 19, 2002).

United Nations
International Environmental Technology Center, United Nations Environmental Programme (UNEP), at unep.or.jp/ietc/Issues/Urban (accessed October 2002).

232

United Nations Population Fund
"State of the World's Population" (2001). Available at www.unfpa.org/ swp/2001/english/index.html (accessed September 21, 2002).

World Commission on Environment and Development (WCED)
Our Common Future. (The Brundtland Report). Oxford, U.K: Oxford University Press, 1987.

World Bank
World Development Report. Oxford, U.K.: Oxford University Press, 1994.

World Bank Group
At www.worldbank/chronologicalarchives (accessed June 2002).

World Resources Institute
"Acid Rain: Downpour in Asia?" (1998a), at www.earthtrends.wri.org (accessed September 23, 2002).

World Resources Institute
"Coral Reefs: Assessing the Threat" (1998b), at www.earthtrends.wri.org (accessed September 23, 2002).

World Resources Institute
"Earth Trends: the Environmental Information Portal" (2001), at www.earthtrends.wri.org (accessed September 23, 2002).

Chapter One: Urban Water Quality, Supply, and Management

Anjos-Barbosa, J.
"Rainwater Harvesting in Situ." Unit for Sustainable Development and Environment, 1995. Available at www.oas.org/usde/publications.

Anonymous
"Meeting the Challenge: Revitalizing the Las Vegas Wash." *Water Engineering and Management* (October 2001).

Anonymous
"New Report Finds Water Efficiency Rules Save Billions of Dollars, Gallons." American Waterworks Association, 2001. Available at www.awwa.org/ Advocacy/pressroom/pr/010618/.cfm.

Anonymous
"Running on Empty." Report for Water World Day, 2001. Teddington, England: Tearfund, 2001.

BIBLIOGRAPHY

Anton, Danilo
Thirsty Cities: Urban Environments and Water Supply in Latin America. Ottawa, Ontario: International Development Research Center, 1993.

Arcata Wildlife Sanctuary
Available at http://www.humboldt.edu/~ere_dept/marsh/ (accessed December 7, 2002).

Barista, Dave
"Living Machine." *Building Design and Construction* 42, no. 4 (April 2001): 30–34.

Beekman, Gertjan
"Water Conservation, Recycling and Reuse." *Water Resources Development* 14, no. 3 (1998): 353–64.

Better Buildings for Greater Vancouver
"Grey-Water Recycling at Quayside Village: The Quayside Village Project," at www.betterbuildings.ca (accessed January 30, 2003).

Biswas, Asit
"Water Management in Latin America and the Caribbean." *Water Resources Development* 14, no. 3 (1998): 293–303.

Biswas, Asit
"Water for Urban Areas of the Developing World." In *Water for Urban Areas: Challenges and Perspectives*, edited by Juhai Vilto and Asit Biswas. New York: United Nations University Press, 2000.

Biswas, Asit, and Abdullah Arar
Treatment and Reuse of Wastewater. London: Butterworths, 1988.

Brown, Lester, Christopher Flavin, and Hillary French
State of the World 2001. New York: W. W. Norton, 2001.

Corbitt, R. A., and P. T. Bowen
"Constructed Wetlands for Wastewater Treatment." In *Applied Wetland Science and Technology*, edited by D. M. Kent. Boca Raton, Fla.: Lewis Publishers, 1994.

Drakakis-Smith, David
"Third World Cities: Sustainable Urban Development." *Urban Studies* 32, nos. 4 and 5 (1995): 657–77.

Earth Summit Watch
Clearing the Water. Washington, D.C.: Earth Summit Watch, 2002.

Falkenmark, Malin
"How Water Is Used." In D. Hinrichsen, *Solutions for a Water-Short World.* Baltimore: Johns Hopkins University School of Public Health, 1998.

Farrell, M., L. van der Hoven, and T. Olsen
"Vermont Rest Area Uses Green Wastewater Treatment System." *Public Roads* 63, no. 6 (May/June 2000): 27–29.

Gearheart, Robert A.
City of Arcata Marsh Pilot Project City of Arcata-Project No. C-06-2270. 1981.

Gleick, P., W. Burns, E. Chalecki, M. Cohen, K. Kao Cushing, A. Mann, R. Reyes, G. Wolff, and A. Wong
The World's Water: The Biennial Report on Freshwater Resources. Washington, D.C.: Island Press, 2002.

Godrej, Dinyar
"Precious Fluid: Challenge Posed by World's Freshwater Crisis." *New Internationalist* 354 (March 2003): 9–12.

Greenpeace
The Environmental Impact of the Car. Washington, D.C.: Greenpeace, 1995.

Grey, D. R. C., D. G. Kinniburgh, J. A. Barker, and J. P. Bloomfield
Strategic Study: Issues and Research Needs. Groundwater Forum Report. London: Foundation for Water Research, 1995.

Haman, D., and D. Brown
Water and Sustainable Urban Development. Gainesville: University of Florida, Institute of Food and Agricultural Sciences, 1994.

International Council for Local Environmental Initiatives
"Rainwater Management." ICLEI Case Study #20, Sumida City, Japan, 1995. Available at www.iclei.org/iclei/casedetail.cfm.

Jacob, J.
Groundwater and Society: Resources, Tensions and Opportunities: Themes in Groundwater Management for the Twenty-First Century. New York: United Nations Department of Economic and Social Affairs, 2000.

Juwarkar, A. S., B. Oke, A. Juwarkar, and S. M. Patnaik
"Domestic Wastewater Treatment through Constructed Wetlands in India." *Water Science Technology* 32, no. 3 (1995): 291–94.

Kadlec, Robert H., and Robert L. Knight
Treatment Wetlands. Boca Raton, Fla.: CRC Press, 1996.

BIBLIOGRAPHY

Kelly, Jane
"USA: Private Firms Belly-Flop in the H20 Biz." *Sacramento Bee* B7 (April 2, 2003).

Kovac, Carl
"Floating Arboretum Cleans Waste Water." *Architectural Record* 188, no. 6 (June 2000): 34–36.

Larsen, T., and W. Gujer
"The Concept of Sustainable Urban Water Management." *Water Science Technology* 35, no. 9 (1997): 3–10.

Lerner, Steve
Eco-Pioneers. Cambridge, Mass.: MIT Press, 1997.

McCully, Patrick
Silenced Rivers: The Ecology and Politics of Large Dams. London: Zed Books, 1996.

Merline, John
"What You Need to Know about Price Controls." *Consumer's Research Magazine* 76, no. 3 (1993): 16–20.

Mitsh, W. J., and J. G. Gosselink
In *Wetland Systems for Water Pollution Control 1994*, edited by H. Brix and R. H. Kadlec. Tarrytown, N.Y.: Pergamon, 1995.

Okun, Daniel
"Urban Water Management in the 21st Century." In *Water Resources Planning and Management*, edited by M. Karamouz. New York: American Society of Civil Engineering, 1992.

Polaris Institute
"Global Water Grab: How Corporations Are Planning to Take Control of Local Water Services" (2000), at www.polarisinsittute.org/pubs/pubs_pdfs/gwg_english.pdf (accessed April 19, 2003).

Postel, Sandra
"Dividing the Waters." *MIT Technology Review* 100, no. 3 (April 1997): 54–65.

Postel, Sandra
"Redesigning Irrigated Agriculture." *State of the World 2000*, edited by Linda Starke. New York: W. W. Norton, 2000.

Postel, Sandra
Pillar of Sand. New York: W. W. Norton, 1999.

Puckett, J., L. Byster, S. Westervelt, R. Gutierrez, S. Davis, A. Hussain, and M. Dutta
Exporting Harm: The High-Tech Trashing of Asia. Seattle, Wa.: Basel Action Network, 2002.

Rainwater Harvesting and Purification System
Available at www.rdrop.com (accessed November 2, 2002).

Rasmussen, Sarah
"Locals Build Wetlands to Treat Leachate." *American City and County* (October 2000): 54.

Riggle, David, and Kevin Gray
"Using Plants to Purify Wastewater." *BioCycle* 40, no. 1 (January 1999): 40–42.

Small Islands Water Information Network
Available at www.siwin.org (accessed December 4, 2001).

Stone, L., and J. Weiss
"Water Efficiency." *Mother Earth News* (April 1995).

Takashi, Asano
"Wastewater Management and Reuse in Mega-cities." In *Water for Urban Areas: Challenges and Perspectives*, edited by J. Vitto and A. Biswas. Tokyo: United Nations University Press, 2000.

Terpstra, P. M. J.
"Sustainable Water Usage Systems: Models for the Sustainable Utilization of Domestic Water in Urban Areas." *Water, Science, Technology* 39, no. 5 (1999): 65–72.

Texas Water Development Board
Texas Guide to Rainwater Harvesting. Austin: Texas Water Development Board in cooperation with the Center for Maximum Potential Building Systems, 2002.

Todd, John
"Greenhouse Treatment of Municipal Sewage." In *Eco-Pioneers*, edited by Steve Lerner. Cambridge, Mass.: MIT Press, 1997.

United Nations
  Groundwater and Society. Department of Economic and Social Affairs, 2000.

United Nations
  Global Environmental Outlook Report. United Nations Environmental and
  Development Programme, 2000.

United Nations
  *Source Book of Alternate Technologies for Freshwater Augmentation in Small Is-
  land Developing States*. United Nations Environmental and Development
  Programme, 2000.

United States Geological Survey (USGS)
  National Water Summary on Wetland Resources. Washington, D.C.: United
  States Geological Survey, 1999. Available at water.usgs.gov/nwsum/
  WSP2425/ (accessed December 10, 2002).

Wallace, Scott
  "Advanced Designs for Constructed Wetlands." *BioCycle* (June 2001): 40–44.

Wolff, G., and P. Gleick
  "The Soft Path for Water." In *The World's Water: The Biennial Report on
  Freshwater Resources*, edited by P. Gleick et al. Washington, D.C.: Island
  Press, 2003.

Wolf, H., A. Amery, and T. Aaron
  Water in the Middle East: A Geography of Peace. Austin: University of Texas
  Press, 2000.

Wren Spaulding, Holly
  "Busting the Water Cartel," at www.corpwatch.org/issues (accessed March
  31, 2003).

Chapter Two: Urban Solid Waste Disposal, Collection, and Management

Ackerman, Frank
  "Waste Management and Climate Change." *Local Environment* 5, no. 2
  (2000): 223–29.

Africano, Sebastian
  On Waste. Unpublished report. San Francisco State University Urban Studies program, 2003.

Anonymous
"A Wall of Waste." *Economist* 321, no. 7735 (November 30, 1991): 73.

Anonymous
"Our Opinion of the Topic of 'Mandatory Deposit.'" *Ratingen* (April 10, 2001).

Aspinwall, R., and J. Cain
"The Changing Mindset in the Management of Waste." *Philosphical Transactions: Mathematical, Physical and Engineering Sciences* 355, no. 1728 (July 1997): 1425–37.

Barista, Dave
"Living Machine." *Building Design and Construction* 42, no. 4 (April 2001): 30–34.

Black Rhinoceros
At www.blackrhinoceros.org/issues/conservation (accessed December 5, 2002).

Blight, G. E., and C. M. Mbande
"Some Problems of Waste Management in Developing Countries." *Journal of Solid Waste Technology and Management* 23, no. 1 (February 1996): 19–27.

Brix, Hans
"Use of Constructed Wetlands in Water Pollution Control: Historical Development, Present Status, and Future Perspectives." *Water, Science and Technology* 30, no. 8 (1994): 209–23.

Blight, G. E., and C. M. Mbande
"Some Problems of Waste Management in Developing Countries" *Journal of Solid Waste Technology and Management* 23, no. 1 (February 1996): 19–27.

Brown, Lester
Eco-Economy: Building an Economy for the Earth. New York: W. W. Norton, 2001.

Center for Health, Environment and Justice
Health Care without Harm. Falls Church, Va.: Center for Health, Environment and Justice, 2002.

Choguill, Charles
"Ten Steps to Sustainable Infrastructure." *Habitat International* 20, no. 3 (1996): 389–404.

Covey, Susan, and Diane Shew
"Building Partnerships—The Ohio Materials Exchange." *Resources, Conservation, and Recycling* 28 (2000): 265–77.

BIBLIOGRAPHY

Drakakis-Smith, David
"Third World Cities: Sustainable Urban Development." *Urban Studies* 32, nos. 4 and 5 (1995): 657–77.

Eighmy, Taylor, and David Kosson
"U.S.A. National Overview of Waste Management." *Waste Management* 16, nos. 5–6 (1996): 361–66.

El Serafy, Salah
"Sustainability, Income Measurement and Growth" In *Environmentally Sustainable Economic Development Building on Brundtland*, edited by Daly Goodland and Salah El Serafy. Environmental Working Paper No. 46. Washington, D.C.: World Bank Environment Department, 1991.

Farrell, M., L. van der Hoven, and T. Olsen
"Vermont Rest Area Uses Green Wastewater Treatment System." *Public Roads* 63, no. 6 (May/June 2000): 27–29.

Furedy, Christine
"Garbage: Exploring Non-conventional Options in Asian Cities." *Environment and Urbanization* 4, no. 2 (1992).

Gardner, Gary, and Payal Sampat
"Making Things Last: Reinventing Our Material Culture." *Futurist* 33, no. 15 (May 1999): 24–25.

Greenpeace
The Environmental Impact of the Car. Washington, D.C.: Greenpeace, 1995.

Hassan, M. N., R. A. Rahman, T. L. Chong, Z. Zakaria, and M. Awang
"Waste Recycling in Malaysia: Problems and Prospects." *Waste Management and Research* 18 (2000): 320–28.

Hassig, Don
"Rural 'Open Waste Burning' Is Extraordinarily Toxic." St. Lawrence Environmental Action, 2002.

Health Alert
"Waste Burning Retards Sex Growth—Study," at www.hain.org (accessed June 28, 2001).

Hufnagel, Casey
"Waste Reduction Taxes." Unpublished case study, Colby College, Waterville, Maine, 1999.

Hwong-wen, Ma, Lai Yen-Ling, and Chang-Chuan Chan
"Transfer of Dioxin Risk between Nine Major Municipal Waste Incinerators in Taiwan." *Environment International* 28 (2002): 103–10.

Ibañez, R., A. Andres, J. R. Viguri, I. Ortiz, and J. A. Irabien
"Characterization and Management of Incinerator Wastes." *Journal of Hazardous Materials* A79 (2000): 215–27.

Josephson, Todd, John Josephson, and Beth Josephson
"The Design of Living Technologies for Waste Treatment." *Ecological Engineering* 6 (1996): 109–36.

Juwarkar, A. S., B. Oke, A. Juwarkar, and S. M. Patnaik
"Domestic Wastewater Treatment through Constructed Wetlands in India." *Water Science Technology* 32, no. 3 (1995): 291–94.

Kovac, Carl
"Floating Arboretum Cleans Waste Water." *Architectural Record* 188, no. 6 (June 2000): 34–36.

Lechner, P., C. Heiss-Ziegler, M. H. Humer, and R. Rynk
"How Composting and Compost Can Optimize Landfilling." *BioCycle* (September 2002).

Mahapatra, Richard
"Down with the Dump." In *Down to Earth*. Delhi, India: Center for Science and the Environment, 2000.

Matthews, Scott
"Disposition and End-of-Life Options for Personal Computers." *Green Design Initiative Technical Report*. Carnegie Mellon University, 1997.

Meadows, Donella
"The City of First Priorities (Curitiba, Brazil)." *Whole Earth Review* 85 (Spring 1995).

Newsday
"Rush to Burn: Solving America's Garbage Crisis?" Washington, D.C.: Island Press, 1989.

Nunan, Fiona
"Urban Organic Waste Markets: Responding to Change in Hubli-Dharwad, India." *Habitat International* 24 (2000): 347–60.

Pacheco, Margarita
"Recycling in Bogota: Developing a Culture for Urban Sustainability." *Environment and Urbanization* 4, no. 2 (October 1992).

Pereira, A., L. Oliveira, and M. Reis
"Waste Recycling and the Sustainable City." In *The Sustainable City: Urban Regeneration and Sustainability*. Southhampton, U.K.: WIT Press, 2000.

Puckett, J., L. Byster, S. Westervelt, R. Gutierrez, S. Davis, A. Hussain, and M. Dutta
Exporting Harm: The High-Tech Trashing of Asia. Seattle, Wa.: Basel Action Network, 2002.

Rasmussen, Sarah
"Locals Build Wetlands to Treat Leachate." *American City and County* (October 2000): 54.

Rogers, Heather, and Cristiane Parenti
"The Hidden Life of Garbage: Why Our Waste Keeps Growing." *Utne* (November/December 2002): 44–48.

Riggle, David, and Kevin Gray
"Using Plants to Purify Wastewater." *BioCycle* 40, no. 1 (January 1999): 40–42.

Sakai, S., S. E. Sawell, A. J. Chandler, and T. T. Eighmy
"World Trends in Municipal Solid Waste Management." *Waste Management* 16, nos. 5–6 (1996): 341.

Secretaria Municipal de Meio Ambiente
Gerenciamento Dos Residuos Solidos Urbanos No Municipio De Curitiba. Curitiba, Brazil: Prefectura Municipal de Curitiba, Departamento de Limpeza Publica, 2000.

Sharma, V., M. Canditelli, F. Fortuna, and G. Cornacchia
"Processing of Urban and Agro-Industrial Residues by Aerobic Composting: Review." *Energy Conservation* 38, no. 5 (1997): 453–78.

Shutes, R. B. E.
"Artificial Wetlands and Water Quality Improvement." *Environment International* 26 (2001): 441–47.

Skena, George
"Packaging: It's in the Box!" *The Technology Teacher* (September/October 1993): 21–36.

Smith, M., J. Whitelegg, and N. Williams
Greening the Built Environment. Washington, D.C.: Earthscan, 1988.

Spowers, Rory
"Dream Machines." *Geographical Research* 73, no. 12 (February 2001): 56.

Tammemagi, H.
The Waste Crisis: Landfills, Incinerators, and the Search for a Sustainable Future. London: Oxford University Press, 1999.

Ueta, K., and H. Koizumi
"Reducing Waste." *Environment* 43, no. 9 (November 2001): 20–33.

United Nations Centre for Human Settlements
Sustainable Human Settlements Development: Implementing Agenda 21. United Nations Centre for Human Settlements, 1994.

United States Environmental Protection Agency (USEPA)
"Analysis of Five Community/Consumer Residential Collections of End-of-Life Electronic and Electrical Equipment" (EPA 901-R-98-003). Washington, D.C.: United States Environmental Protection Agency, 1998.

Urban Development Sector Unit East Asia and Pacific Region
What a Waste: Solid Waste Management in Asia. Washington, D.C.: World Bank, 1999.

Veggie Van Organization
At www.veggievan.org (accessed March 16, 1999).

Wei, Meng-Shiun, and Kuo-Hei Huang
"Recycling and Reuse of Industrial Wastes in Taiwan." *Waste Management* 21 (2001): 93–97.

Wilson, David
"Stick or Carrot? The Use of Policy Measures to Move Waste Management up the Hierarchy." *Waste Management and Research* 14 (1996): 385–98.

World Bank
What a Waste: Solid Waste Management in Asia. Washington, D.C.: World Bank, Urban Development Sector Unit, East Asia and Pacific Region, 1999.

Zurbrugg, Chris
"Decentralized Composting in India: Lessons Learned." Paper presented at the WEDC Conference, Sustainable Environmental Sanitation and Water Services, Calcutta, India, 2002.

Chapter Three: Urban Energy Supply and Management

Adam, Jim
"Energetic Challenges." *Our Planet* 12, no. 3 (2002): 15.

Africano, Sebastian, Mia Bookoff, and Morgan Crowell
Household Solar Panel Roof System. Unpublished report. San Francisco State University Urban Studies program, 2002.

Anonymous
"Zurich: Managing the Right Combination of Public Transport," at www.Eauc.de/winuwd/45 (accessed March 2002).

Auken, Svend
"Winds of Change." *Our Planet* 12, no. 3 (2002): 24–25.

Bale, Ross, and Lea Hoffman
Wind Energy: A Case Study of Middelgrunden. Unpublished report. San Francisco State University Urban Studies program, 2002.

Barton, H., and N. Bruder
A Guide to Local Environmental Auditing. London: Earthscan, 1995.

Bartone, C., J. Bernstein, J. Leitmann, and J. Eigen
"Toward Environmental Strategies for Cities: Policy Considerations from Urban Environmental Management in Developing Countries." UNDP/UNCHS (Habitat) World Bank Urban Management Program (UMP). Washington, D.C.: World Bank, 1994.

Bin Gadhi, S., and M. Mukbel
"A Review of Renewable Energy Activities in Yemen." *Renewable Energy* 14, nos. 1–4 (1998): 459–65.

Brown, Lester
Eco-Economy: Building an Economy for the Earth. New York: W. W. Norton, 2001.

California Integrated Waste Management Board
"Green Building Design and Construction," at www.ciwmb.ca.gov/GreenBuilding (accessed November 2002).

Cavallo, A, S. Hock, and D. Smith
"Wind Energy: Technology and Economics." *The Energy-Environment Connection,* edited by Jack Hollander. Washington, D.C.: Island Press, 1992.

Citizens for a Better Environment
"Checklist for Environmentally Responsible Design and Construction." Available at www.buildinggreen.com/ebn/checklist.html (accessed November 2002).

Clini, Corrado
"Power to the People." *Our Planet* 12, no. 3 (2002): 19–20.

County of San Mateo
"Recycle Works." Available at www.recycleworks.org.

Columbo, Umberto
"Development and the Global Environment." In *The Energy-Environment Connection*, edited by Jack Hollander. Washington, D.C.: Island Press, 1992.

Devencenzi, Tony
"Green Building and Design." Unpublished report. San Francisco State University Urban Studies program, 2002.

Ediger, Volkan, and Elcin Kentel
"Renewable Energy Potential as an Alternative to Fossil Fuels in Turkey." *Energy Conversion and Management* 40 (1999): 743–55.

Gibbs, David
"Integrating Sustainable Development and Economic Restructuring: A Role for Regulation Theory?" *Geoforum* 27, no. 1 (1996): 1–10.

Green Building Store
Available at www.greenbuildingstore.co.uk.

Grubb, M., and N. Meyer
"Wind Energy: Resources, Systems, and Regional Strategies." In *The Energy-Environment Connection*, edited by Jack Hollander. Washington, D.C.: Island Press, 1992.

Hollander, Jack, ed.
The Energy-Environment Connection. Washington, D.C.: Island Press, 1992.

Hughart, D.
Prospects for Traditional and Non-conventional Energy Sources in Developing Countries. Washington, D.C.: World Bank, 1979.

Johansson, T., H. Kelly, A. Reddy, and R. Williams
"Renewable Fuels and Electricity for a Growing World Economy: Defining and Achieving the Potential." In *The Energy-Environment Connection*, edited by Jack Hollander. Washington, D.C.: Island Press, 1992.

BIBLIOGRAPHY

Lean, Geoffrey
"Energy." *Our Planet* 12, no. 3 (2002): 16.

Leggett, Jeremy
"Rising Sun." *Our Planet* 12, no. 3 (2002): 15.

Pasztor, Janos, and Lars Kristoferson
"Biomass Energy." In *The Energy-Environment Connection*, edited by Jack Hollander. Washington, D.C.: Island Press, 1992.

Peet, John
Energy and the Ecological Economics of Sustainability. Washington, D.C.: Island Press, 1992.

Petesch, Patti
North-South Environmental Strategies, Costs and Bargains. Washington, D.C.: Overseas Development Council, 1992.

Philip, Joseph
"Solar Thermal Technologies in the United States." *Solar Magazine* (April 2001). Available at www.solarserve.de/solarmagazine (accessed February 2, 2003).

Rain Forest Action Network
Drilling to the Ends of the Earth. Berkeley, Calif.: Project Underground, 1998.

Roussely, Francois.
"Meeting Social Needs." *Our Planet* 12, no. 3 (2002): 8–9.

Scott, Aldous
"How Solar Cells Work" (2002), at www.howstuffworks (accessed January 2003).

Smith, M., J. Whitelegg, and N. Williams
Greening the Built Environment. Washington, D.C.: Earthscan, 1988.

Tickell, Joshua, and Kia Tickell
From the Fryer to the Fuel Tank: How to Make Cheap, Clean Fuel from Free Vegetable Oil. Tallahassee, Fla.: Tickell Energy Consulting, 1999.

Union of Concerned Scientists
"Powerful Solutions: Seven Ways to Switch America to Renewable Electricity" (1999), at www.ucsusa.org/clean_energy (accessed July 2003).

Whipple, Dan
"Web Hoster Uses Solar-Powered Server." *Interactive Week* 8, no. 11 (2001): 50.

White, Rodney
"The International Transfer of Urban Technology: Does the North Have Anything to Offer for the Global Environmental Crisis?" *Environment and Urbanization* 4, no. 2 (October 1992).

World Resources Institute
"Table ERC.2 Energy Consumption by Source" (2001), at www.earth-trends.org (accessed February 2, 2003).

www.solarengineering.co.za/biogas_floating drum

Chapter Four: Urban Transportation Planning and Management

Abdi, S.
"Rickshaw Ban Marks End of Road for the City's Symbol." *South China Morning Post* (April 19, 2002), 11.

Advocacy Institute
Oil and Transportation Environment and Energy Study Institute Fact Sheet, cited in *Draining the Tank: Transportation and Energy Consumption in the United States*. National Resources Defense Council, 2002.

Agarwal, M. K.
"Urban Transportation: Some Aspects and Prospects." *Indian Highways* 24, no. 6 (June 1996): 45–49.

Akinbami, J., and S. Fadare
"Strategies for Sustainable Urban and Transport Development in Nigeria." *Transport Policy* 4, no. 4 (1997): 237–45.

Anonymous
"Two Wheels or Four Wheels?" *China Daily* (November 20, 2002): 9–11.

Anonymous
"Tools for a Sustainable Community," at www.workbike.org (accessed December 2001).

Anonymous
"Construction Ministry Plans to Support Construction of Bicycle-only Roadway in Central Tokyo Area: Bicycle-Friendly Environment Creation Projects in the Offing," at www.jbpi.or.jp/english/b.news/enews1.html.

BIBLIOGRAPHY

Anonymous
"Bicycles Used in Tokyo's Government District for Cleaner Air," at www.jbpi.or.jp/english/b.news/top_1.html.

Anonymous
"New Bicycle Parking System Proving Popular in Nishinomiya," at www.jbpi.or.jp/english/b.news/enews6.html.

Argalis, A., L. Baltioa, I. Zarumba, and D. Liepioo
"Transport Policy in Riga." In *The Sustainable City: Urban Regeneration and Sustainability*. Southhampton, U.K.: WIT Press, 2000.

Armstrong-Wright, Alan
Public Transport in Third World Cities. London: Department of Transport, 1997.

Blowers, Andrew
"We Can't Go On As We Are: The Social Impact of Trends." In Transportation in *Urban Transport*, edited by H. K. Blessington. London: Thomas Telford, 1995.

Brown, Lester, Christopher Flavin, and Hillary French
State of the World 2001. New York: W. W. Norton, 2001.

Center for Sustainable Transportation
Definition and Vision of Sustainable Transportation. Toronto: Center for Sustainable Transportation, 1997.

Center for Sustainable Transportation
Sustainable Transportation: Reflections on the Movement of People and of Freight, with Special Attention to the Role of the Private Automobile. Toronto: Center for Sustainable Transportation, 1998.

Clark, W., and M. Kuijpers-Linde
"Commuting in Restructuring Urban Regions." *Urban Studies* 31, no. 3 (April 1994).

Cleary, J., and H. McClintock
"The Nottingham Cycle-Friendly Employers Project: Lessons for Encouraging Cycle Commuting." *Transport Policy* 7, no. 2 (April 2000): 217–22.

Cooper, J., T. Ryley, and A. Smyth
"Contemporary Lifestyles and the Implications for Sustainable Development Policy: Lessons from the UK's Most Car Dependent City, Belfast." *Cities* 18, no. 2 (2001): 103–13.

Crane, Randall
The Impacts of Urban Form on Travel: A Critical Review. Cambridge, Mass.: Lincoln Institute of Land Policy, 1999.

DeCorla-Souza, Patrick
"The Impacts of Alternative Urban Development Patterns on Highway System Performance." *Public Roads* 56, no. 2 (September 1992): 72–81.

Dittmar, Hank
"A Broader Context for Transportation Planning." *Journal of the American Planning Association* 61, no. 1 (1995): 7–13.

Durning, Alan
The Car and the City. Seattle, Wa.: Northwest Environmental Watch, 1996.

Ecology Center
Personal interview with Dave Williamson, April 2003.

European Commission
Good Practices in Urban Development. Berlin: European Academy of the Urban Environment, 2002.

Evans, R., S. Guy, and S. Marvin
"Views of the City: Multiple Pathways to Sustainable Transport Futures." *Local Environment* 6, no. 2 (2001): 121–33.

Everett, Lauren
"DaimlerChrysler: Corporate Environmental Report." Donald Bren School of Environmental Science & Management, Fall 2000.

Frank, Lawrence, and Peter Engelke
"The Built Environment and Human Activity Patterns, Exploring the Impacts of Urban Form on Public Health." *Journal of Planning Literature* 16, no. 2 (November 2001.): 202–18.

Gardner, Gary
"Cities Turning to Bicycles to Cut Costs, Pollution, and Crime." Press release, August 26, 1998. Available at www.worldwatch.org/press/news.

Greenpeace
The Environmental Impact of the Car. Washington, D.C.: Greenpeace, 1995.

Guy, S., and S. Marvin
"Understanding Sustainable Cities: Competing Urban Futures." *European Urban and Regional Studies* 6, no. 3 (1999): 268–75.

BIBLIOGRAPHY

Hook, W.
"Mahal Cycle Taxi Improvement Project." Paper presented at the Conference on Public-Private Partnerships in the Transport Sector, Jakarta, Indonesia, June 1999.

Hook, W., and M. Replogle
"Motorization and Non-motorized Tranport in Asia." *Land Use Policy* 13, no. 1 (1996): 69–84.

Iijima, Masako
"Running Rings around Pollution: Pedal Power Rickshaws are Rolling into Action to Help Save the Taj Mahal from Pollution." *Birmingham Post* (March 25, 2000), 57–58.

Ingram, Gregory
"Patterns of Metropolitan Development: What Have We Learned?" *Urban Studies* 35, no. 7 (June 1998): 1019–36.

International Bicycle Fund
"America: Bike, Non-motorized and Sustainable Transport—Caribbean, North, Central, Latin and South" (2001a), available at www.ibike.org/america.

International Bicycle Fund
"Poland's Bicycle Policy" (2001b), available at www.ibike.org/poland-law.

Kahn, Joseph
"Today's China, in a Rush, Has No Time for Bikes." *New York Times* (September 6, 2002), 4.

Kenworthy, Jeffrey, and Felix Laube
"Patterns of Automobile Dependence in Cities: An International Overview." Transportation Research Part A 33 (1999): 691–723.

Litman, Todd
Reinventing Transportation: Exploring the Paradigm Shift Needed to Reconcile Transportation and Sustainability Objectives. Victoria, Canada: Victoria Transport Policy Institute, 1999.

Mass Transit
"New Park 'n Rides and Transit Center Key to Houston's METRO's Expansion Plans." *Mass Transit* 25, no. 4 (July/August 1999): 64–67.

McClintock, H., ed.
The Bicycle and City Traffic. London: Belhaven, 1992.

McClintock, H.
"Lessons for Encouraging Cycle Commuting: The Nottingham Cycle-Friendly Employers Project." *Local Environment* 5, no. 2 (May 2000): 217–23.

Meadows, Donella
"The City of First Priorities (Curitiba, Brazil)." *Whole Earth Review* 85 (Spring 1995).

Meurs, Henk, and Rinus Haaijer
"Spatial Structure and Mobility." *Transportation Research* (2001): 429–46.

Moore, T., and P. Thorsnes
The Transportation/Land Use Connection. Chicago: American Planning Association, 1994. Available at www.planning.org.

National Biodiesel Board
"Biodiesel Basics." Available at www.biodiesel.org/resources/biodiesel_basics (accessed 2002).

National Resources Defense Council (NRDC)
"Clean Air & Energy: Transportation" (2002). Available at www.nrdc.org/air/transportation (accessed 2002).

O'Meara Sheehan, Molly
"Making Better Transportation Choices." In *State of the World 2001*, edited by Linda Starke. New York: W. W. Norton, 2001.

Pedal Express
Personal interviews with David Cohen and Shane Rhodes. Pedal Express Collective, February 2003.

Pope, Chris
"Take Me to the Taj." *Professional Engineering* (2001): 44–47.

Pucher, John
"Capitalism, Socialism, and Urban Transportation: Policies and Travel Behavior in the East and West." *APA Journal* 56, no. 3 (Summer 1990): 278–96.

Pucher, John, and Lewis Dijkstra
"Making Walking and Cycling Safer: Lessons from Europe." *Transportation Quarterly* 54, no. 3 (Summer 2000): 25–50.

Rabinovitch, Jonas
"Innovative Land Use and Public Transport Policy." *Land Use Policy* 13, no. 1 (1996): 51–67.

Rabinovitch, Jonas, and Josef Leitman
"Urban Planning in Curitiba." *Scientific American* (March 1996): 46–53.

Rebelo, Jorge
"Essentials for Sustainable Urban Transport in Brazil's Large Metropolitan Areas" (2002). Available at www.worldbank.org/html/fpd/transport/urb-strans/tr-plan.htm.

Renzi, Shanna, and Robert Crawford
"Powering the Next Generation Automobile: DaimlerChrysler's Venture into Fuel Cell Technology." *Corporate Environmental Strategy* 7 (2000): 38–50.

Replogie, Michael
"Bicycles as Transportation Policy." In *Case Study of Japan Bicycle Oriented Transportation Policies and Land Use Planning*, edited by Khury Brown. Unpublished report, San Francisco State University, 2002.

Rietveld, Piet
"The Accessibility of Railway Stations: The Role of the Bicycle in the Netherlands." *Transportation Research* D5 (2000): 71–75.

Sen, J.
"The Sha Fu of Calcutta: Past, Present and Future of Hand-rickshaw Pullers of Calcutta: Is a Civilized Transition Possible?" *Bulletin of Concerned Asian Scholars* 30 (1998): 37–49.

Sirkis, A.
"Bike Networking in Rio: The Challenges for Non-motorized Transport in an Automobile-Dominated Government Culture." *Local Environment* 5, no. 1 (2000): 83-95.

Smith, H., and J. Raemaekers
"Land Use Pattern and Transport in Curitiba." *Land Use Policy* 15, no. 3 (1998): 233–51.

Sperling, Daniel
Future Drive: Electric Vehicles and Sustainable Transportation. Washington, D.C.: Island Press, 1995.

Spowers, R.
"Dream Machines." *Geographical Research* 73, no. 12 (February 2001): 56.

Starke, Linda, ed.
State of the World 2001. New York: W. W. Norton, 2001.

Taylor, B., P. Haas, B. Boyd, D. Baldwin Hess, H. Iseki, and A. Yoh
"Increasing Transit Ridership: Lessons from the Most Successful Transit Systems in the 1990s." San Jose, Calif.: Mineta Transporation Institute, 2002.

Thein Durning, Alan
The Car and the City. Seattle, Wa.: Northwest Environmental Watch, 1996.

Tickell, Joshua, and Kaia Tickell
From the Fryer to the Fuel Tank: How to Make Cheap, Clean Fuel from Free Vegetable Oil. Ashland, Ohio: BookMasters, 1999.

Tolley, R., L. Lumsdon, and K. Bickerstaff
"The Future of Walking in Europe: A Delphi Project to Identify Expert Opinion in Future Walking Scenarios." *Transport Policy* 8 (2001): 307–15.

United States Environmental Protection Agency (USEPA)
"Clean Alternative Fuels: Methanol" (EPA 420-F-00-040). Washington, D.C.: United States Environmental Protection Agency, 2001.

Wadhwa, L. C.
"Sustainable Transportation: The Key to Sustainable Cities." In *The Sustainable City: Urban Regeneration and Sustainability.* Southhampton, U.K.: WIT Press, 2000.

Wegener, M.
"Accessibility and Development Impacts." In *Transport and Urban Development,* edited by D. Banister. London: Routledge, 1995.

Weyrich, Paul, and William Lind
Conservatives and Mass Transit: Is It Time for a New Look? Free Congress Foundation, 1996.

Whitelegg, John, and Nick Williams
"Non-motorized Transport and Sustainable Development: Evidence from Calcutta." *Local Environment* 5, no. 1 (2000): 7–18.

Winner, Cherie
"Bike It Instead." *Current Health* 22, no. 2 (October 1995): 20–22.

Workbike Research
At www.workbike.org, 2001 (accessed 2001).

Worldwatch Institute
Vital Signs 2001: The Trends That Are Shaping Our Future. New York: W. W. Norton, 2001.

Chapter Five: Urban Food Production

Anonymous
"Roots of Change: Agriculture, Ecology and Health in California." Report for the Funders Agriculture Working Group, San Francisco, 2001.

Anonymous
"Are Pesticides Hazardous to Our Health?" *Journal of Pesticide Reform* 19, no. 2 (Summer 1999). Available at www.pesticidewatch.org (accessed 2001).

Armar-Klemesu, M., and D. Maxwell
"Urban Agriculture as an Asset Strategy: Supplementing Income and Diets." In *Growing Cities, Growing Food: Urban Agriculture on the Policy Agenda. A Reader on Urban Agriculture*, ed. N. Bakker, M. Dubbeling, S. Gündel, U. Sabel-Koschella, and H. de Zeeuw. Feldafing, Germany: Deutsche Stiftung für internationale Entwicklung, 2000.

Bello, Waldon
Dark Victory: The United States and Global Poverty. Oakland, Calif.: Food First Books, 1998.

Brown, Lester
"Eradicating Hunger: A Growing Challenge." In *State of the World 2001*, edited by Linda Starke. New York: W. W. Norton, 2001.

Conway, Gordon
"Food for All in the 21st Century." *Environment* 42, no. 1 (January/February 2000).

Cook, C. D., and J. Rogers
"Community Food Security: A Growing Movement." *Pesticide Campaigner* 6, no. 1 (1996): 7.

de Zeeuw, Henk, and Marielle Dubbeling
"First Bulletin on Urban Agriculture in Europe." *City Farmer* (May 1997).

Eberlee, John
"Chasing Away Hunger." *Farming in the City* 21, no. 3 (October 1993).

Foeken, D., and M. Mwangi
Farming in the City of Nairobi. ASC Working Paper No. 30. Leiden: African Studies Center, 1998.

Food and Agriculture Organization of the United Nations (FAO)
"Good Agricultural Practices," June 2002. Available at www.fao.org.

Food and Agriculture Organization of the United Nations (FAO)
Agriculture 21 (July/August 2003). Available at www.fao.org.

Foodmiles
"The Food Miles Report: The Dangers of Long-Distance Food Transport."
Report published by the SAFE Alliance, London, October 1994.

Gardner, G., and B. Halweil
"Nourishing the Underfed and Overfed." In *State of the World*, edited by
Linda Starke. New York: W. W. Norton, 2000.

Garnett, Tara
"Urban Agriculture in London: Rethinking Our Food Economy." In *Grow-
ing Cities, Growing Food: Urban Agriculture on the Policy Agenda. A Reader on
Urban Agriculture*, ed. N. Bakker, M. Dubbeling, S. Gündel, U. Sabel-
Koschella, and H. de Zeeuw. Feldafing, Germany: Deutsche Stiftung für in-
ternationale Entwicklung, 2000.

Gonzalez Novo, Mario, and Catherine Murphy
"Urban Agriculture in the City of Havana: A Popular Response to a Crisis."
In *Growing Cities, Growing Food: Urban Agriculture on the Policy Agenda. A
Reader on Urban Agriculture*, ed. N. Bakker, M. Dubbeling, S. Gündel, U.
Sabel-Koschella, and H. de Zeeuw. Feldafing, Germany: Deutsche Stiftung
für internationale Entwicklung, 2000.

Graham, Elizabeth
"Farming in the Built Environment." In *For Hunger Proof Cities: Sustainable
Urban Food Systems*, edited by M. Koc, R. MacRae, L. Mougeot, and J.
Welsh. International Development Research Centre (IDRC), 1999. Avail-
able at ruaf.org (accessed March 2003).

Howe, Joel, and Paul Wheeler
"Urban Food Growing: The Experience of Two U.K. Cities." *Sustainable Development* 7, no. 1 (1999): 13–24.

Jacobi, P., J. Amend, and S. Kiango
"Urban Agriculture in Dar Es Salaam: Providing an Indispensable Part of the
Diet." In *Growing Cities, Growing Food: Urban Agriculture on the Policy
Agenda. A Reader on Urban Agriculture*, ed. N. Bakker, M. Dubbeling, S.
Gündel, U. Sabel-Koschella, and H. de Zeeuw. Feldafing, Germany:
Deutsche Stiftung für internationale Entwicklung, 2000.

Kneen, Brewster
"CSA Roots in Japan." In *Context: A Quarterly of Humane Sustainable Culture*
(Fall 1995). Available at www.context.org (accessed July 2003).

Kreinecker, Peter
"La Paz: Urban Agriculture in Harsh Ecological Conditions." In *Growing Cities, Growing Food: Urban Agriculture on the Policy Agenda. A Reader on Urban Agriculture*, ed. N. Bakker, M. Dubbeling, S. Gündel, U. Sabel-Koschella, and H. de Zeeuw. Feldafing, Germany: Deutsche Stiftung für internationale Entwicklung, 2000.

Lachance, Andre
"A Plot of One's Own in West African Cities." International Development Research Centre (IDRC), Resources Book Report 21, no. 3 (October 1993). Available at www.idrc.ca/books (accessed September 1999).

Mbiba, Beacon
Urban Agriculture in Zimbabwe. Brookfield, Vt.: Avebury, 1995.

Memon, Pilar Ali, and Dianne Lee-Smith
Urban Farming in Africa: The Case of Kampala, Uganda, and Nairobi. Nairobi, Kenya: ACTS Press, African Center for Technology Studies, 1993.

Mougeot, Luc
"Urban Food Production: Evolution, Official Support, and Significance." International Development Research Centre (IDRC), Cities Feeding People CFP Report, 1994. Available at www.idrc.ca/cfp (accessed September 1999).

Murphy, Catherine
Cultivating Havana: Urban Agriculture and Food Security in the Years of Crisis. Oakland, Calif.: Institute for Food and Development Policy, 1999.

Petts, James
"Edible Buildings: Benefits, Challenges, and Limitations." Available at www.sustainweb.org/pdf/edible_buildings.pdf (accessed October 2002).

Pinderhughes, Raquel
"Democratizing Environmental Assets: The Role of Urban Gardens and Farms in Reducing Poverty." In *Natural Assets: Democratizing Environmental Ownership*, edited by J. K. Boyce and B. G. Shelley. Washington, D.C.: Island Press, 2003.

Pinderhughes, Raquel, Catherine Murphy, and Mario Gonzalez-Novo
"Urban Agriculture in Havana, Cuba." In *Down to Earth*. New Delhi, India: Centre for Science and the Environment, 2001.

Postel, Sandra
"Dividing the Waters." *Technology Review* 100, no. 3 (April 1997): 54–65.

Postel, Sandra
"Redesigning Irrigated Agriculture." *State of the World 2000*, edited by Linda Starke. New York: W. W. Norton, 2000.

Pothukuchi, K., and J. Kaufman
"The Food System: A Stranger to the Planning Field." *American Planning Association Journal* 66, no. 2 (2000).

Potutan, G. E., W. H. Schnitzler, J. M. Arnado, L. G. Janubas, and R. J. Holmer
"Urban Agriculture in Cagayan De Oro: A Favourable Response of City Government and NGOs." In *Growing Cities, Growing Food: Urban Agriculture on the Policy Agenda. A Reader on Urban Agriculture*, ed. N. Bakker, M. Dubbeling, S. Gündel, U. Sabel-Koschella, and H. de Zeeuw. Feldafing, Germany: Deutsche Stiftung für internationale Entwicklung, 2000.

Purnomohadi, Ning
"Urban Agriculture as an Alternative Strategy to Face the Economic Crisis." In *Growing Cities, Growing Food: Urban Agriculture on the Policy Agenda. A Reader on Urban Agriculture*, ed. N. Bakker, M. Dubbeling, S. Gündel, U. Sabel-Koschella, and H. de Zeeuw. Feldafing, Germany: Deutsche Stiftung für internationale Entwicklung, 2000.

Rifken, Jeremy
"Foreword." In *Rainforest in Your Kitchen: The Hidden Connection between Extinction and Your Supermarket* by Martin Teitel. Washington, D.C.: Island Press, 1992.

Rodrigues, M. S., and J. M. Lopez-Real
"Urban Organic Wastes, Urban Health and Sustainable Urban and Peri-urban Agriculture: Linking Urban and Rural by Composting." *Urban Agriculture Notes* (1999). Available at www.cityfarmer.org/urbanwastes.html.

Rokadi, Carole
"Urban Agriculture: Research Questions and Zambian Evidence." *Journal of Modern African Studies* 26, no. 3 (November 1988): 495–515.

Schurmann, Franz
"Can Cities Feed Themselves? Worldwide Turn to Urban Gardening Signals Hope." *Jinn*, Pacific News Service, June 3, 1996. Available at www.pacific-news.org/jinn/stories/2.12/960603-habitat.html.

Schurmann, Franz
"China's Government Could Regret Its Popular Revolution against the Land." *Pacific News Service* (July 26, 2001).

BIBLIOGRAPHY

Shiva, Vandana
Stolen Harvest: The Hijacking of the Global Food Supply. Cambridge, Mass.: South End Press, 2000.

Smit, Jac
"What Would the World Be Like in the 21st Century If Cities Were Nutritionally Self-Reliant?" *City Farmer* (April 1996).

Smit, Jac, and Joe Nasr
"Urban Agriculture for Sustainable Cities: Using Wastes and Idle Land and Water Bodies as Resources." *Environment and Urbanization* 4, no. 2 (1992).

Smit, Jac, and Joe Nasr
"Farming in Cities." *In Context: A Quarterly Journal of Humane Sustainable Culture* (Fall 1995): 29.

Smit, J., A. Rattu, and J. Nasr
Urban Agriculture: Food, Jobs and Sustainable Cities, vol. 1. United Nations Development Program Publications, 1996.

Sommers, Paul, and Jae Smith
"Promoting Urban Agriculture: A Strategy Framework for Planners in North America, Europe, and Asia." International Development Research Centre (IDRC), Cities Feeding People (CFP) Report Series #9 (1994). Available at www.idrc.ca/cfp (accessed September 1999).

Stren, R., and R. White
African Cities in Crisis: Managing Rapid Urban Growth. Boulder, Colo.: Westview, 1992.

Teitel, Martin
Rainforest in Your Kitchen: The Hidden Connection between Extinction and Your Supermarket. Washington, D.C.: Island Press, 1992.

Tripp, A. M.
"The Informal Economy, Labour and the State in Tanzania." *Comparative Politics* 22, no. 3 (1990): 253–64.

United Nations
Food and Agriculture Organization Agenda 21. United Nations Development Program (UNDP), 1996.

Yeung, Yue-Man
"Urban Agriculture: Three Cities in Asia." *United Nations Works in Progress* 10, no. 1 (1986): 7.

Yi-Zhoang, Cai, and Zhang Zhangen
"Shanghai: Trends towards Specialized and Capital-Intensive Urban Agriculture." In *Growing Cities, Growing Food: Urban Agriculture on the Policy Agenda. A Reader on Urban Agriculture*, ed. N. Bakker, M. Dubbeling, S. Gündel, U. Sabel-Koschella, and H. de Zeeuw. Feldafing, Germany: Deutsche Stiftung für internationale Entwicklung, 2000.

Yoveva, A., B. Gocheva, G. Voykova, B. Borissov, and A. Spassov
"Sofia: Urban Agriculture in an Economy in Transition." In *Growing Cities, Growing Food: Urban Agriculture on the Policy Agenda. A Reader on Urban Agriculture*, ed. N. Bakker, M. Dubbeling, S. Gündel, U. Sabel-Koschella, and H. de Zeeuw. Feldafing, Germany: Deutsche Stiftung für internationale Entwicklung, 2000.

Chapter Six: Toward Sustainable Development Planning in Cities

Anonymous
Introduction in "Sustainable Cities: Meeting Needs, Reducing Resource Use and Recycling, Reuse and Reclamation." *Environment and Urbanization* 4, no. 2 (1992).

Briassoulis, Helen
"Who Plans Whose Sustainability? Alternative Roles for Planners." *Journal of Environmental Planning and Management* 42, no. 6 (1999): 889–902.

Choguill, Charles
"Ten Steps to Sustainable Infrastructure." *Habitat International* 20, no. 3 (1996): 389–404.

Durning, Alan
How Much Is Enough: The Consumer Society and the Future of the Earth. New York: W. W. Norton, 1992.

Hamm, Bernd, and Pandurang Muttagi
"Introduction." In *Understanding Sustainable Development and the Future of Cities*, edited by B. Hamm and P. Muttagi. London: Intermediate Technology Publications, 1998.

Henrique Cardoso, Fernando
"Changing the Paradigm." *Our Planet* 13, no. 2 (2002): 6–7.

BIBLIOGRAPHY

Herfindahl, Orris C., and Allen J. Kneese
Quality of the Environment: An Economic Approach to Some Problems in Using Land, Water & Air. Baltimore: Johns Hopkins University Press, 1965.

Hollantai, Vladimir
"Russia." *Whole Earth* (Spring 1999): 96–97.

Mbeki, Thabo
"Agenda of Hope." *Our Planet* 13, no. 2 (2002): 13–14.

Moody-Stuart, Mark
"Breaking the Grid Lock." *Our Planet* 13, no. 2 (2002): 13–14.

Moosa Valli, Mohammed
"African Renaissance." *Our Planet* 13, no. 2 (2002): 13–14.

Pothukuchi, K., and J. Kaufman
"The Food System: A Stranger to the Planning Field." *American Planning Association Journal* 66, no. 2 (2000).

Rees, William
"Understanding Sustainable Development." In *Sustainable Development and the Future of Cities*, edited by B. Hamm and P. Muttagi. London: Intermediate Technology Publications, 1998.

Repetto, R.
World Enough and Time. New Haven, Conn.: Yale University Press, 1986.

World Commission on Environment and Development (WCED)
Our Common Future. (The Brundtland Report). Oxford, U.K: Oxford University Press, 1987.

INDEX

ABOUT THE AUTHOR

Raquel Pinderhughes is professor of urban studies and environmental studies at San Francisco State University, where she teaches courses in the area of urban environmental planning and policy. Her areas of expertise include sustainable development, sustainable urban infrastructure planning and management, appropriate technology, environmental inequities, environmental justice, urban agriculture, local food systems, and urban poverty. She has conducted research on sustainable development planning and appropriate technologies in Cuba, Brazil, India, Spain, and the United States. In addition, she has conducted research on the community level impacts of social inequality and poverty in the United States. Her research in this area has been focused on the impact of race, ethnicity, and class on environmental quality in residential communities; inequalities in local food systems; the social and environmental benefits of urban agriculture; the role of urban agriculture in reducing poverty; and the impacts of poverty on Latino families and communities.

She has received numerous awards and honors for excellence in teaching. Most of her courses include applied assignments. Students in her courses have designed and constructed bicycle cargo systems; rainwater catchment systems; seed starting greenhouses; solar food dryers, radios, and lights; and many other appropriate technologies. Students have also produced an environmental audit of San Francisco State University; cradle to grave analyses focused on the social and environmental impacts of the exploitation and use of the world's most important natural resources; and a how-to manual that takes readers through their home, room by room, informing them about how they can affordably reduce their use of natural resources and create a more sustainable and healthy urban home.

For several years, she taught an international seminar on urban environmental planning that took students to study in Havana, Cuba.

Prof. Pinderhughes is also the director of the SFSU/Delancey Street College Program; a program that provides ex-felons and drug addicts the opportunity to pursue an SFSU bachelor's degree on site at the Delancey Street facility in San Francisco. She currently serves on Advisory Boards for the Ecology Center, Prevention Institute, and the city of San Francisco's Public Health Department. Previous appointments include serving as an Environmental Commissioner for the city of Berkeley and on advisory boards for Urban Habitat, the city of San Francisco's Sustainable City Project, and the state of California's Comparative Risk Project.